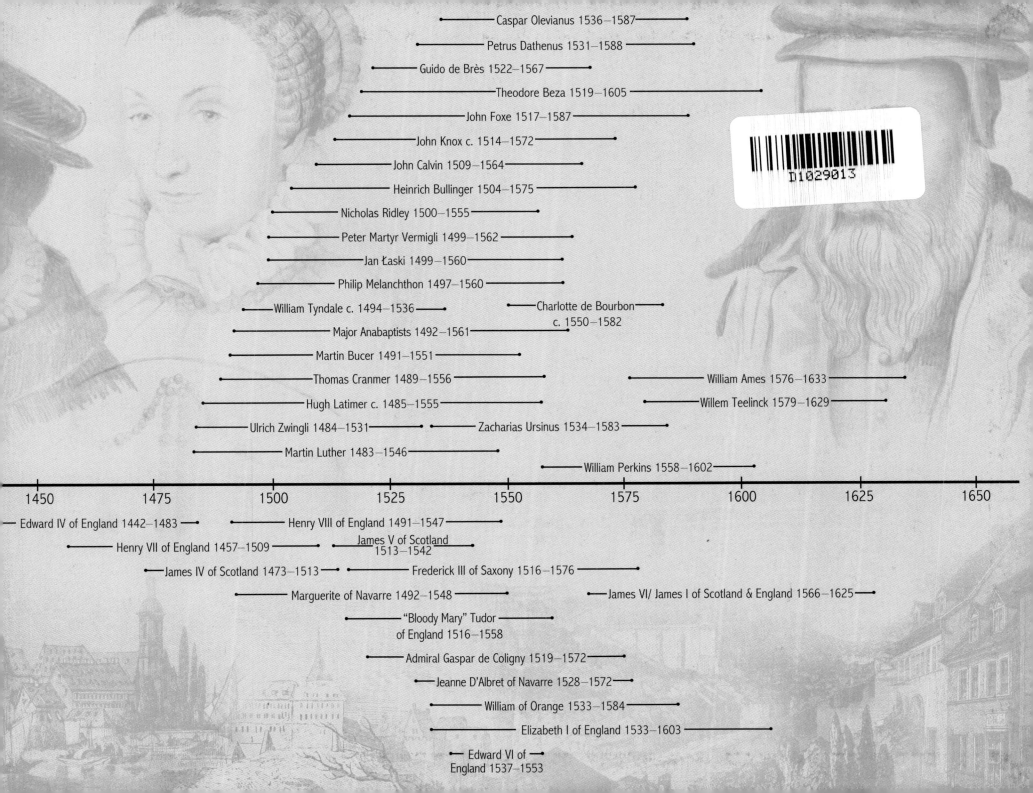

Caspar Olevianus 1536–1587

Petrus Dathenus 1531–1588

Guido de Brès 1522–1567

Theodore Beza 1519–1605

John Foxe 1517–1587

John Knox c. 1514–1572

John Calvin 1509–1564

Heinrich Bullinger 1504–1575

Nicholas Ridley 1500–1555

Peter Martyr Vermigli 1499–1562

Jan Łaski 1499–1560

Philip Melanchthon 1497–1560

William Tyndale c. 1494–1536

Charlotte de Bourbon c. 1550–1582

Major Anabaptists 1492–1561

Martin Bucer 1491–1551

Thomas Cranmer 1489–1556

William Ames 1576–1633

Hugh Latimer c. 1485–1555

Willem Teelinck 1579–1629

Ulrich Zwingli 1484–1531

Zacharias Ursinus 1534–1583

Martin Luther 1483–1546

William Perkins 1558–1602

1450   1475   1500   1525   1550   1575   1600   1625   1650

Edward IV of England 1442–1483

Henry VIII of England 1491–1547

Henry VII of England 1457–1509

James V of Scotland 1513–1542

James IV of Scotland 1473–1513

Frederick III of Saxony 1516–1576

Marguerite of Navarre 1492–1548

James VI/ James I of Scotland & England 1566–1625

"Bloody Mary" Tudor of England 1516–1558

Admiral Gaspar de Coligny 1519–1572

Jeanne D'Albret of Navarre 1528–1572

William of Orange 1533–1584

Elizabeth I of England 1533–1603

Edward VI of England 1537–1553

This beautifully written and illustrated volume, co-authored by Diana Kleyn and Joel Beeke, is a joy to read and deserves a place in any home where the triumphs of the Reformation are held dear. It provides a sure resource for inquiring young minds to capture the thrill of God's work in the lives of men and women primarily in the sixteenth century. Reformation Heroes *is a magnificent achievement.*

— Dr. Derek Thomas, John E. Richards Professor of Theology,
Reformed Theological Seminary, Jackson, Mississippi

Living as we do in a generation so wrapped up in the present, we need tools, wisdom, and skill to impress upon the young of our day and in our churches—for our church youth are not immune to the follies of the age—that study of the Christian past is worthwhile and deeply rewarding. Here is one such tool. The authors are to be warmly commended for giving our young people fresh access to the riches of the Reformation, namely, God's saints who did such great exploits for the kingdom of the Lord Christ. These men and women were not perfect—and their flaws are not overlooked—but they were "sold out" for Christ and Scripture-truth. And in our degenerate day, we need such models held before our young people—just as what is done with the saints of Hebrews 11—to encourage them to run the Christian race and find at the very end the Lord Jesus—the sum and substance of all that is best in the history of the Reformation.

— Dr. Michael Haykin, Professor of Church History,
Southern Baptist Theological Seminary,
Louisville, Kentucky

Reformation
HEROES

Reformation HEROES

A Simple, Illustrated Overview of People
Who Assisted in the Great Work of the Reformation

Second Edition, with Study Questions

by Diana Kleyn with Joel R. Beeke

Illustrated by Caffy Whitney and others
Based on Richard Newton's *The Reformation and Its Heroes*

Reformation Heritage Books
Grand Rapids, Michigan

Published by
Reformation Heritage Books
3070 29th St. SE
Grand Rapids, MI 49512
616-977-0889
e-mail: orders@heritagebooks.org
website: www.heritagebooks.org

Printed in the United States of America
23 24 25 26 27 28/13 12 11 10 9 8 7

Library of Congress Cataloging-in-Publication Data

Kleyn, Diana.
Reformation heroes : a simple, illustrated overview of people who
assisted in the great work of the Reformation / by Diana Kleyn, with
Joel R. Beeke ; based on Richard Newton's The Reformation and its
heroes. — 2nd ed., with study questions.
     p. cm.
 Includes bibliographical references and index.
 ISBN 978-1-60178-064-5 (hardcover : alk. paper)
 1. Reformation—Biography. I. Beeke, Joel R., 1952- II. Newton,
Richard, 1813-1887. Reformation and its heroes. III. Title.
 BR315.K54 2009
 270.6092'2—dc22
 [B]
                                        2009017797

Cover artwork by Caffy Whitney: Hugh Latimer and Nicholas Ridley being burned at the stake.
For additional artwork by Caffy Whitney, see pages 52, 62, 87, 106, 108, 116, 130, 134, 151, 160, 168, 171, 183, 187.

For additional Reformed literature, request a free book list
from Reformation Heritage Books at the above address.

To my parents,

Liz and Murray Sommer,

who taught me to value the
scriptural doctrines
rediscovered during the
Reformation
— DK

With heartfelt appreciation to

Gary and Linda den Hollander,

quality and faithful friends for twenty-five years,
quiet and effective workers in God's kingdom,
a quick and meticulous typesetting/proofreading team
— JRB

Table of Contents

Introduction

Since the close of the New Testament history and the founding of the Christian church, no more-important event has taken place than the great Reformation of the sixteenth century. Martin Luther wrote his ninety-five theses almost five hundred years ago. This caused the Reformation to take firm root.

The Reformation did not happen all at once. As you read this book, you will learn that the Lord used some people to plant the seeds of church reform (see chapters 1–4) long before Martin Luther posted the ninety-five theses on the church doors of Wittenberg on October 31, 1517. The story of Luther and the ninety-five theses is well known (see chapter 5). We trust you will find it interesting and instructive to read about other events and people contributing to the Reformation—some well-known and others not so well-known—most of whom are Reformation heroes. They form the bulk of this book (see chapters 6–31). To provide a fuller picture of the many-sided Reformation, chapters are also included on the Anabaptist and Counter Reformation movements (see chapters 32–33). Finally, the book concludes with a brief summary of the influence of the Reformation in different areas of life.

Because this book is written for older children and teens, a glossary is included which can be found in Appendix E. Any time you are not sure of the meaning of a word, check the glossary in the back of the book. This will give you the meaning of the word in the context of the chapter you are reading. Also, most quotations have been simplified so that you can understand what was said, since much of the language of long ago was flowery and consisted of long sentences. The sources have been given, however, in case you would like to find the original quotes.

This book serves as an update, rewrite, and expansion of Richard Newton's *The Reformation and Its Heroes* (1897). We have also relied fairly extensively on the *Oxford Dictionary of National Biography* (2004) for our final authority on various issues concerning facts and dates. Additional sources are noted in the text and in the bibliography.

The purpose of this book is threefold: first, to teach a general knowledge of the Reformation and the events leading up to it. Second, because young people often lack helpful mentors and role models, we wish to set forth accurate life stories of Reformers who are still genuine heroes and helpful mentors for us today. Third, we hope you also gain a deeper respect for the doctrines of the Reformation, as well as for the freedom we enjoy to worship God according to Scripture. Many people suffered and even gave their lives so that the gospel would be proclaimed and read everywhere. We have a rich heritage and much to be thankful for. Let us pray that the God of the Reformation may once again reform and revive His church through the lives of godly men and women who live for His glory. May you, dear children and young people, be among them.

Finally, we wish to thank seminarian Maarten Kuivenhoven for his valuable editing of this book and his work on the thorough bibliography which is designed also for adults who wish to study the Reformation in greater depth; Michael Haykin for his helpful suggestions on Chapter 32 for this second edition; Sharla Kattenberg, Kate DeVries, Gary den Hollander, and Martha Fisher for their proofreading; Linda den Hollander for her typesetting; Caffy Whitney for her artwork on the cover and throughout the book; and Amy Zevenbergen for her cover design and work on the illustrations. We also thank our spouses, Chris Kleyn and Mary Beeke, for their love and patience as this book moved rather laboriously through several drafts. May God graciously bless them for their servant hearts and kindness.

— DK/JRB

~ 1 ~

Peter Waldo

(c. 1140 – c. 1217)

"How can I become righteous before God?"

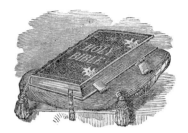

The city of Lyons, France

In the middle of the twelfth century, a wealthy merchant by the name of Peter Waldo (or Peter Valdes) lived in Lyons (Lē-ŏn), France. His house stood on a piece of land near the place where the Rhone[1] and the Saone[2] Rivers meet. The walls of the city were old and gray, the streets narrow and shadowed by tall houses on either side. The city of Lyons was famous for its commerce (buying and selling), so the wharves on both rivers were always busy. Lyons was most famous for its silk. In many homes, the clicking sound of the loom was heard. Numerous trees had been planted outside the city walls. On these trees, silk worms were bred, and the cocoons were used for making silk.

Waldo is awakened to spiritual life

Peter Waldo had been very successful in his business, but he was not selfish or greedy. He was known in Lyons for his kindness and generosity. One day, something happened that made him feel concerned not only for the physical well-being of the people in his city, but also for their spiritual well-being. Waldo was visiting some of his friends. After supper, one of the men suddenly fell down and died. This made a tremendous impression on Waldo.

---

1. The Rhone River is a major European river about 500 miles long. It begins at the Rhone Glacier in the Swiss Alps and flows through Lake Geneva, then southward through France to the Mediterranean Sea.

2. The Saone River is about 270 miles long. It begins in eastern France and joins the Rhone River at Lyons.

He began to seek for truth. He saw people living sinful lives. He noticed others trying to ease their guilty consciences by doing penance. Waldo also did penance for his sins, but it did not give him any peace. He asked the priests, "How can I become righteous before God?" The priests, however, could not answer this question. Waldo knew he was a sinner; his conscience told him so. He knew he was not ready to die, but when he asked the priests what he had to do to be saved, he was not satisfied with their answers.

He discovers the Bible

The Bible held the answers to Waldo's questions, but he did not own a Bible. Rich as he was, he did not have the greatest of treasures. The few copies of the Bible which did exist in those days were kept in libraries that common people were not allowed to visit. Besides, they were written in Latin, and few people could read even their own language, let alone Latin. Even if a person could read Latin, Bibles were very rare.

Soon afterward, Waldo read some books written by someone who lived shortly after the time of the apostles. In these books, he found many passages that quoted the New Testament. This brought him comfort, and he realized that the answers to all his questions were to be found in God's Word. Reading these passages of Scripture made him eager to buy the entire Bible.

After some time, Waldo was finally able to buy a Bible. It cost him a lot of money, but he didn't mind, for in its pages he found the way of salvation. He learned that he could only approach God through the Mediator, Jesus Christ, and that God requires a humble, contrite heart, as well as obedience. The Lord graciously moved Waldo to receive salvation on His terms. Before, he was confused and troubled; now he was peaceful and glad. He felt like a new man. The burden had been lifted from his soul. He had light and comfort, for he had found mercy through faith in Jesus Christ, the Savior of sinners.

Poverty

Waldo heard about a young man named Alexis. This young man had been very rich, but he had given all his riches to the poor. This young man had done what Jesus told the rich young ruler to do in Matthew 19:21: "If thou wilt be perfect, go and sell that thou hast, and give to the poor, and thou shalt have treasure in heaven: and come and follow me." Waldo believed that God wanted him to do the same thing, so he gave his money and possessions to the poor and lived a simple life.

Concern for others

Waldo had been known for his kindness to all, but now he became more concerned about the souls of the people. The Bible had taught him how he must be saved, and now he longed to tell others this good news. He observed the people, who were deceived by the priests, trying to pay for their sins without the Lord Jesus Christ. Seeing this made him weep. He began to visit people, telling them what God says in His Word. He told them that God requires only repentance and faith in His Son; their good works could not save them. He urged them to come to Jesus by faith and have their sins washed away in His blood.

Waldo held many meetings with the poor in their cottages. He visited the sick and the dying, and held meetings in the woods with people who were as confused as he had been. In his sermons, Waldo taught them the truth and spoke out against the worldliness of the Roman Catholic priests. He prayed with the people and gave them food and clothing if they needed it. He was so concerned for their souls as well as their physical needs, it is no wonder the people loved him.

The Bible translated into French

Still, there was something that Waldo longed for. He wished that the Bible would be translated into the language of the people. Very few people in France could read or understand Latin, which was the language of the Bible as well as all church services. The church did not want the Bible to be written in the language of the people. They told the people that only the priests were wise enough to understand the Bible and that the common people wouldn't be able to understand it anyway. Waldo disagreed. He believed that the people should be able to read the Bible and that as many people as possible should have their own Bibles. We are not sure if Waldo himself translated the Bible into French, or if he hired people to do it for him. Most likely, he and some others worked on it together.

It was a huge undertaking, but after having read the Bible himself, Waldo was convinced that it was necessary. Finally, it was finished. This was the first translation of the Bible into a modern language. What a blessed gift this was

Peter Waldo teaching

to the people of France! Still, it could not be distributed to very many people, because the printing press had not yet been invented. Each copy had to be handwritten! This took many long hours, and that meant that a complete copy of the Bible was very expensive. Most people could not afford this, but Waldo was so eager to teach the people the way of salvation that he freely gave away many copies of the New Testament and separate books of the Bible. Many people read the Bible for the first time in their lives because of his efforts.

The poor men of Lyons

Waldo not only had the Bible translated, but he also formed a missionary society. Many people who had been brought to love the Savior through the work of the Holy Spirit were sent out, two by two, into the area all around Lyons. They carried their books with them, even venturing into other countries. Many were led to a knowledge of the truth through the humble work of these "poor men of Lyons," as they were called. These poor men of Lyons took a vow of poverty. Waldo believed it was beneficial to be poor, as Jesus Himself was when He lived on earth.

These men visited all kinds of people. They would travel as peddlers, carrying a box of things to sell. Peddlers were people who traveled the countryside with various items they had for sale. When they entered people's homes, especially those of the rich, they would tell them they had something for sale that was more valuable than anything else. Of course, people would want to know what it was, and the peddler would show them a Bible or a New Testament, or even just one book of the Bible. Then they would explain why this book was so valuable. In this way, the Bible found a place in the homes and hearts of many people.

The church opposes Waldo

You must not think that the pope and the priests thought Waldo and the poor men of Lyons were doing a good deed. In 1179, Waldo sent some of his poor men to the pope to ask for permission to preach. The pope granted them permission to preach if the archbishop also agreed. When Waldo asked the archbishop for permission to continue preaching, the archbishop responded, "If you continue to preach, I will have you condemned as a heretic and burned at the stake."

"How can I be silent in a matter that concerns the souls of men?" replied Waldo boldly. The archbishop repeated his stern warning and let him go.

When the archbishop heard that Waldo continued to teach the people, he sent some of his men to arrest him. These men were afraid of the citizens of Lyons, however, for they knew how much they loved Waldo. For three years, the people of Lyons hid him.

In 1184, Pope Lucius III anathemized Peter Waldo and the poor men of Lyons, which means he proclaimed that they were accursed. He ordered the archbishop of Lyons to stop Waldo from preaching and giving out Bibles to the people. The archbishop was eager to obey. Waldo fled from the city because it was no longer safe for him. He went from place to place, and everywhere he went, he taught people about the Bible. God blessed his efforts, and many people were saved.

Waldo and his friends were treated badly by their enemies. In those days, people were especially superstitious, and they did not trust these men who taught that the Roman Catholic Church was wrong. So they called them "sorcerers" (wizards) or "tur-lupines" (people who live with wolves). The term "poor men of Lyons" came to mean something bad. Often Waldo and his men could find no place to spend the night and had to sleep in the forest. What the author of the letter to the Hebrews wrote about the prophets can also be said of them: "They wandered about in sheepskins and goatskins; being destitute, afflicted, tormented; (of whom the world was not worthy:) they wandered in deserts, and in mountains, and in dens and caves of the earth" (Hebrews 11:37b–38).

In 1194, another pope, Alfonso II, made a proclamation that anyone who protected, fed, or even listened to Waldo's followers would be punished. Some of these Christians were burned at the stake, but even while they were being burned, they praised God for the privilege of working and suffering for Him who had suffered and died on the cross for them. Once, thirty-five Christian men and women were burned in one fire, and, another time, eighteen were burned at the stake. Hundreds of Christians were killed for their faith. God's truth, however, cannot be burned or destroyed. God Himself makes sure of that. In spite of the anger of their enemies, Waldo and his missionaries spread God's Word. People were converted, and many Bibles and New Testaments were sold.

The Waldensians

Because of fierce persecution, many of the poor men of Lyons fled to other countries, and so the gospel spread, just as it had when the apostles were scattered during the persecution in Jerusalem. Trying to find safety, some of Waldo's followers later joined with a group of people who had never agreed with the Roman Catholic Church. They shared Waldo's beliefs and were willing to work together in spreading the gospel during this time of persecution. This group of followers was almost unknown to the world, a "little flock" dwelling alone in the lovely, quiet valleys of Piedmont. Sometimes persecutors would seek them out to imprison or kill some of them, but there was always a "remnant" that continued to be faithful to the truth. This remnant began to be called "the Waldensians" (or "the Vaudois") after Peter Waldo (Valdes).

In spite of being pursued, Waldo's enemies did not succeed in killing him. God protected him so that he was able to travel to several countries to preach the gospel. He finally went to live in Bohemia, where he died peacefully around the year 1217.

After Waldo's death, the Waldensians increasingly organized themselves apart from the Roman Catholic Church by means of informal meetings in different areas. They ignored the church's decrees and appointed their own ministers. They taught that sacraments administered by priests who lived in sin were not valid. They also refused to pray for the dead and to worship saints and relics. And

The Waldensian Seal

they refused to take oaths or to fight in wars. In these ways, they distanced themselves from both church and society.

The Waldensians grew rapidly, especially among the poor. They spread first throughout southern France and Spain, and then into Germany. Persecution in these countries, however, forced them into the mountainous valleys of Italy. Though their numbers dwindled in France and Spain, they soon spread from Germany into Bohemia, Poland, and Hungary. In Bohemia, Waldensian preachers later became associated with the followers of John Huss, called the Hussites. The major difference between the two movements is that the Waldensians rejected the church's authority whereas the Hussites accepted that authority in principle though they disagreed with much of what the church said and did.

The efforts of Waldo and his followers were the seeds of the Reformation. Five years after the Reformation was born in 1517, the Waldensians made contact with Martin Luther. A little later they approached the southern German and Swiss Reformers. In 1532, they invited some Protestant representatives, including William Farel and Anthony Saunier, to attend one of their more official gatherings, similar to what we would call a synod or an assembly. At that gathering, they adopted a new Confession of Faith, which included the doctrine of predestination. They also cut all ties with the Roman Catholic Church and decided that ministers could marry.

For a while, the Waldensians enjoyed some measure of freedom to worship. During that time, they built many places of worship, which they called "temples." When Carlo Emmanuel II, Duke of Savoy, attacked them in the seventeenth century, Oliver Cromwell intervened on their behalf. This provided them about twenty years of liberty. In 1685, however, when the Edict of Nantes, which allowed for religious liberty, was revoked, many Waldensians were forced to cross the mountains under terrible conditions to find refuge in Switzerland. Though their outward conditions improved in the eighteenth century, it was not until 1848 that Charles Albert[1] gave them real religious and political freedom.

---

1. Charles Albert (Italian: Carlo Alberto Amedeo di Savoia; 1798–1849) was the King of Sardinia from 1831 to 1849. Sardinia is the second largest island in the Mediterranean Sea (after Sicily). Charles Albert was the son of Carlo Emanuele, Duke of Savoy (1770–1800).

Today, the membership of the Waldensians numbers about 20,000. Since 1920, they have trained their ministers at their own theological school in Rome. Their theology, however, is not well thought out, and it departs from biblical, Reformed theology at several points. For example, today most Waldensians embrace the Arminian doctrine of free will.

God touched one man, Peter Waldo, who in turn was graciously used to touch the hearts of hundreds of others. His obedience to God's calling was a great blessing to many people.

~ 2 ~

John Wycliffe

(c. 1324–1384)

Wycliffe was certainly one of the most important forerunners of the Reformation. This is why he is referred to as the Morning Star of the Reformation. His influence on the Reformers was very great.

The morning star of the Reformation

Before the sun rises in the morning to drive away the darkness of the night, a bright star often shines beautifully in the eastern sky. We call it the morning star. It tells us that the sun will soon appear above the horizon. The Reformation was like the sun rising on the church after the long night. John Wycliffe was born during a time of great spiritual darkness. He has been called the morning star of the Reformation because God used him to shine rays of light into the spiritual darkness of England and much of Europe. He was not actually one of the Reformers, but he, like Peter Waldo, helped prepare the way for the Reformation.

Wycliffe's birth

John Wycliffe was born in a village called Ipreswel, near the town of Richmond, in Yorkshire in about 1324, almost two hundred years before the Reformation took place.

His last name has been spelled many different ways and is pronounced either Wî-klĭf or Wī-klĭf.

The Plague

In 1349, when he was about twenty-five years old, the plague swept through England. This fearful plague started in Asia and spread westwards across Europe. By August of that year, it had reached England. Because of the dark blotches on the sick person's skin, it was called "the Black Death." People were terrified of this sickness. The plague was responsible for the death of about one third of the population. It left a deep impression on young Wycliffe. Merle d'Aubigne records, "This visitation of the Almighty sounded like the trumpet of the judgment day in the heart of Wycliffe." Desperately, he studied the Word of God, seeking refuge from the judgment to come. He spent hours in prayer, asking God to show him what to do with his life. He mentions the plague several times in his writings.

His studies and work as a minister and a debater

Wycliffe studied at Merton College at Oxford, first as a student and then as a teacher. He had many talents and gifts and quickly gained a reputation of being an excellent scholar. At Merton College, there was a godly professor named Thomas Bradwardine. This professor taught that God alone is able to save men from their sins by His sovereign grace. This teaching was blessed to young Wycliffe's heart. He began to love the Scriptures and studied them gladly. Eventually, he became a doctor of theology in 1372.

After entering the ministry, he moved three times. His last move was to a little town called Lutterworth. Here he spent the last ten years of his life, and this is the place with which his name is most often connected. Lutterworth is a small market town in the central part of England, about eighty miles from London. It stands on a hill overlooking the Swift River.

Wycliffe was a great preacher. He studied the Bible very carefully and loved to preach the gospel. He preached with a clarity, faithfulness, and power that were unusual in those days. Crowds came to hear him. His great piety gave power to what he said. His preaching came to the attention of the king, Edward III, who was glad to hear him. It was not unusual for the pope and the king to be at odds with one another, and in Wycliffe's day it was no different. It used to be that the king was required to collect money from the church and then send it to Rome, where the pope lived. When King Edward III heard that Wycliffe taught that the king should not have to do this anymore, he was pleased. He supported Wycliffe.

Wycliffe was an effective debater as well as a preacher. A debater is someone who debates—that is, he discusses something with someone who has a different point of view from his own. The monks, priests, and friars of the church went around the country teaching the people all kinds of wrong doctrines. Wycliffe bravely debated with these men whenever he met with them. He also wrote many tracts about the errors of the church. His friends copied out these tracts and gave them to many people.

Wycliffe speaks against the monks and friars

At this time in England, there were many monks and friars. Monks were men who lived alone or separate from other people. Their homes were called monasteries, where a large number of monks lived together. "Friars" means "brothers." They were monks who were dependent on begging for their food. Instead of working for an income, they dressed as beggars and traveled all over the country, forcing their way into the houses of rich and poor, living without paying for things, and taking all the money they could get. They were supposed to live in poverty and be humble, as those who are "poor in spirit" and "the meek of the earth," but they spent so much time begging that they actually became wealthy. They wore expensive clothes and ate fine food. Their homes were beautiful, and they did not care to help the poor. Like the Pharisees, they pretended to be better and holier than others, although their lives were full of evil. They taught that those who belonged to their order, or group, were sure to be saved.

When Wycliffe saw the behavior of the friars, his heart was grieved. The best way he knew to oppose them was to write a book against them. He used some harsh words when he described the friars, calling them "the pests of society, the enemies of religion, and the promoters of every crime." The friars, of course, were very angry when they read this and wanted to have him sentenced to death. But Wycliffe continued to write and preach against them. He worked so hard that his health began to suffer.

Wycliffe summoned to appear before the Roman Catholic Church

The Roman Catholic Church was alarmed at the accusations against their clergy. Wycliffe openly spoke against the pope and against the sins of the church. The church was afraid the people would believe Wycliffe. They charged Wycliffe with heresy and summoned him to appear in St. Paul's Cathedral in London. A huge crowd gathered to watch the proceedings

Begging Friars

on February 19, 1377. Two influential men accompanied Wycliffe into the cathedral: Lord Percy, marshal of England, and John of Gaunt, Duke of Lancaster. The Roman Catholic clergy brought many false accusations against Wycliffe. They wanted to get authority to stop him from preaching and have him imprisoned or put to death. Angry words were exchanged between these men and the Roman Catholic clergy. The crowd joined in the uproar that followed. The two men who were with Wycliffe escaped during the commotion. Wycliffe's case was dismissed, although he was warned not to preach against the Roman Catholic Church. Wycliffe, however, continued his preaching. Boldly, he stated that the pope was antichrist. The pope claimed to be the supreme ruler of the church on earth. Wycliffe said that such a claim was against the Scriptures: only Christ is King of His church.

In 1377, Wycliffe was denounced as a heretic and was summoned to another meeting in London. This time Wycliffe was not accompanied by his influential friends, but there were many people present who favored his teachings. They surrounded the church in protest and forced their way into the meeting, determined to protect their beloved pastor and friend. In the midst of this uproar, a message from Joan, the queen-mother, silenced the men who wanted to harm him. Joan, mother of Richard II and mother-in-law of Anne of Bohemia (of whom you will read in the next chapter) greatly admired Wycliffe and his teachings. She sent a message to stop the meeting. She forbade them to have this meeting and stated that Wycliffe was not the detestable heretic they said he was. The men were afraid to proceed with the meeting, and Wycliffe was free to go. The enemies of God's Word could not harm Wycliffe.

Wycliffe resolved more than ever to spread the gospel wherever he could. He endured many great trials. The times in which he lived were very unsettled and troubled. The bishops and other leading persons in the church disliked him very much because he preached against their errors.

Illness

Once, Wycliffe became very ill, and it seemed as if he was going to die. The Roman Catholic clergy was glad to hear that their enemy might die. Some of the "Begging Friars" came to see him. Wycliffe had said many severe things against them, and they asked him to take back all that he had said. They tried to frighten him by telling him that God would punish him eternally by sending him to hell for his heresy. He listened to them quietly for some time, then he

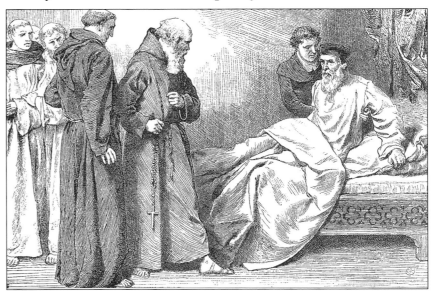

Wycliffe and the Friars

motioned to his friends to help him sit up. Looking intently at the friars, he said, "I shall not die, but live and declare the errors and sins of you wicked men more than ever!" Alarmed at his courage, the friars fled from the room.

His teachings

Wycliffe was born at a time when the power of the Roman Catholic Church was very great. There was no true preaching of the Word of God. Most people never saw a Bible, let alone one written in English, and even if they had seen one, they probably would not have been able to read it.[1] Even many of the wealthy could not write their own names. Often only one person in a whole town could read and write. It is easy to understand, then, why there was such little knowledge of the truth of God's Word.

The priests taught that people could earn forgiveness of sins by doing penance, buying indulgences (promises of forgiveness), or going on pilgrimages. In every area of life, the church exercised enormous control. Wycliffe taught that a sinful man could not save himself and that mercy was only to be found through faith in the blood and righteousness of Jesus Christ. The priests taught that images ought to be worshiped, but Wycliffe said that the worship of images was idolatry and that saints and angels were not to be prayed to, for "there is but one mediator between God and men" (1 Timothy 2:5). Because Wycliffe so boldly opposed the doctrines of the church, the priests and bishops hated Wycliffe.

---

1. Margaret Shand (http://www.epc.org.au/start/literature/bb/wycliffe. html), drawn from "John Wycliffe," in *The Burning Bush* (Sydney: Evangelical Presbyterian Church of Australia, 1998).

In his own village, however, he was much loved. He was often seen with a portion of his handwritten Bible under his arm, his staff in hand, visiting the people in order to share the Word of God with them. Rich and poor were glad when he came to visit. He was the friend of all; he was ready to teach, comfort, and pray with anyone in his community. Continually he sought the good of his flock and for this the people loved him.

Wycliffe spoke against the doctrine of transubstantiation. This doctrine teaches that in the Lord's Supper, the bread and wine actually change into the body and blood of Jesus. Wycliffe said this was not true. How could it be that people who partake of the Lord's Supper are actually eating and drinking the body and blood of the Lord Jesus Christ? Wycliffe taught that Christ's body and blood are *represented* by the bread and the wine. This "new" doctrine taught by Wycliffe made some people uncomfortable and angry. Even King Edward III did not want to support Wycliffe anymore. He thought Wycliffe had gone too far. Many of the teachers, professors, and students at Oxford University also disagreed with Wycliffe, choosing rather to adhere to the doctrines of the Roman Catholic Church.

The Earthquake Council

In 1381, the peasants revolted. Wycliffe was blamed for this uprising, although he had nothing to do with it. He was simply teaching the people about God's Word; he was not teaching rebellion and warfare. Because of all the unrest, another meeting was called. It became known as the Earthquake Council, because an earthquake occurred while the meeting was taking place. Wycliffe's friends believed God was showing His anger toward His enemies and hoped

Wycliffe tried at Oxford

it would help thwart his enemies from carrying out their evil plans. However, the meeting proceeded, and Wycliffe's doctrines and writings were condemned anyway.

Summoned again

In November 1382, Wycliffe was summoned before a council in Oxford. The university that had educated him now turned on him. He bravely spoke against the errors of the church. Wycliffe was weak due to his life of trials and ill health, but he was not afraid to speak the truth boldly. When he was finished, he simply said, "The truth shall prevail!" He then turned and left. No one dared to stop him.

Fewer and fewer people supported Wycliffe as he continued preaching and teaching. He must have been lonely at times, but he clung to his God and continued boldly in his attacks on the errors of the Roman Catholic Church. He used strong language that offended even some of his friends. In speaking about the Roman Catholic doctrine of transubstantiation, he said, "How can you, O priest, who are only a man, make your Maker? What? The thing that grows in the fields today—the ear of wheat which you pluck today, shall that be God tomorrow?[2] As you cannot make the works which He made, how can you make Him who made the works? Woe to the adulterous generation that believes the words of the pope rather than of the gospel!"

He translates the Bible into English

Wycliffe's greatest work was his translation of the Scriptures. Before his time, there was no complete English translation of the Bible. Parts of the Bible had been translated into English, but not the complete Bible. Wycliffe believed every person should have a copy of the Bible. Two hundred years after Waldo translated the Bible into French, God helped Wycliffe and a team of academic helpers translate the Bible from Latin into English. It was a very great work. Imagine copying out by hand the Bible as we know it today! With much prayer and patience, Wycliffe and his friends kept working on translating God's blessed Word for the people of England in their own language. As he worked, Wycliffe found instruction and comfort for his soul while providing for the spiritual good of many others. Finally, in 1380, the last verse of the New Testament was translated.

Perhaps you would like to try to read a passage of what Wycliffe's translation would have looked like. The people at that time spoke very different English from the English we speak today. To compare this passage with the one in your Bible, look at John 5:2–9.

and in ierusalem is a waischynge place / that
in ebrewe is named bethsaida / and hath fyue
porchis / in these laie a greete multitude of sike
men / blinde / crokid / and drie / abidynge the
mouynge of the watir / for the aungel of the lord
came doun certeyn tymes in to the watir / and
the watir was moued / and he that first cam
down in to the sistterne aftir the mouynge of the
watir was made hool of what euer sikenesse he
was holden / and a man was there hauynge eiyte
and thritti yeer his sikeness / and whanne ihesus
hadde seen hym liggynge and hadde knowen
/ that he hadde myche tyme / he seith to him /
wolt thou be made hool / the sike man answerid

---

2. Wycliffe was referring to the wafer baked from wheat, which the Roman Catholic Church taught became the actual body of Christ during celebration of the Lord's Supper.

to hym / lord i haue no man that whanne the
watir is moued to putte me in to the cisterne /
for the while i come / another goith doun bifor
me / ihesus seith to hym / rise up / take thi bed
and go / and anoon the man was made hool / and
tooke up his bedde and wente forth / and it was
saboth in that dai /

Did you notice that no capital letters are used and that the spellings of words are not only different from ours, but not always consistent? If you were to hear someone speak English as the people spoke it in the fourteenth century, you would hardly be able to understand it. Wycliffe's friend, Nicholas Hereford, helped with the translation of the Old Testament for the last three years of Wycliffe's life, and then he supervised the task until it was completed around the year 1388, more than three years after Wycliffe's death.

The Roman Catholic Church, of course, was not pleased with either the translation or the distribution of God's Word to the people. They said that it was casting pearls before swine when the common people read the Scriptures. They believed it was heresy to speak the words of Scripture in the English language. They told the people that they must trust the church's interpretation of the Bible rather than their own.

The Lollards

In addition to preaching and writing a large number of books on a great variety of subjects ranging from theology to philosophy and logic, Wycliffe trained a large number of men to help him in carrying on his call for reform. These men were also poor, like the poor men of Lyons, and went

Wycliffe and the Lollards

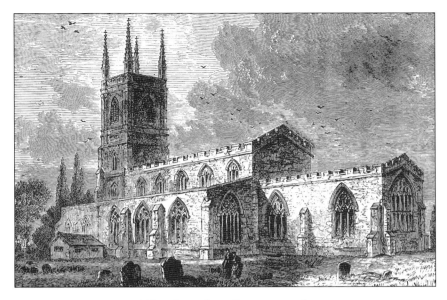

The church at Lutterworth

all over the country, preaching the gospel in churchyards, at fairs, in marketplaces, in the streets, and wherever they could get people to come and hear them. Sometimes these men were called Lollards. In 1401, the Lollards were condemned by the pope as heretics, and some were burned at the stake.

His death

In spite of all his trials and persecutions, Wycliffe lived until the age of sixty. While he was preaching in his church at Lutterworth, he was seized with paralysis, which means he was not able to move. Today, the doctors might have called it a stroke. The attack was so severe that he was unable to speak and was utterly helpless. He lived two days after this; then he died a calm and peaceful death on December 31, 1384.

Wycliffe was buried in the graveyard of his church at Lutterworth. Forty-four years after his death, his enemies dug up his bones, burned them to ashes, and threw the ashes into the Swift River. Afterward, someone said that just as Wycliffe's ashes were thrown into the river that eventually flows into the ocean, so the Word of God which he preached and translated will make its way all over the world. "Surely the wrath of man shall praise thee: the remainder of wrath shalt thou restrain" (Psalm 76:10).

Though he never came to a clear understanding of the Reformation doctrine of justification by faith alone, Wycliffe was certainly one of the most important forerunners of the Reformation. This is why he is referred to as the Morning Star of the Reformation. His influence on the Reformers was very great. He especially influenced John Huss through the Lollards and the call for reform in Bohemia. The authority of the Bible, the importance of predestination, and the biblical doctrine of the Lord's Supper are several areas in particular that lie close to the heart of the Reformation. Wycliffe's contributions in teaching and writing about these doctrines can scarcely be overestimated.

Wycliffe's writings are still being studied today. The Wycliffe Society was founded in 1882 for the purpose of translating his writings into English. Between 1883 and 1921, they translated thirty-five of his books, but they never finished the task.

~ 3 ~

Anne of Bohemia

(c. 1366–1394)

Queen of Richard II

Wycliffe was delighted to hear that the queen loved to read and study the Scriptures. He compared her to Mary, who sat at Jesus' feet to listen to what He had to say.

Her family

Anne of Bohemia[1] lived during the time of John Wycliffe and was a help to him and the Reformation. She was the eldest daughter of the Emperor Charles IV and the sister of King Wenceslaus, King of Bohemia and Emperor of Germany. Her mother was the fourth wife of Charles IV; the daughter of Beleslaus, Duke of Pomerania; and the granddaughter of Cassimir the Great, King of Poland. Anne was born in Prague, Bohemia, around the year 1366.

Her youth

Anne was taught the truths of Scripture from her youth. In Bohemia at that time, there were several ministers to whom the people listened eagerly. Their names were John Melice, Conrad Strickna, and Matthias Janovius. Anne was an intelligent young lady and asked many questions about the Scriptures and the truths in its pages. The Lord blessed her studies, and she not only learned much about the Scriptures and the errors of the church, but she loved the Author of the Scriptures.

Her marriage to Richard II

Richard II was the son of Edward, Prince of Wales. Sometimes he was called the Black Prince, because he wore dark-colored armor. His mother was Joan, of whom you read in the previous chapter. Richard was born in Bourdeaux,

---

1. Bohemia is in the present-day Czech Republic.

France, in 1367. His father died in 1376 and his grandfather the following year, so Richard became king at the young age of ten.

When he was thirteen years old, he heard about Anne of Bohemia and thought she would be a good wife for him. In January 1382, when they were fifteen years old, Anne and Richard were married in St. Stephen's Chapel, Westminster. Although she had never met Richard, Anne had heard that the writings of John Wycliffe had begun a revival in England, so that fact encouraged her to go there to marry King Richard.

Anne as queen

Anne took friends and servants who were true believers with her to England. The people of England loved her immediately. She was gentle and kind. She tried to help the poor, the orphans, and widows. It is said that as many as six thousand people ate at the royal table every day, most of whom were poor! She thought about how Jesus had compassion on the crowds and fed them miraculously so that they wouldn't be hungry. Christians want to be like their Master, so that is why Anne wanted to help the needy. It is no wonder the people called her "good Queen Anne." King Richard was pleased with this kind queen and loved her very much.

In England, Anne continued to read and study the Scriptures. She had copies of the gospels in three languages: Bohemian, English, and Latin. In those days, even a page of Scripture was a treasure. Few people had ever seen a page or a book of the Bible. The young queen was happy to have the gospels in these three languages.

Queen Anne was not afraid to talk about the Bible. She once spoke with Arundel, the Archbishop of York, and told him how she loved to read the Bible. Arundel, like most Roman Catholics in those days, did not appreciate the Bible and did not want people to read it. He was alarmed to hear that the queen owned copies of the gospels which she was reading, but he could say nothing since she was the queen of England.

Her friendship with Wycliffe

Wycliffe was delighted to hear that the queen loved to read and study the Scriptures. He compared her to Mary, who sat at Jesus' feet to listen to what He had to say. He was encouraged that she was reading an English translation of the gospels.

Queen Anne gave her protection to Wycliffe, since he had many enemies. Often she would go to her husband and gently plead with him on his behalf. She would read passages of Scripture to him, such as Matthew 23:34–35: "Wherefore, behold, I send unto you prophets, and wise men, and scribes: and some of them ye shall kill and crucify; and some of them shall ye scourge in your synagogues, and persecute them from city to city: that upon you may come all the righteous blood shed upon the earth, from the blood of righteous Abel unto the blood of Zacharias son of Barachias, whom ye slew between the temple and the altar." King Richard did not want to be guilty of killing one of God's prophets, so he listened to the words of his loving wife. Sadly, Wycliffe lived only three years after Queen Anne came to live in England.

Her early death

In the spring of 1394, Queen Anne became ill of the plague. She weakened rapidly, and on June 7, she died. She was only twenty-seven years old. The King was devastated, and the people mourned deeply. It is said that Richard destroyed Sheen Palace where she had died. She is buried at Westminster, where Richard had a beautiful tomb made. Richard had a life of trouble, losing his crown and being imprisoned. If only he had fled to the Savior, he would have had a place of refuge! He died in 1400. Some years later he was buried beside his beloved Anne.

The Lord had His divine purpose in Queen Anne's life as well as in her death. After the young queen's death, many of her friends and servants returned to Bohemia. They took with them the translations of the gospels and some of the writings of Wycliffe that had been so treasured by Queen Anne. Some of these friends and servants had known the queen since she was a child and had learned many things about the Bible from her. Some of her friends remained in England to attend Oxford University, telling others what they had heard and learned from Queen Anne. The friends who returned to Bohemia told the people there about their beloved queen, and what she had taught them from Scripture. So the seeds of the Reformation were spread throughout Bohemia and England with the blessing of the Lord.

~ 4 ~

John Huss

❖

(1372–1415)

In the midst of all his trouble and suffering, he found peace and comfort in his Savior.

Peter Waldo lived in France; John Wycliffe lived in England. Through Queen Anne, the Lord brought the seeds of the Reformation to Bohemia, the same country in which John Huss was born.

Huss's birth and education

John Huss was born about the year 1372, which means he was about twelve years old when Wycliffe died. He was born in the little town of Husinetz, in southern Bohemia. His father died when he was just a little boy. Although his mother was poor, she was determined to send him to school. Through God's providence, a nobleman kindly paid for Huss's education. Later, Huss became a servant to one of the masters, or professors, at the Charles University of Prague. In return for serving the master, he was allowed to borrow his books. He made good use of this privilege and studied diligently. When he was twenty-six years old, Huss became a priest and a professor of divinity at the University of Prague, which was an unusually high and honored position for such a young man.

He is converted

At the time, Huss was still a Roman Catholic and dedicated to the teachings of the church. In God's gracious providence, someone gave him some of Wycliffe's writings. His interest was aroused, and he began to study the Bible. He soon discovered that Wycliffe was right in his teachings, and Huss embraced most of them. He became troubled about his sins and spent much of his time studying the Scriptures and reading the works of Wycliffe in search of the solution. The Holy Spirit opened his eyes to see the Savior, who is the only remedy for sin. By faith, he trusted in the sacrifice of Christ Jesus, and his sins were forgiven.

He becomes a preacher

In 1402, Huss was asked to be the preacher at Bethlehem Chapel in Prague, which became the center of the Czech reform movement. Like Wycliffe, Huss began to preach and write against the errors he saw in the church. His clear, powerful preaching was easily understood. People began to consider seriously what he was telling them, and many believed his teachings.

Friends of the Roman Catholic Church became alarmed. In 1403, a public meeting was called for the purpose of condemning the doctrines of Wycliffe. Huss and his friends tried to prevent this, but they did not succeed. Two groups were now formed: one was made up of the friends of Huss, and the other of the friends of the pope and the church. This was the beginning of pre-Reformation times in that part of the world.

Opposition

The bishops tried to stop Huss from preaching, but the Queen of Bohemia was his friend and attended his church. She and her husband protected Huss. The bishops wrote to

John Huss

the pope, accusing Huss of being a heretic. In 1409, the pope told the archbishop of Prague to root out heresy in his area, so the archbishop forbade Huss from preaching and ordered that his books be destroyed. The Roman Catholics collected a pile of about two hundred books of Huss and Wycliffe and made a bonfire with them. Huss continued to preach, however, and plenty of books survived, so that the work went on in spite of all the efforts of the pope and the bishops.

The leaders of the church tried many different plans to stop Huss from spreading the gospel. In 1410, they excommunicated him, but Huss boldly continued to attack papal politics. The church put one of his friends in prison as a warning to the courageous preacher. When Huss spoke against the sale of indulgences, the pope ordered all public worship services to stop as long as Huss remained in the city. So Huss left Prague in 1412. Instead, he preached in towns and villages, in fields and forests, so that the gospel was spread even further, reaching the ears of people who did not normally attend church.

Summoned to Constance

When the pope heard that the doctrines of Huss were spreading rapidly, he attempted to stop them in another way. He wrote to the emperor of Germany and told him to call a council of bishops and educated men to meet in Constance. The emperor ordered Huss to appear before this council. Huss's friends would not let him go until the emperor gave

The city of Constance

him a "safe conduct," which was a promise that he would be protected and allowed to return home in safety whatever the result of the trial might be.

Relying on this promise of the German emperor, Huss went to the council in the fall of 1414. When he left his friends, he spoke to them one last time: "You know that I have taught you the truth. Continue in the truth, and trust in the mercy of God. Beware of false teachers. I am going to this great assembly, where the Lord will give me grace to endure trials, imprisonment, and if it be His will, even the most dreadful death. Whatever happens, our joy will be great when we meet in the everlasting mansions."

Imprisoned

When Huss arrived at Constance, he sent a message to the pope that he was ready to meet all the charges laid against him. The pope's response was to cast Huss into a dark and filthy dungeon by the side of a river. The dungeon was part of a Dominican monastery located on the Rhine River. How could the pope break his word like that? Hadn't he promised Huss that he would be safe? The pope, however, told himself that it is no sin to break a promise to a heretic.

Some time later, Huss was examined by the council. He appeared thin and sickly because of his sufferings in the miserable dungeon. He was not given a fair trial; he was treated as a condemned heretic and sent to another prison. During the day he was kept in chains in his cell, and at night he was fastened to the wall. For at least six months he was kept prisoner in this castle. During this time, his enemies tried to force him to say that he had been wrong in his teachings. But Huss's answer was, "God will not permit me to deny His truth." In the midst of all his trouble and suffering, he found peace and comfort in his Savior.

Condemned

On July 6, 1415, Huss was summoned before the council once again. The emperor looked regal and distinguished with his crown on his head and his scepter carried before him. Around him stood his princes and nobles; the cardinals and bishops were there to pronounce the sentence of death on the prisoner. They placed Huss on a high platform so that he might be seen by the whole assembly. A band of soldiers stood guard around him. He knew that his life was in danger, but he also knew that his God and Savior would hear and

They mocked Huss, placing a paper crown on his head.

all my confidence and hope in God my Savior. I know He will never take from me the cup of salvation, but that by His grace I shall drink of it today in His kingdom."

The hearts of these nobles and clergy had no pity for their suffering prisoner. They mocked him, placing on his head a paper crown, about two feet high, on which were painted three devils, as well as the words, "Arch-heretic," which means "greatest enemy of the truth." Huss calmly answered his tormenters, "My Lord Jesus bore a painful crown of thorns for me, a poor sinner, and died the shameful death of the cross. Therefore, for His sake, I will cheerfully bear this lighter crown."

"Now we deliver your soul to Satan and to hell!" cried the bishops.

"But I," responded Huss, "commit my soul to my gracious Lord, Jesus Christ."

Then he was led out to the place of execution in a meadow outside the city. Eight hundred soldiers guarded him—a large army to guard a poor, unarmed man! The crowd of people was so large that the guards had to shut the gates of the city, so that only some of the people could leave. Everyone wanted a glimpse of this "heretic."

Huss was calm and even joyful on the way to his death. As he passed the archbishop's palace, seeing his enemies burning copies of the fifteen books he had written, he sadly surveyed their useless attempts to stop the spreading of God's Word. A little further on, he cried out, "O Jesus Christ, the Son of the living God, have pity upon me," and other similar prayers. The people who followed began to say to each other, "We don't know what the teachings of this man are, but all we hear from him are holy words and Christian prayers!"

help him. Falling on his knees, he prayed for strength that he might be faithful to the end.

After his enemies accused him of heresy, sentence was passed upon him that he should be burned. His answer was a prayer: "O Lord God," he cried, "I beseech Thee, for Thy mercy's sake, pardon all my enemies, for Thou knowest that I have been falsely accused, and unjustly condemned. But do Thou forgive this sin."

Again Huss's enemies loudly accused him, calling him "Judas, the betrayer of the Lord." To this he replied, "I place

When he arrived at the spot where he would die, Huss fell on his knees, lifted up his eyes to heaven, and praying aloud, repeated these words: "Into Thine hands I commit my spirit; Thou hast redeemed me, O Lord God of truth." After a short pause, he began to pray again, "Lord Jesus, I cheerfully suffer this terrible and cruel death, for the sake of Thy holy gospel, and the preaching of Thy sacred Word. Do Thou forgive my enemies the crime they are committing."

The executioners made him walk three times around the pile of wood. Then Huss asked if he could speak to his jailers, and when they allowed him to do so he said, "I thank you most sincerely for all the kindness you have shown me, for you have behaved to me more as brothers than as guards. Know also that my trust in my Savior is unshaken, for whose sake I willingly suffer this death, being assured that I shall be with Him this day in paradise."

His death

The executioners then took him and bound him to the stake with wet ropes. They fastened around his neck a rusty

John Huss being burned at the stake

chain. Next, they heaped straw and wood around him up to his neck. The pile was lighted, and the flames began to wrap around the body of the martyr. Instead of screams of agony, the people heard singing. In the midst of his pain, John Huss was singing praises to God! So this faithful servant of God entered into eternal glory.

After his death, Huss's enemies gathered up his ashes and threw them into the Rhine River to show their hatred toward him. Huss's friends were outraged at this and decided to go to war against them. The people of Bohemia gathered under the leadership of a man named Ziska. This war lasted fifteen long years. Finally in 1421, Ziska was killed. It is a sad thing that the followers of Huss were not in agreement among themselves. Some were tired of fighting and went back to the Roman Catholic Church. Others remained faithful to the teachings of Huss. These followers were later called the Bohemian or Moravian brethren.

Huss's teaching was a mixture of biblical, evangelical doctrine and traditional Roman Catholic doctrine. On the one hand, he stressed the need to be saved by faith alone through Jesus Christ and to read and live according to the Scriptures. To help the people, he revised a Czech translation of the Bible. His stress on preaching and the universal priesthood of all believers—that is, that all God's people bear the office of believers in this world—would later become major hallmarks of the Protestant Reformation. Huss encouraged congregational singing at worship services, even writing out many songs himself. He also spoke out strongly against the immorality and worldliness of the clergy and the worship of the pope. In these ways and others, Huss helped restore a biblical vision of the church that focused on Christ's teachings and example of purity.

On the other hand, Huss still accepted the Roman Catholic doctrine of purgatory and held a view of the sacraments that would be similar to Luther's. He had a profound impact on the Reformation, particularly through Luther, who once claimed, rather exaggeratedly, that none of his teaching was new, for he had learned it all from Huss.

~ 5 ~

Martin Luther

(1483–1546)

Luther was studying the book of Romans, and when he came to verse 17 of the first chapter, he suddenly understood! "The just shall live by faith," it said. Now he saw it clearly! Salvation is by faith in Jesus Christ, not by anything we can do.

So far, we have talked about those whom God used to prepare the way for the Reformation. Just as morning comes slowly, so the Lord is never in a hurry with His plans. His timing is always perfect. As the sun rises gradually to give us light and warmth, so the Lord gradually prepares and carries on all His work. This is also the way in which the Reformation was brought about. There were many years of preparation.

His youth

The best-known Reformer whom God used to usher in the Reformation is Martin Luther. He was born in a small town called Eisleben on November 10, 1483. He was named Martin for the simple reason that the day on which he was born was called St. Martin's Day in the Roman Catholic Church. It is said that his father prayed aloud at the bedside of his newborn son, asking God to grant him grace, that he might become known for learning and piety.

Shortly after Martin was born, his family moved to Mansfeld, where his father, Hans, owned a small business mining copper-bearing shale. This eased some of the harsh poverty the family had endured. Hans Luther determined to give his son a good education. Martin's teachers certainly taught him his subjects, but educators in those days were very harsh. They believed that beating boys was the best way to make them learn. Poor Martin once received fifteen whippings in a single day at school!

The house where Luther was born

His studies

Young Martin attended the village school of Mansfeld. After that, he most likely attended the Cathedral School at Magdeburg to continue his studies. Many of the students were poor and not well provided for. Luther was one of these boys. Often they went from door to door begging for some food. At Christmas time, they would sing carols as a way to earn their food. Sometimes people were kind and gave them something to eat, but many times the boys were scolded and chased away.

After a short time at Magdeburg, Martin's father transferred him to Eisenach, where he studied for four years at the Georgenschule. Here also, Luther had to beg for food with the other poor scholars. One day after being sent away from several houses, Luther was discouraged. Feeling faint with hunger, he wondered if he should give up studying and go to work with his father in the mines. But the door of the next home opened, and the kind lady of the house called to him. Her name was Ursula Cotta. She felt sorry for him and gave him a good meal. She told him to come back often. This woman and her family cheerfully provided for many of Luther's needs.

When he was eighteen, Luther went to university in the town of Erfurt and began to study law. The University of Erfurt was one of the oldest and most famous universities in Germany at the time. His father worked hard to pay for Martin's education. He was very proud of his son, and although he knew it would cost a great deal of money, he was willing to pay it because he wanted his son to become a famous lawyer. Here, young Luther spent about seven years in study. He learned quickly and soon became one of the best students in the university.

One of Luther's favorite things to do when his work was done for the day was to go to the library to read. One day, to his delight, he discovered a copy of the Latin Bible. It was the first time he had ever seen a Bible! He had heard the priests recite several passages of Scripture but never realized the Bible was such a big book. As he carefully turned the pages, he came across the story of Samuel and his mother Hannah. With joy and delight Luther read this story. What a wonderful Book this was! He would have loved to have a copy of his own, but books were scarce, and it seemed impossible that he would ever own one.

He becomes a monk

Not long after this, Luther decided to give up the study of law and to begin the study of theology, which literally means "the study of God." Two things happened that led him to this decision. One of these was the sudden death of a friend whom he loved very much. When he heard of it, he asked himself, "What would become of me if I were to die suddenly?"

About the same time, during the summer of 1505, while returning to Erfurt after visiting his parents, he was overtaken by a violent storm. Suddenly, a lightning bolt fell almost at his feet. Overcome with fear, he dropped to his knees and prayed to Saint Anne to save him. When he arose unhurt, he believed that the saint had saved him. He felt he had to do something to show his gratitude, so he said, "I must become holy." He made a vow that he would change his life and become a priest.

These two events transformed his life. His friends were surprised. His father was not pleased: he had worked so hard for Martin's education! He had hoped that Martin would make himself known in the world and perhaps become rich as well as famous as a doctor of law. Now all these hopes were dashed when Martin entered the monastery. Monks were not respected very much in that time. People knew that many of the monks led lives of luxury—wealth they had taken from the people. Martin's father believed that his son had broken the fifth commandment: "Honor thy father and thy mother" (Exodus 20:12a).

Convinced it was the right thing to do, Luther left the university and entered the monastery of the Observant Augustinian Friars in Erfurt on July 17, 1505. Monks were supposed to live very strict lives, and they professed to be very religious. The Bible Luther had read at college had made him think seriously about God and his soul, but like the Ethiopian eunuch in Acts 8, he needed someone to explain the Scriptures to him.

He tries to find peace

Luther tried to win God's favor by praying and fasting often. He whipped himself and lived in a cell that had no heat. He slept very little and recited many prayers. He tried to think of every sin he had committed so that he could do penance for them all, but that did not make him feel any better. He did not know that a sinner can only be saved through faith in Jesus Christ. He did not know about the love of God. Rather, whenever he heard about God, he was afraid. Luther's trust was not in the Savior, but in saints and angels, good works, doing penance, and paying for his own sins. Luther, along with other Roman Catholics, had been taught that God was so holy that He could only be approached through the saints. No one had told him that the sacrifice of the Lord Jesus Christ alone can satisfy God's justice.

The monks with whom Luther lived knew even less than he did. They were more interested in his physical labor than in his spiritual welfare. They made him stand watch at the gates, sweep the church, help in the kitchen, and clean the rooms. When he finished his chores, they often said to him, "Go with your bag into the town." That meant he had to beg for food for the monks living in the monastery. For these monks, living in a monastery meant observing a religion based on a long list of do's and don'ts. They did not understand that serving God is a matter of the heart.

Most monks and other clergy members of the Roman Catholic Church did not think much about their souls. They obeyed the rules because it was required of them by the church. But most often, their obedience was done out of a sense of duty. In addition, it is sad to say that most of the clergy lived a wicked life even though they professed to serve God. They seemed pious during religious ceremonies, but their lifestyles were full of sin and injustice.

Luther, however, was different. The Holy Spirit would not allow him to be like the others. For that reason, he could find no peace in the monastery and its rituals. "What will deliver me from my sins and make me holy?" he sighed. "How shall I make peace with a just God? How shall I appear before Him?" He could find no answers.

Some of the other monks thought he was foolish, but some were sympathetic. One old monk in particular pitied Luther. When Luther did not come out of his cell for a whole day, this monk became concerned. Knowing his love of music, the monk took some of the choir boys and knocked at the door of Luther's cell. When there was no response, he became alarmed and broke open the door. There was Luther, unconscious on the floor. They tried to arouse him but could not. So the monk asked the boys to sing. Finally Luther regained consciousness. As much as he tried, he simply could not find peace.

After he had been in the monastery for some time, Luther came across another copy of the Bible. He could not take it to his cell because it was chained to the wall. Anytime he could slip away unnoticed, however, he would read this precious book and even memorize long passages.

Johann von Staupitz

Johann von Staupitz, vicar of the German Observant Augustinian Friars, came to visit the monastery where Luther lived. When he saw how sickly Luther looked, he asked, "Why are you so sad, brother Martin?"

"I do not know what will become of me," answered Luther. "I promise God I will do better, but I find it is useless to make promises to God because sin is stronger than I am."

Von Staupitz did not fully understand the struggle Luther was experiencing, but he wanted to help him. "My friend," replied von Staupitz, "look at the wounds of Jesus Christ and think of why He came into the world."

Though von Staupitz pointed him in the right direction, Luther was afraid of God and of His Son Jesus. He thought of God only as one who punishes sin. Von Staupitz tried to encourage Luther. "God is not angry with you. Christ Jesus does not want to terrify you; He comforts those in trouble and distress. He became man to give you the promise of deliverance. By His stripes we are healed. By His blood our sins are washed away. Love Him who first loved you." But Luther didn't understand.

He becomes a priest

Luther was ordained a priest on May 2, 1507, when he was twenty-three years old. He began to do as much good as he could by visiting the poor and preaching and teaching as well as he knew how. Being a priest meant that he could perform the sacrament of the mass. He listened to people as they confessed their sins to him. He would sit in a little room that had a curtain between the priest and the person confessing his or her sins. Then Luther would have to decide what the punishment for the sins would be. Perhaps he would tell them to recite the Lord's Prayer twenty-five times, or give an offering to the church, or fast for three days. When the person had completed the penance, Luther could tell them their sins were forgiven. This was one of the tasks of the priest.

Wittenberg

In 1508, he was invited by Frederick, Prince of Saxony, to move to the town of Wittenberg to become a professor of moral philosophy in the university there. A chapel was part of the university campus, and Luther was asked to take his turn with other professors to preach to the monks, professors, students, and townspeople who came to listen. Before long, Luther became popular as a teacher and a preacher in the university. Later he became a preacher in the town church of Wittenberg. He preached at this church for the rest of his life. When he first began his teaching and preaching, however, he did not yet understand the gospel of Jesus Christ.

A visit to Rome

One thing that opened Luther's eyes to see the great errors of the church was his trip to the city of Rome in 1510. The pope lives there at the Vatican, the headquarters of the Roman Catholic Church. Luther expected to find the church very pure, and the priests, bishops, and cardinals to be godly men. He looked forward to having spiritual conversations and receiving guidance from these high-ranking religious leaders. He was, however, greatly disappointed. He found that Rome was one of the most corrupt places he had ever visited. The church was full of all sorts of errors and sin. Most of the priests were self-serving men who did not seem to believe the things they were teaching the people.

In a chapel connected with one of the main churches in Rome, there is a flight of white marble steps called the *Scala Sancta*, which means "holy stairs." The priests claimed that these stairs were the very same stairs Jesus climbed when He went from Pilate's judgment hall to Calvary, and that an angel transferred them from Jerusalem to Rome. They also informed the people that whoever went up these stairs on his knees would have all his sins forgiven. Tradition says that Luther went up these steps on his knees, praying and kissing each step. How Luther hoped to find peace for his troubled soul! But his hopes were cruelly dashed. He did not understand why he could not find peace. The Lord had a reason for all of this unrest, however. He was showing Luther his own sin, the wickedness of the church, and the necessity of finding salvation only in Christ. The Lord was graciously leading him, even though Luther believed God was full of wrath and ready to destroy him.

When Luther returned to Wittenberg, he continued to teach his students and to preach in the chapel that was part of the castle of Wittenberg. In his room, he continued to study, pray, and fast. In 1512, he attained his doctoral degree. But he still had no rest for his soul. No matter how he studied, prayed, and punished himself, he never felt as though his sins were forgiven.

The just shall live by faith

Finally, a breakthrough came. Luther was studying the book of Romans, and when he came to verse 17 of the first chapter, he suddenly understood! "The just shall live by faith," it said. Now he saw it clearly! Salvation is by faith in Jesus Christ, not by anything we can do.

Luther's life proves this to us. For years he tried to pay for his sin through his own merits, but he never found rest for his soul. Now, however, the Holy Spirit opened his eyes, and he saw that he could find forgiveness only because of what Jesus Christ had done. Now he understood that God was not an angry God, eager to destroy him, but a patient and loving Father who had sent His only Son to suffer and die for the sins of His people. In Christ's righteousness, God's wrath was satisfied, and sinners who believed in Christ by the grace of the Holy Spirit were saved. Luther was so overjoyed with his new discovery that he later wrote that he felt as if his soul went through the open gates of a heavenly paradise.

Luther became a changed man. He no longer tried to pay for his own sins, but he trusted in his Savior. Now he wanted to obey God, not out of fear, but out of love. His teaching and his preaching also changed. He told people what he had discovered in God's Word. His preaching and teaching were full of the righteousness and love of Christ Jesus.

Johann Tetzel

At last, the time came when God called Luther to begin the work of the Reformation. It began when the church sold indulgences in Wittenberg. Indulgences were pieces of paper signed or stamped with the pope's name. An indulgence declared that the person who bought that piece of paper had all his sins forgiven, even the sins he would commit in the future! He did not have to do penance for his sins; the paper was enough. When a man named Johann Tetzel came to sell indulgences in Luther's area, Luther spoke out against this practice.

Tetzel set up a table in the town square. Some of the monks who were with him set up a red flag that had the pope's coat of arms on it, and then they seated themselves behind the table. "Come near," shouted Tetzel, "and I will give you indulgences, letters sealed by the pope. Even the sins you do in the future shall all be forgiven you. Repentance is not necessary. What's more, these letters will not only save the living, but also the dead! The very moment the money clinks against the bottom of the chest, the soul escapes from purgatory, and flies up to heaven. Bring your money! Bring your money!" A popular rhyme in those days ran:

When the coin in the coffer rings,
The soul from purgatory springs.

Purgatory, the Roman Catholics believed, was a place of punishment where souls were purged, or cleansed, by fire from sin. They said the soul had to remain in purgatory until it was ready to go to heaven. Of course, Tetzel and the pope were wrong. It was all a terrible lie. Money and pieces of paper cannot save people from their sins. Besides, the money collected from the sale of indulgences was being used by the pope and the clergy to build beautiful churches and to live in luxury themselves.

Luther was determined to stop this corrupt sale of indulgences. He spoke and preached against it. He proved from the Bible that this practice was false. He clearly and boldly declared that man can only be saved by the atoning blood of the Lord Jesus Christ.

The ninety-five theses

Because of Tetzel's sale of indulgences, Luther wrote ninety-five theses, or statements, that explained that salvation was only in Christ. They also explained what was wrong in the church. He took this paper and nailed it to the church door in Wittenberg on October 31, 1517. The Lord used the ninety-five theses to begin the Reformation. The theses were written in Latin, but within weeks people translated them into German and nearly every European language so people all over Europe could understand them. People had become more and more dissatisfied with the doctrines and practices of the Roman Catholic Church. Eagerly they read Luther's theses. Many people agreed with Luther. The corruption must be stopped; the truth must be proclaimed. The Reformation had truly begun!

At first, Tetzel, the bishops, and the pope ignored Luther's protest, thinking it would pass, but when they realized that more and more people agreed with Luther, they began to worry. Soon they became angry, because people were not buying as many indulgences as before, and that meant less money for them.

Luther summoned by the pope

Some time after this, Luther received a letter from the pope. The pope ordered him to stop preaching against the church and to retract what he had been saying and writing. Luther wrote back immediately saying he could not comply with this order. In reply, the pope

Martin Luther

— 31 —

demanded that Luther go to Rome to meet with him there. Luther's friends couldn't help but remember what had happened to John Huss. The pope had also ordered Huss to appear before him, and he had been captured and killed even though he had been promised the pope's protection. For this reason, Luther refused to go to Rome.

The pope tried another plan. He wrote to Frederick the Wise, the Elector of Saxony, telling Frederick that he had to send Luther to Rome. But Frederick the Wise, who was Luther's friend, asked the pope to send representatives to Germany to deal with Luther. Meetings with Cardinal Cajetan in October 1518, and Karl von Militz in January 1519, failed to get Luther to recant. These papal delegates tried to force Luther to take back everything he said against Roman Catholic teaching, but it soon became clear that Luther knew much more about the Bible than they did. He refused to retract anything he had said or written since it was based on God's Word.

Realizing these men were terribly angry with him and that he was now in danger, Luther left the city during the night. His friends helped him escape because they feared the pope and his men would probably try to arrest him and put him in prison. God protected His brave servant because there was still much work for him to do.

Johann Eck

Johann Eck was a man who defended the church. He wrote booklets against Luther, saying that he was a heretic just like John Huss. Eck and Luther had debates, discussing the differences between their beliefs. At one debate in Leipzig in the summer of 1519, Eck got Luther to say that the pope was in error. Luther stated that Scripture is the Word of God and there are no mistakes in God's Word. If there is a disagreement between the pope and the Bible, we must agree with God's Word rather than the pope's. Eck thought he had won the debate when he got Luther to say that he believed the pope was not the supreme truth, but many people believed Luther was the real winner because he boldly stated the truth.

Luther burning the papal bull

Luther burns the papal bull

When Eck went back to Rome, he persuaded Pope Leo X to accuse Luther of being a heretic. With Eck's prodding, the pope threatened to excommunicate Luther. In the summer of 1520, Luther was ordered to go to Rome and retract everything he had said and written against the doctrines of the church. He had sixty days to do so. The pope added that if Luther refused, he would be persecuted in this life and in the life to come. This letter from the pope was called a papal bull ("bull" comes from a Latin word meaning "seal," so "papal bull" means "a special document or command from the pope").

Although Luther did reply to the pope, he also made his convictions clear in another way. On December 10, 1520, he and his friends made a fire and burned the papal bull. He also burned a book which taught that the pope was the supreme ruler of the church. This was an obvious insult to the pope, but Luther refused to listen to people who did not obey God and who wanted him to disobey God, too. By this action, he cut himself off from the church. He was excommunicated on January 3, 1521. No longer was he a member of this church. Many people in Wittenberg were glad; they agreed with Martin Luther.

Important writings

During 1520, Luther completed three important books in which he stated his views. In the first, *Address to the Christian Nobility of the German Nation,* he urged the German princes to reform the church and society since the Roman Catholic Church was in such a sad state of corruption. In *A Prelude Concerning the Babylonian Captivity of the Church,* he attacked the church's theology of sacraments. Luther maintained there were only two sacraments, baptism and the Lord's Supper, or at most three, with penance possibly qualifying as a third; the Roman Catholic Church taught that there were seven. He also denied the doctrine of transubstantiation. The third pamphlet, *On the Freedom of a Christian Man*, defined Luther's position on justification and good works.

The Diet of Worms

In the early 1520s, Luther and his friends continued to preach and teach the gospel. By way of Luther's preaching and writing, the doctrines of the Bible were spreading rapidly. Many people in Germany, Switzerland, France, England, and other countries were leaving the Roman Catholic Church and joining the church of the Protestants. The pope was alarmed. He had not been able to stop Luther. God had given Luther powerful friends who stood by him and protected him.

The pope met with Charles V, the emperor of Germany, and together they decided to call a meeting. This meeting was called the Diet of Worms. "Diet" means "meeting," and Worms was the name of the city where the meeting was held. Luther was summoned to appear before this Diet. The pope and the emperor hoped to do one of two things: either they would get Luther to recant, or else they would get the authority of this Diet to put him to death.

Martin Luther's friends were frightened. Even though Luther had been given a safe conduct, again they couldn't help but think about John Huss. He also had been given the pope's promise that he would be protected, but he had been burned at the stake. Luther, however, assured them that he was not afraid. He believed the Lord wanted him to go to

Luther's triumphal progress to Worms

Worms. "Even if there were as many devils in Worms as there are tiles on the rooftops, I must go," he said firmly.

The Diet of Worms, held on April 18, 1521, was a grand assembly. Princes, rulers, and many important people were present. Emperor Charles V and his brother, the Archduke Ferdinand, were there. Also present was the Archbishop of Treves, who represented the pope. The chancellor of the archbishop asked Luther questions during the trial. Some of Luther's friends were there, too. Frederick the Wise, the Elector of Saxony, was one of the most powerful of the German princes. In the great hall in the palace in which the Diet was held, a crowd of thousands of people had gathered as well.

When Luther entered, there was great excitement. Everyone wanted to see him. The archbishop's chancellor stood up and said in a loud, clear voice that there were two questions Luther had to answer. Pointing to some books on a table, he asked Luther, "Did you write those books?"

Luther asked what the titles were. When he recognized the titles, he answered, "Yes, I wrote them."

"Will you retract everything in these books that is against the Church of Rome?" was the next question.

Luther asked for some time to think and pray before answering this question. The emperor told him he would have until the next day.

When the Diet met again the following day, Luther was asked to give his answer. He made a long speech, first in German, then in Latin. In this speech, he said that if it could be proven that anything in his books was not in agreement with the Scriptures, he would at once retract it, but if not, he could take back nothing. When they urged him again to take back his writings, he repeated what he

Luther at the Diet of Worms

had said before. Then he said, "Unless I am convinced by testimonies of the Scriptures or by clear arguments that I am in error—for popes and councils have often erred and contradicted themselves—I cannot withdraw, for I am subject to the Scriptures I have quoted; my conscience is captive to the Word of God. It is unsafe and dangerous to do anything against one's conscience." He concluded with these famous words, "Here I stand; I cannot do otherwise. God help me! Amen!"

Luther's friends rejoiced, but his enemies were angry. They tried to convince the emperor to break his promise of safe conduct. But the emperor was afraid that the people would revolt if he did so. Instead, he ordered Luther to leave the city at once. As soon as Luther left, however, the emperor declared that anyone was allowed to kill him. The pope also stated that Luther was forbidden to preach and all his writings must be burned. This declaration was called the Edict of Worms.

The castle at Wartburg

Luther is captured

On the way home from Worms, Luther had an unsettling experience. His friends found out that there was a plan to capture him, so they made plans of their own. As Luther was riding homeward through the forest, several masked, armed men suddenly opened the door of the carriage in which he rode, pulled him out, placed him on a horse, and rode away with him. They rode a long time, until they came to the castle of Wartburg. At first Luther did not realize who his captors were. You can imagine how relieved he was when he discovered they were his friends! Frederick the Wise had arranged his capture and hid him in the castle for almost a year.

During this time, Luther wrote a series of pamphlets attacking Roman Catholic practices and began his German translation of the Bible. The translation of the New Testament was finished in the autumn of 1522, but it wasn't until 1542 that Luther, with the help of friends, completed the translation of the entire Bible. He also wrote letters to other friends, but he did not sign his name on them. His friends knew then that Luther was safe, though they had no idea where he was or who had "captured" him.

While Luther was at Wartburg Castle, there was unrest in Wittenberg. Some people who claimed to follow Luther destroyed images, artwork, altars, and crucifixes. This type of destruction is called iconoclasm. While Luther *did* speak against the wrongs of the Roman Catholic Church, he did *not* believe in riots and destruction. In March 1522, Luther went back to Wittenberg, though it meant he put himself in danger of being arrested and killed. He believed he was needed in Wittenberg, and he began to preach and teach the people as soon as he arrived there. He told them that

Luther translating the Bible in the Wartburg

such behavior was not according to Scripture, neither was it honoring to God. Thankfully, the people listened to him, and things settled down again.

God gives Luther a wife

The Roman Catholic Church taught that it was sinful for a priest to marry. When Luther began to study the Bible, he

Catherine von Bora

Do you know the songs "Away in a Manger" and "A Mighty Fortress is Our God"? Luther wrote these songs, as well as more than 125 hymns. In 1524, he published the first German hymnbook. It contained only eight hymns, but each time it was printed more hymns were added. The German people loved to sing these hymns with their families or as they went about their daily activities.

Luther and Zwingli on the Lord's Supper

In 1529, Philip of Hesse, one of the Protestant princes of Germany, arranged for a meeting with the leading theologians of Switzerland and Germany. He wanted them to reach an agreement about the doctrines of the Lord's Supper. This meeting was held in Marburg. Luther and Philip Melanchthon, who was Luther's greatest helper and an able theologian, represented Luther's teaching that although the bread and wine do not literally change into the body and blood of the Lord Jesus, He is still physically present in, with, and under the bread. Ulrich Zwingli, the leading Reformer in Switzerland, who took his friend Johannes Œcolampadius,[1] supported the belief that the sacrament of the Lord's Supper is only a memorial to the death of the Lord Jesus. Sad to say, each side was unwilling to compromise. When they parted ways, Luther refused to shake Zwingli's hand as a brother in Christ. Zwingli was grieved over this. Sometimes God's people have differences of opinion and differences in their beliefs, and often hard feelings result. This is not what God

discovered that God had never made such a law. On June 13, 1525, Luther married Catherine von Bora. Two years earlier, Catherine (or Katie, as Luther fondly called her) and several other women had escaped from a convent. Luther and his wife loved each other very much, and they were a good help to each other. The Lord blessed them with six children. One of the children, Magdalena, died on September 20, 1542, at the age of thirteen. Luther and his family were very sad, but they also rejoiced, knowing that this child was taken to heaven to be with her Savior forever.

Luther loved children and wrote a catechism for them, as well as many songs. Some of them are still sung today.

---

1. Œcolampadius (1482–1531), which means "burning lamp" in Latin, was born in Hussgen, Germany. He left the monastery after reading Luther's writings and went to Basel, where he preached and wrote about the truths of Scripture. He agreed with Zwingli's view of the Lord's Supper. In 1518, he helped Erasmus in writing his Greek New Testament.

teaches. Paul says in 1 Corinthians 1:10, "Now I beseech you, brethren, by the name of our Lord Jesus Christ, that ye all speak the same thing, and that there be no divisions among you; but that ye be perfectly joined together in the same mind and in the same judgment."

His work and hospitality

In 1537, and again in 1541, Luther became so ill that his family and friends feared he would die. The Lord restored him to health, however, and enabled him to continue in his work. He lectured, preached, attended conferences, and wrote books and tracts. He and his wife Katie were well known for their hospitality. Even though they themselves often had little money, they welcomed anyone in need. Meals were usually times of lively conversation, as visitors talked with Luther about Scripture and its doctrines.

His death

Early in 1546, Luther wrote to a friend that he felt "old, spent, worn, weary, and cold, and had but one eye to see with." Feeling this way, he left for Eisleben to try to help some people settle a dispute over land, despite the cold winter weather. On his journey he became sicker and lay suffering in his hometown for several days. His beloved Katie was far away. Only his sons Martin and Paul had accompanied him on his trip. He did have friends surrounding him, however, in his last days. One of his friends, Justus Jonas, asked Luther, "Reverend Father, will you stand by Christ and the doctrine you have preached?" The dying Reformer roused himself to firmly answer "yes." His last words were, "Father, into Thy hands I commend my spirit." He died on February 18, 1546. His body was taken to Wittenberg and buried in the churchyard. This was the same church where Luther had posted his famous ninety-five theses for all to read.

Luther was sixty-three years old when he died. He faced many trials and difficulties in his life; many times his enemies had tried to condemn him to death and silence him, but God enabled Luther to continue the blessed work of the Reformation. Many times he was sad and discouraged; the devil tried to make him fall and give up, but the Lord always helped Luther in his work so that he persevered until the end.

Throughout his life, Luther maintained a very heavy workload: teaching, writing books, organizing the new Protestant church, and providing overall leadership for the German Reformation. Luther never viewed himself as the founder of a new church body, however. In 1522, when his followers first began to use his name to identify themselves, he was not pleased. He wrote: "Let us abolish all party names and call ourselves Christians after Him whose teaching we hold.... I hold, together with the universal church, the one universal teaching of Christ, who is our only master." His goal was to reform and restore the church so that it would be true to the biblical teaching of salvation by gracious faith alone. Little could he realize the impact he would have on Protestantism around the world, and that more biographies—well over one thousand by now—would be written about his life than any other person in history except the Lord Jesus.

~ 6 ~

Philip Melanchthon

◆◆◆

(1497–1560)

His greatest treasure was a copy of the Latin Bible given to him by Dr. Johannes Reuchlin. He carried it with him everywhere and read it as often as he could. The precious Word of God took hold of Melanchthon, and the Holy Spirit blessed it.

His family

Philip Melanchthon (Me-lank'-thən) was a close friend of Luther and a great help to him in the important work he had to do. Melanchthon was born thirteen years after Luther in a little town named Bretten, in Germany, on February 16, 1497. Melanchthon was the eldest son of George and Barbara Schwartzerel. So, when he was young, his last name was actually Schwartzerel. He studied under a relative named Reuchlin, who changed Philip's last name to Melanchthon, the Greek version of Schwartzerel, which means "black earth." His father was an armorer, which is someone who makes or repairs armor. His mother was the daughter of a well-to-do merchant.

His education

Philip's grandfather, Hans Reuter, noticed that Philip was a bright child and hired a tutor for him and his brothers. John Hungar made the boys work very hard, but he was kind, and the children learned much under his teaching.

When Philip was only ten years old, both his father and grandfather died in October 1507. His dying father gave the family these parting words: "I have seen many changes in my life, and there are greater changes coming soon. May God preserve you all through whatever comes! And you, Philip, my boy, be sure to live righteously and in God's fear."

Soon after his father died, Philip was sent to Pforzheim, along with his younger brother, George, and his cousin, John Reuter. His teacher was a very kind man named Dr. George Simler. While studying at Pforzheim, young

Philip Melanchthon

Melanchthon found a friend in his uncle, the famous Dr. Johannes Reuchlin. Philip and some of the other students often visited him. Dr. Reuchlin was one of the most learned men in Germany and enjoyed having the boys come to visit. They had scholarly discussions, and he allowed the boys to borrow his books.

In the autumn of 1509, Melanchthon left Pforzheim to go to Heidelberg University. There he became the best scholar in his class. He graduated from the university when he was only fourteen years old! In September 1512, he went to the University of Tübingen. The home of Dr. Reuchlin was not far away, so Melanchthon visited his uncle as often as

he could. He also spent many evenings reading and talking with his friends. One of these friends was John Hussgen, later known as Johannes Œcolampadius.

At Tübingen, Melanchthon was introduced to Luther's writings. He was fascinated. His greatest treasure, however, was a copy of the Latin Bible given to him by Dr. Reuchlin. He carried it with him everywhere and read it as often as he could. The precious Word of God took hold of Melanchthon, and the Holy Spirit blessed it.

Dr. Reuchlin was also a child of God and suffered for it. When a monk urged the people to burn all Hebrew books except the Old Testament, Dr. Reuchlin raised his voice in disapproval. The monks hated him because of this and wanted to have him killed. God protected his faithful servant, however, and his life was spared. Melanchthon defended his uncle in a paper he wrote entitled, *Epistolæ Clarorum Virorum,* which means *Letters of Famous Men.* Because of this, Dr. Reuchlin's enemies hated Melanchthon, too. They wrote nasty things against him which hurt, but he continued steadfast. In 1514, Melanchthon attained his master's degree from Tübingen when he was sixteen years old.

In 1518, the Elector of Saxony, Frederick, asked Dr. Reuchlin if he knew any professors who could teach at his new University of Wittenberg. Frederick needed someone to teach Hebrew and someone to teach Greek. He suggested Melanchthon for the position of professor of Greek at the University of Wittenberg. Melanchthon accepted, and there he met Luther.

Melanchthon soon became known as one of the most educated men of that age. He could speak and write as well in Greek as he could in his own native German language. He also studied the Bible constantly. Although he was never ordained as a priest or a minister, he lectured on theology and wrote many sermons to help other men preach better. Because of his learning and writing ability, he was a great help to Luther, even assisting him to sharpen and fine-tune his theology. Melanchthon provided considerable assistance to Luther at the Leipzig disputation in 1519. Two years later, he wrote *Loci Communes*, the first Protestant systematic theology and a fine statement of Luther's main ideas. It sold well due to its clear style and peaceful tone.

His friendship with Luther

The friendship Melanchthon shared with Luther can be compared to the friendship David had with Jonathan (1 Samuel 18:1). Melanchthon said of his dear friend, "I love Luther's studies, the sacred science he pursues, and the man himself above all that is on earth, and I embrace him with all my heart. I would rather die than be separated from him."[1]

Luther appreciated Melanchthon as a friend and partner in the work of the Reformation. When Luther was hiding in the Wartburg Castle, he wrote a letter to his beloved friend when he thought he and Melanchthon might be killed for their faith. "If I perish, the gospel will lose nothing. You will succeed me, as Elisha succeeded Elijah, with a double portion of my spirit." Remembering Melanchthon's timid nature, he added, "Minister of the Word! Keep the walls and towers of Jerusalem till our enemies shall strike you down. We stand alone; after they destroy me, they will strike you down, but the truth of God will yet prevail."

---

1. Dr. Macaulay, *Luther Anecdotes: Memorable Sayings and Doings of Martin Luther, Gathered from his Books, Letters, and History; and Illustrating his Life and Work* (London: The Religious Tract Society, n.d.), 95.

His character

God's children do not all have the same personalities. Christians love the Lord Jesus and try to be like Him, but they show this in different ways. When the grace of God enters the hearts of His children, it makes them Christians according to their personalities and characteristics. Luther's character was rough, sharp, and sometimes harsh. When he became a Christian, he always had a certain roughness about him. Melanchthon's character was mild, gentle, and loving. When he became a Christian, his piety was of this gentle, lamb-like kind. Luther was more like Peter, who was often quite blunt, while Melanchthon was more like the loving John. If he and Luther had been the same, they could never have accomplished the great work before them that the Lord called them to do. If Melanchthon had been like Luther, they would have spoiled many things by haste and harshness, and if Luther had been like Melanchthon, neither of them would have had the boldness and strength to do what had to be done. Melanchthon was like oil on the wheels of the Reformation that made everything turn more smoothly.

Family life

Luther decided that it would be good for his friend to have a wife. Following Luther's advice, Melanchthon married Katharine Krapp on November 25, 1520. He lived happily with his wife for thirty-seven years until she died in 1557, three years before his own death. He loved his wife very much. "I cannot begin to express what an unexpected gift my wife was, or how little I am worthy of her," wrote Melanchthon, "but she is a wonderful mixture of natural and spiritual blessings. I would hardly have dared to ask God for a better wife."[2]

Both Philip and Katharine were kind and generous to the poor. They had many visitors and they warmly welcomed them all. Although they were poor, they were eager to share what they had.

The Lord blessed Philip and Katharine with four children: Anna, Philip, George, and Magdalena. George died when he was a little boy. Melanchthon used to call his home his "little church." Sometimes, when visitors would come to visit Melanchthon, they would find this learned professor sitting on the floor playing with his children.

Illness

In 1536, Melanchthon became very ill. A message was sent to Luther saying that his friend was dying. Luther rode night and day until he reached Weimar, where Melanchthon lay ill. It seemed Melanchthon would soon die. His eyes were already dim; reason, speech, sight, and hearing were gone. His face was thin and hollow-looking. He did not notice anyone around him and could no longer eat or drink. Luther was shocked as he gazed at his friend and exclaimed, "God forbid!"

Luther walked over to the window, where he earnestly pleaded with God for the life of his friend. "I cast my burden down before His door," Luther said later, "and besieged His ear with every promise He has made about prayer, which I recalled from the Holy Scripture."

---

2. George Wilson, *Philip Melanchthon, 1497–1560* (London: The Religious Tract Society, 1897), 69–70.

He then took his friend by the hand, saying, "Be of good cheer, my friend Philip; you will not die."

Melanchthon began to recover consciousness, but for a long time he could not utter a single word. At last he turned his face to Luther and pleaded with him not to try to keep him on earth. "I am now on a good journey," said Melanchthon, "I beg you, let me continue. Nothing better than this can happen to me."

"It cannot be, Philip," answered Luther, "you must serve our God a little longer yet."

Melanchthon continued to revive, and Luther asked someone to prepare some food, which he himself brought to the sick man. Melanchthon, however, did not want to eat. Then Luther said, "Hear me, Philip, you must eat, or I must excommunicate you." With these words, spoken lovingly in jest, he urged Melanchthon to eat. He ate, and slowly, his strength returned.

Afterwards, Melanchthon said that if Luther had not come to him then, he would certainly have died. He also said that as he lay apparently dying, the words came before him as clearly as if they had been written on a wall, "I shall not die, but live, and declare the works of the Lord" (Psalm 118:17). These words brought him great comfort.

Since Melanchthon was away from home when he had become ill, his wife and children were very worried about him. Luther visited them to ease their fears and told them Melanchthon was recovering. In a letter to his faithful friend, Melanchthon later wrote, "I thank you heartily, my best and dearest pastor, that during my absence you have comforted me in so Christian a manner, and that in my home my wife has been aided by your counsels. I have been restored from death to life by the power of God. This is the testimony of all who were with me. Oh, that I might thank God aright and live to His glory. I commend myself and the church of Christ to your prayers."

His work

Melanchthon attended many debates and conferences. He wrote many papers. When Luther couldn't be at the Diet of Augsburg, Melanchthon was there instead. He prepared a confessional statement that was discussed in great detail. The first part of the document talked about the doctrines of the Reformation. The second part pointed out the errors of the Roman Catholic Church. Luther provided some of the material included in the document, but Melanchthon was its primary author. This document was accepted as the Augsburg Confession in 1530, and together with Melanchthon's Apology of 1531 and Wittenberg Concord of 1536, these documents became key statements of Lutheran belief.

Even the quiet Melanchthon received criticism. Melanchthon was a peace-loving man and did his best to smooth over differences. He tried his best to help people with differing opinions and persuasions to understand each other and to reach an agreement. At times, however, Melanchthon wavered too much on some of the doctrines of the Reformation, especially after Luther's death. Often disappointed by the arguments and unpleasantness between people of differing views, Melanchthon once wrote, "These things I did for the best. I trusted that people would understand what I meant. I expected, indeed, too much; but I would have died rather than betrayed the truth or wounded my kind brethren. Why have I, born for my Greek studies and for the humble pursuits of the scholar, been set in the high places of theological debates and war? If only Doctor Martin had been with us, for he would have saved it all!"[3]

At one of the many conferences Melanchthon attended, he met John Calvin. They became good friends. Calvin appreciated the work Melanchthon was doing for the Reformation, although he was disappointed that Melanchthon compromised too much at times.

His death

Returning one day from a trip in 1560, Melanchthon caught a cold. He never recovered. A few days before he died, he wrote down some reasons why he would be happy to die:

> Thou shalt say farewell to sin;
> Thou shalt be set free from miseries
> And from the spiteful fury of theologians.
> Thou shalt come into the Eternal Light.
> Thou shalt see God.
> Thou shalt look into the face of the Son of God.
> Thou shalt learn those secret things
> Too difficult to be understood—
> Why we are created as we are;
> How in Christ the two natures are united.

On the afternoon of April 19, as Melanchthon lay almost unconscious, his son-in-law bent over him and asked him if he wanted anything. "Nothing except heaven; ask me no more," he replied. He died quietly a few hours later, and was buried near his beloved friend, Martin Luther.

---

3. Wilson, *Melanchthon*, 121.

After his death, Calvin wrote,

> O Philip Melanchthon, now you live at the right hand of God with Christ, waiting for us in heaven till we are gathered with you into blessed rest. So often, when you were weary with work and frustration, you leaned your head upon my bosom, and said, "Would to God, would to God that I might die upon that bosom!" As for me, later, a hundred times I wished that God would have allowed us to be together more often. Certainly, you would have been bolder to face struggles, more courageous to despise envy and slander. Then, also the ill-will of many whose rude boldness increased in proportion to what they called your cowardice would have been suppressed.[4]

---

4. C. G. McCrie, *Beza's "Icones": Contemporary Portraits of Reformers of Religion and Letters* (London: The Religious Tract Society, 1909), 62–63.

~ 7 ~

The Protest at Speyer

(1529)

This protest was important for several reasons. First, it showed the selflessness of the German princes.... Second, it was important because it gave to the friends of the Reformation the name by which they have become known. The word "Protestant" comes from the word "protest."

An important event in connection with the Reformation was the "protest at Speyer." Speyer, or Spires, is an old town in Bavaria, Germany. It is situated on the Rhine River[1] and is one of the oldest towns in Germany. It is a walled town with gates and towers. In Luther's time, it was a place of great trade and wealth. It had a large palace belonging to the emperors of Germany. There is also a large cathedral where many of the emperors were buried.

Martin Luther had been declared a heretic by the pope and the emperor after he burned the papal bull on December 10, 1520. Shortly after this, he was excommunicated. At the Diet of Worms in April 1521, Luther was asked to recant and retract his writings. His response was his famous statement, "Here I stand; I cannot do otherwise. God help me! Amen!" The result of this firm stance was that Charles V signed a document which outlawed Luther. This document was called the Edict of Worms, dated April 19, 1521. Luther's friends hid him in the Wartburg Castle to keep him safe from his enemies.

The Roman Catholic Church could not stop the light of the Reformation from shining into the darkness of error, however, and Luther continued to write; more and more people came to embrace the light of the gospel. When Luther returned to Wittenberg in 1522, it was a time of political and religious unrest. Many people were opposed to the ban on Luther and his teachings and writings. In 1526, Charles V called for an Imperial Diet of Speyer to try to settle some of the unrest. At this diet, which opened on June 25, the ban on Luther

---

1. The Rhine River originates in the Swiss Alps. It is 820 miles long, the longest river in Western Europe.

was lifted after much discussion. Surprisingly, the same emperor who had branded Luther a heretic now granted a measure of religious freedom to the German people; each prince could decide for himself what he thought was best for the people in his province as far as religion was concerned. This law had been passed by Luther's friends and was a great help to the cause of the Reformation.

This freedom was cut short, however, by the Diet of Speyer three years later. The Reformation was spreading at an alarming rate. The pope, the Roman Catholic leaders, and Charles V decided that something had to be done to stop it.

Diet at Speyer

The Diet of Speyer was called by Emperor Charles V on March 15, 1529. The emperor himself did not attend the meeting, but he sent his younger brother, Ferdinand,[2] to take his place. At this meeting, it became clear that the Roman Catholics would no longer tolerate the teachings of the Reformation. Ferdinand tried to get a new law passed that would repeal the decision that the Diet had made in 1526 that allowed religious freedom. He wanted a law passed that would forbid anyone to preach or believe the doctrines that Luther taught. Melanchthon observed, "We are regarded as the curse of the earth; but Christ will look down on His poor people, and will preserve them."

Most German princes, however, were friends of Luther and the Reformation. They opposed the pope and Ferdinand so strongly that this new law could not be passed.

---

2. Ferdinand I was emperor of Germany from 1558–64 and king of Bohemia and Hungary from 1526–64.

When the friends of the pope realized this fact, they proposed a law stating that a person could believe what he wanted, but he should not be allowed to make a change in his religion. The Roman Catholics believed this would be an effective way to stop the spread of the Reformation. The friends of the Reformation objected, arguing that such a law would bring strife and controversy into Germany, whereas the last three years had been peaceful. Ferdinand and the Roman Catholic princes tried to persuade those who objected, but they would not submit. Finally, Ferdinand announced that his decision was made: they must submit to his authority and the pope's; Roman Catholicism was to be the religion of the land. He then left the meeting and refused to listen to any requests to change his mind.

The protest written

Six reforming princes and fourteen cities met together to talk about this tragic law that was intended to stop the spread of the Reformation. They drafted a protest for themselves, their subjects, and all who then or in the future would believe in the Word of God. They said to each other, "We will obey the emperor in everything that maintains peace and the honor of God, but we cannot give up the truths of the Bible or the true worship of God."

One of the five princes signing the Protestation at Speyer in April 1529 was Philip, the 25-year-old landgrave (a count or prince in Germany) of Hesse. He was among the most committed of Luther's supporters, founding in Marburg in 1527 the first Protestant university. Another of these princes was John, Elector of Saxony, known as John the Steadfast or John the Constant (1468–1532). He became the Elector of Saxony in 1525 when his brother Frederick III, also known as

John the Steadfast, Elector of Saxony

Frederick the Wise, died. His name "The Steadfast" indicates his unwavering faith in God and his protection of those who helped the Protestant Reformation.

At this Diet, John the Steadfast was requested to read the letter of protest before those in attendance. This is what the letter said:

> We are resolved, with the grace of God, to maintain the pure preaching of God's holy Word, such as is contained in the biblical books of the Old and New

Testaments, without adding anything to it that may be contrary to it. This word is the only truth; it is the sure rule of all doctrine and of all life, and can never fail or deceive us. He who builds on this foundation shall stand against all the powers of hell, while all the human vanities that are set up against it shall fall before the face of God.

> For these reasons, most dear lords and friends, we earnestly entreat you to weigh carefully our grievances and our motives. If you do not yield to our request, we protest before God, our only Creator, Preserver, and Redeemer and Savior, who will one day be our Judge, as well as before all men and all creatures, that we, for us and our people, neither consent nor adhere in any manner whatsoever to the proposed decree in anything that is contrary to God, to His holy Word, to our right conscience, and to the salvation of souls.

This protest also stated,

> There is no true preaching or doctrine but that which conforms to the Word of God. The Lord forbids the teaching of any other faith. Each text of the holy and divine Scriptures should be explained by other texts. This Holy Book is in all things necessary for the Christian and easy to be understood. It shines clearly in its own light, and is found to enlighten the darkness. We are determined by God's grace and aid to abide by God's Word alone, to maintain the pure preaching of God's only Word, as it is

The protest at Speyer

the face of God. We therefore reject the yoke that is imposed upon us.

This protest was important for several reasons. First, it showed the selflessness of the German princes. They did not say to themselves, "Well, *we* belong to the Reformation, so it doesn't affect *us*." Rather, they thought of others. They saw that this new law was intended to stop others from joining the Reformation, so they took a stand in favor of religious freedom. The salvation of souls was more important to them than their own safety.

Second, it was important because it gave to the friends of the Reformation the name by which they have become known. The word "Protestant" comes from the word "protest." The English word originally meant "resolute confession, solemn declaration." The princes were standing for the truth of God's Word against the corruption of the Roman Catholic Church.

The Diet of Augsburg and the Augsburg Confession

Since Ferdinand did not want to hear any more from these German princes, the protest was sent to Emperor Charles V. He made an attempt to resolve this matter at the Diet of Augsburg in June 1530. Melanchthon and Luther were the main authors of a statement describing the views of the Reformation. They bolstered these views with Scripture. This statement of faith, now known as the Augsburg Confession, was accepted by the Protestant princes, and they signed their names to it.

Luther had been declared a heretic and an outlaw and was therefore unable to attend. His place was taken by Philip

contained in the Scriptures of the Old and New Testaments, without anything added thereto. This Word alone should be preached, and nothing that is contrary to it. It is the only truth. It is the sure rule of all Christian doctrine and life and can never fail or deceive us. He who builds on this foundation shall stand against all the powers of hell, whilst all the vanities that are set up against it shall fall before

Melanchthon. While Melanchthon and the princes were gathered at Augsburg, Luther prayed at least three hours each day. In the privacy of his chamber, he was overheard pouring out his soul before God as if speaking to a friend.

On the day of the meeting, the Confession was read before Charles V. The emperor had demanded that the Confession be read in Latin, but John, Elector of Saxony, objected, saying that they were Germans and the Confession should be read in German. So the truth of the Scriptures was clearly proclaimed in the language of the people, and the errors of the Roman Catholic Church noted.

The Confession made a great impact on all who heard it. Some of the princes' eyes were opened and they began to understand that the Reformation was true, since it was based solely on Scripture. Even John Eck, the opponent of Martin Luther, had to admit that he could not refute this confession with Scripture, but only with the writings of the Roman Catholic clergy. Emperor Charles V could find no words to declare the confession unscriptural. Though Luther could not be there, he rejoiced.

Although the Augsburg Confession made an impression, the Diet did not want to accept this document, since it spoke against the Roman Catholic Church. They decided to give the Protestants time to retract their confession. A statement was written that by April 1531 all Protestant princes and cities must recant from the Lutheran faith.

If the Roman Catholic Church thought that the Protestants would yield to their pressure, they were mistaken. The Protestant princes and some of the cities united to protect each other. This became known as the League of Schmalkald. Though there was tension between the two groups, there was no outright war until after Luther's death in 1546.

In 1547, in the battle of Mühlberg, Charles V gained the victory, and Philip of Hesse was imprisoned for five years. In 1555, another Diet gathered at Augsburg. By this time, both the Roman Catholics and the Protestants were willing to come to an agreement. This agreement, known as the Peace of Augsburg, allowed each prince and city to choose between Roman Catholicism and Lutheranism.

The conflict between truth and error continued over the years. This conflict will not end until the Lord Jesus Christ returns on the clouds to judge the living and the dead. Jesus told His disciples, "And ye shall be hated of all men for my name's sake: but he that endureth to the end shall be saved" (Matthew 10:22).

~ 8 ~

Martin Bucer

(1491–1551)

People respected his simple lifestyle, his godly walk, his patience in sickness, and his faithfulness in his many labors.

Martin Bucer was a leading figure in the European and English Reformation movements. Born at Schlettstadt, Germany, in 1491, Martin Bucer's name originally was Martin Kuhorn. Later his name was changed to Butzer or Bucer, which means "cleanser." Can you guess why his friends gave him this name?

At the young age of seven, Bucer studied at a Dominican monastery, officially entering it when he was fifteen or sixteen, around the year 1506. He was a good student and had a gift for public speaking. His teachers noticed his intelligence and good study habits, and they encouraged him to continue his studies. He was sent to Heidelberg to study Hebrew, Greek, philosophy, and theology. While in Heidelberg, Bucer came across the writings of Erasmus. Erasmus criticized many of the errors of the Roman Catholic Church, but he never actually broke from the church. Heidelberg is also where Bucer met Luther, who came to the city in 1518.

Luther's ninety-five theses made a great impact on the people, and Bucer was eager to read these statements as well. What he read made him question the Roman Catholic teaching. He began to read more of Luther's writing. When Luther made his bold stand at the Diet of Worms in 1521, Bucer was there supporting him. Bucer did not immediately leave Roman Catholicism, but he carefully studied Scripture and the writings of the Reformers. Several years later, convinced that the Reformers were correct, he embraced their teaching and wrote a book called *Summary*, explaining and defending the Protestant faith, especially the doctrine of justification by faith alone. Soon Bucer was one of the leading Protestant ministers in southern Germany. The Lord had important work for him to do. He was present at most of the important meetings that took place in that time, wrote numerous books, and became chaplain to the elector of the Palatinate. Bucer refused to sign a document that attempted to get the Roman Catholics and the Protestants to compromise in order to reconcile some of their differences. He received Calvin heartily in Strasbourg after Calvin was banished from Geneva in 1538. For the last two years of his life, Bucer taught theology at Cambridge University in England at the request of Archbishop Cranmer. There he played a significant role in the reform of the *Book of Common Prayer*, published after his death in 1552.

Like Melanchthon, Bucer's character was peace-loving and mild. He tried to help Luther and Zwingli come to an agreement about their differences. But the result was that neither side trusted him. They felt the differences were too great to reconcile. "How can this man be friends of people on both sides?" people wondered. "He must not be very firm in his faith." Bucer was not without friends and supporters, however. He was recognized at the University of Cambridge for his learning. People respected his simple lifestyle, his godly walk, his patience in sickness, and his faithfulness in his many labors.[1]

---

1. Thomas Fuller, *Abel Redevivus; or, the Dead Yet Speaking. The Lives and Deaths of the Modern Divines* (London: William Tegg, 1867), 1:186.

Martin Bucer

When he was in England, Bucer was often very cold. The damp climate was not good for his health. Young King Edward VI was concerned and kindly sent him money to buy a good stove!

While Bucer was traveling with his friend Paulus Fagius,[2] both men became ill. Fagius died first. A pastor-friend came to visit him on one occasion before a church service and told him that he would pray for him. Bucer answered with a prayer of his own: "Forsake me not, O Lord, in the time of my old age, and when my strength fails me." After church, the pastor returned and learned that the doctors dared not give him any more medication due to his great weakness. Bucer was not alarmed. Simply and trustingly he responded, "He, He it is that ruleth, and governeth all things." Bucer died quietly on February 27, 1551, at the age of sixty-one.

Bucer is perhaps best remembered for his contribution to the Reformation's understanding of the doctrine of the church. Six years after he died, his views were published in his most important book, *De Regno Christi* (The Reign of Christ). His emphasis on the church and the Holy Spirit's role in it influenced Calvin, as did his mediating role in developing the doctrine of the sacraments. Bucer felt that Luther went too far in stating that Christ was physically present in the Lord's Supper, and that Zwingli did not go far enough by treating the Supper only as a memorial. Like Calvin, he insisted that the Lord's Supper was a real means of grace (against Zwingli) and, at the same time, was essentially spiritual (against Luther).

---

2. Paulus Fagius (1504–1550) was a pastor in Germany. He also wrote several helpful books. Answering Thomas Cranmer's call, he went to England to help with the Reformation there. When Queen Mary came to the throne, she ordered his bones to be dug up and burned.

~ 9 ~

Ulrich Zwingli

(1484–1531)

He grieved over the sin and corruption of the clergy, over the ignorance and disregard for God's Word on the part of the people, and over the disrespect for God and His law.

What Luther was to the German Reformation, Ulrich Zwingli was to the Swiss Reformation. The Lord used Zwingli greatly to spread the gospel in Switzerland and beyond.

His family

Zwingli was born on January 1, 1484—only weeks after Luther—in a high alpine valley in Wildhaus, Switzerland. The town was reached by means of a steep mountain path through forests and meadows. The village was situated about two thousand feet above Zurich Lake. On the outskirts of the village was a log cabin where the Zwingli family lived.

The Zwinglis were a devoted Roman Catholic family. Ulrich's father was a shepherd and the village bailiff. He was loved and respected by all who knew him. He had eight sons and two daughters; of these ten children, Ulrich, or Huldrych, was the third. In his early boyhood, Ulrich kept his father's sheep. His mother used to tell her children stories from the Bible, while his father told them stories connected with the history of Switzerland. Thus, a love for the Bible, the Roman Catholic Church, and his native land grew in Ulrich's heart.

His studies

Because Zwingli's father believed his third child was destined for a higher calling than caring for sheep, he sent him at a young age to Wesen to study. He stayed there in the household of his uncle from 1489 to 1494. Young Zwingli

Zwingli when he was a child

many learned men. One of these well-known scholars was Desiderius Erasmus. Born in the Low Countries around 1466, Erasmus taught at Cambridge University in England for a time. Erasmus was aware of problems in the Roman Catholic Church, but he never broke from it.

Zwingli was a diligent student and was loved by his teachers. In 1496, he went to study in Berne under an eminent scholar, Heinrich Woelflin. However, Zwingli's father heard that his son's teachers were urging him to become a monk, so he sent a message telling him he must leave Berne for Vienna.

In 1498, Zwingli went to Vienna for a short time to study philosophy. He then went back to the University of Basel, where he graduated in 1502. In the humanist tradition, Zwingli was taught Greek, Hebrew, and Latin, which allowed him to read the Bible in its original languages. This helped him greatly in his understanding of scriptural doctrine and truths. His studies eventually led him, like Luther, to his belief in the doctrine of Scripture alone and justification by faith alone.

A priest and a soldier

Near Zwingli's hometown of Wildhaus was the town of Glarus. Since they had no priest, the people of Glarus asked Zwingli to be their priest. He agreed to this request. The ceremony in which he was installed as priest of the Roman Catholic Church took place in the church in Constance, the same church where Huss had been condemned to death.

After being in Glarus for a short time, Zwingli became a soldier and joined his fellow countrymen in fighting against France. He then returned to Glarus, where he again carried out the duties of a priest. While in Glarus, he continued to

was fond of books and enjoyed studying, so he progressed rapidly in his studies.

He went to St. Theodore's School in Basel when he was ten years old. Basel was famous for its scholars in that day, and Zwingli felt privileged to come into contact with

Ulrich Zwingli

study the Bible and began to see the importance of Scripture over the traditions of the Roman Catholic Church. The pope claimed to be infallible or without error when he spoke officially on behalf of the church, but Zwingli began to see that the church did not abide by the truths of Scripture. More and more, the Holy Spirit opened Zwingli's eyes to the errors of Rome. He grieved over the sin and corruption of the clergy, over the ignorance and disregard for God's Word on the part of the people, and over the disrespect for God and His law. The Holy Spirit was working a love for God and for His Word in the heart of the priest of Glarus. Zwingli became alarmed. He wondered how the church could survive if it was so corrupt. The more he studied Scripture, the more he realized how far the church had wandered from the truth. He decided to go to Basel and seek answers.

At Basel, Zwingli met Erasmus again. He was impressed with Erasmus's knowledge and respect for God's Word. But Erasmus did not push very hard for change, nor did he like debate and argument. He tried to be a friend to everyone, but in the end, he was distrusted by both Protestants and Roman Catholics.

His conversion

Shortly after Zwingli returned to Glarus, he became a soldier once again, this time to help Italy fight against France. Sin, war, and injustice: religion had an impact on everything. Zwingli was losing faith in his once-loved church.

When he returned to Glarus, people noticed a change in him. He preached powerfully from the Scriptures, expounding its blessed truths. He did not so much denounce the Roman Catholic Church as he held up the Word of God as the only supreme truth. The people at Glarus loved

Zwingli and were sad when he accepted a call as priest at Einsiedeln in 1516.

Einsiedeln

Einsiedeln was an important medieval pilgrimage site. During this time Zwingli met many pilgrims who were searching for inward peace. One reason so many pilgrims visited this mountain village is the story that was told about it. It was said that in the days of Charlemagne, long ago, a hermit prayed to an image of Mary that stood in Einsiedeln. As he bowed in prayer, he was cruelly murdered. The murder was discovered and the murderers punished. A church was built on the site in honor of the murdered hermit. It was said that Christ and His angels came to consecrate the church. How could they be sure that Jesus Himself came down to the church? They discovered a stone that they imagined had the hand print of the Savior pressed into it. The pope declared the site to be holy. Forgiveness of sins was promised by the pope to anyone who made the trip to this shrine called Our Lady of the Hermits. Each year a special festival was celebrated that drew many pilgrims to Einsiedeln.

Although we know this story is false, Zwingli had grown up in the Roman Catholic Church and had simply believed all these stories and doctrines. To question the church was a sin. The Holy Spirit continued His work in Zwingli's heart so that he understood it was foolish to teach that all these people had to travel so far, often in pain or in poverty, to gain forgiveness of sins. Did God require many sacrifices for sin?

Here in Einsiedeln, the Lord continued His preparation of Zwingli for the great work He had planned for His servant. Zwingli continued to study the Scriptures and memorized most of the New Testament as well as large portions of

Zwingli comforting the sick

the Old Testament. Boldly, he began to preach what he discovered in the Bible. "*Christ* is our sacrifice," he said. "We don't need other sacrifices for sin." He also declared, "God is everywhere. It is not necessary to travel great distances to find Him." As is always the case when the gospel is preached, some believed, "but some doubted" (Matthew 28:17).

Zurich

In 1519, Zwingli became pastor of the church in Zurich, a large city in Switzerland. In his first sermon to his new congregation, he said, "To Christ will I lead you: He is the source of salvation. His word is the only food I wish to nourish your hearts and lives with."

After he had been preaching for some time, someone said to him, "Master Ulrich, they tell me you have gone along with the new error, and that you must certainly be a Lutheran."

Zwingli replied, "I learned the doctrines that I teach and preach from the Greek New Testament before I ever heard the name of Luther. I preach as Paul writes; why do you not then call me a Paulinian? Yes, I preach the word of Christ; why do you not rather call me a Christian?"

While in Zurich, Zwingli became convinced that the Roman Catholic Church was teaching many false doctrines and rules. He spoke strongly against indulgences, just as Luther did. He removed the images, altars, and relics from the church. Relics are items that the Roman Catholic Church believed to be sacred. The church might have a small piece of wood and say it was a splinter of the cross; or some hair, which they said was a lock of Peter's hair. People would treat these items as holy things, often traveling long distances to see them.

In 1523, Zwingli wrote sixty-seven articles, or theses, promoting Protestant truths and showing what was wrong in the church. (These theses were even more Christ-centered than Luther's ninety-five theses were.) This led to a debate in the city of Zurich. Zwingli defended his beliefs, clearly stating why the Roman Catholic Church was wrong. He told the audience that salvation is by faith alone, and he pointed out how far the church had strayed from this truth. Zwingli won the debate; no one could successfully argue against him. The Lord blessed Zwingli and his work so that many reforms were made in the city of Zurich.

Zwingli was also used by God to write several books and tracts refuting Roman Catholic doctrine and practice. *To Allow Priests to Marry, or at Least Wink at their Marriages* was written in 1522. In this tract, Zwingli argued that priests should be allowed to marry, because the Bible supported marriage. In forbidding priests to marry, the church created many problems for the priests. Zwingli wanted this to change by allowing them to marry. Zwingli also wrote several tracts against the Roman Catholic view of the Lord's Supper, teaching his own view that the Lord's Supper was a memorial of the Lord's death.

Luther and Zwingli

Luther and Zwingli wrote letters back and forth between them. They had much in common, but they also had their differences. In 1529, they decided to meet at Marburg with some of their friends to discuss these differences. The meeting became known as the Marburg Colloquy.[1] Philip Melanchthon was also at the meeting. His kind manner was a peaceable influence, and the two Reformers agreed on fourteen points. But on one point they could not agree. Luther believed that the body of Christ is physically present in the bread and the wine at the Lord's Supper. Zwingli, however,

---

1. "Colloquy" means conversation, debate, or discussion. It comes from the Latin *loqui*, "to speak."

believed that the bread and the wine are only symbols of the body and blood of Jesus. Because of this difference, sad to say, Luther refused to shake Zwingli's hand as a sign of brotherhood, causing Zwingli to shed tears.

Because of this difference in the teachings of Luther and Zwingli, Protestantism was split into two kinds of churches. The Lutheran Church followed Luther's teachings, and the Reformed Church in Switzerland followed Zwingli's teachings. Much of Switzerland accepted Zwingli's doctrines, but some parts remained Roman Catholic. Persecution broke out and there was a threat of war, but this was avoided temporarily when the Roman Catholics and the Protestants promised not to fight against each other.

Killed in battle

When the Roman Catholics continued to persecute the Protestants, however, war broke out. In 1531, a large army of Catholics invaded Zurich. Quickly, the followers of Zwingli gathered together to defend themselves. Zwingli also joined, not as a soldier, but as a chaplain. He cared for the wounded and comforted the dying. About five hundred of Zwingli's followers died in the battle.

Zwingli himself was also killed. As he knelt over a wounded soldier, telling him about Jesus Christ, he was wounded. A soldier approached him and asked Zwingli if he wanted him to get a priest so that he could make his final confession. Zwingli refused. When the soldier realized that Zwingli was a Protestant, he killed him with his sword. His body was then cut in pieces, burned, and his ashes scattered. He was only forty-seven years old, but the Lord wanted His brave and faithful servant to come and live with Him forever in heaven.

Zwingli's death on the battlefield

~ 10 ~

Heinrich Bullinger

(1504–1575)

One of Bullinger's major contributions to the Reformation was his help in writing the Reformed confessions of Switzerland.

Heinrich Bullinger was born in Bremgarten, Switzerland on July 18, 1504. There are two interesting facts known about his childhood, both involving God's sparing mercy. When he was an infant, a serious plague broke out. Many people died, and the family worried that their young child would die, too. But God kept him safe. When he was a little older, he had a terrible accident. It is not known exactly what happened, but young Heinrich fell and received a bad wound in his throat. He could not eat for five days, and the danger of infection was great. God, however, had a plan for this boy, and so his life was spared once again. God wanted to use him to further the Reformation.

Bullinger's father was a parish priest of great learning, and he wished his son to begin his education at an early age. There was a school near his home, and at five years of age, Heinrich was sent to this school. At age twelve, Heinrich was sent to Emmerich in Rhenish Prussia[1] to study. This town was well known for its many learned scholars. Although his parents were not poor, they sent him off with only one extra set of clothes, and while he was at school, they seldom sent him any money. His father believed that this was for his own good, and that poverty would make him kind and helpful to the poor. Like Luther, Bullinger had to sing and beg for his food.

Bullinger moved to Cologne at age fifteen to continue his schooling. He studied Greek and Latin, as well as literature and science. In the privacy of his room, however, Bullinger eagerly read the writings of the early church fathers,

---

1. Prussia was a former German state. "Rhenish" pertains to the Rhine River or the lands bordering on it.

as well as those of Luther, Melanchthon, and Zwingli. The Lord blessed him with a new heart, and Bullinger became a Protestant.

Bullinger's first job was teaching school at an abbey in Kappel, which was near Zurich. In 1529, he returned to his hometown, Bremgarten, to be a minister. He spent much time in prayer and studying the Scriptures to seek out its truths. In his preaching, he pointed out the errors of the Roman Catholic Church, as well as those of the Anabaptists, who, in several ways, went beyond the Reformers in their teachings. After Zwingli died in 1531, the people of Zurich called Bullinger to be their pastor. He remained in Zurich for forty years, carrying on the work of the Reformation in Switzerland that Zwingli had begun.

Bullinger was a kind, friendly man who welcomed many Christians into his home. When Queen Mary began persecuting the Protestants in England, he helped many of those who fled to Switzerland. After these people returned to England, he kept contact with them through letters. He also wrote many of the Reformers, such as Bucer, Melanchthon, Calvin, Beza, Peter Martyr, and other people who helped in the great work of the Reformation.

Bullinger was a man who did not like the unkind feelings some people held toward each other when they did not agree on matters. He was grieved when Luther and Zwingli spoke angry words and wrote bitter things to each other. Although he himself did not agree with Luther's teaching on the Lord's Supper, he treated Luther and other Christians kindly and lovingly.

Bullinger wrote a few hundred books, including major studies on providence, justification, the nature of the Scriptures, and the history of the Reformation. He also wrote several commentaries on Bible books and numerous books against different errors. The best summary of his teaching is his *Decades*, which consists of five groups of ten sermons each that preach through all the major teachings of the Reformed faith. Published from 1549 to 1551, the *Decades* were soon translated into English, Dutch, and French. In England, they easily outsold Calvin's *Institutes*. They also were used in England as required reading for all ministers who had not obtained a master's degree in theology.

One of Bullinger's major contributions to the Reformation was his help in writing the Reformed confessions of Switzerland. He was one of the writers of the first Helvetic Confession, published in 1536, and he wrote the Second Helvetic Confession (1566) on his own. Also, he helped John Calvin with a pamphlet called *Concensus Tigurinus*, which examined the doctrine of the Lord's Supper. He wrote many tracts about the errors of the Roman Catholic Church. He also wrote against the errors of the Anabaptists, who troubled the congregation at Bremgarten. Then, of course, there was the ongoing tension between the Lutherans and the Calvinists, in which his wise advice was continually sought.

In 1561, Bullinger became very ill with a pestilence that invaded Tigurum (Zurich) where he was attending the Council of Trent. He thought he was going to die, so he asked the ministers of the city to come to his bedside so he could say good-bye to them. However, his time on earth was not finished yet. God completely restored his health so that he could continue his work.

During the persecution of the Protestants in France, Bullinger took up collections in various churches to send relief to the suffering Christians who fled France, leaving behind their homes and possessions. Bullinger worked hard

Heinrich Bullinger

to teach people the truth of Scripture. He tried hard to keep error out of the Protestant churches. He loved God's Word and labored faithfully for many years in God's service.

In 1575, Bullinger became seriously ill again. He had much pain, but instead of complaining, he prayed this prayer: "If it seems good unto Almighty God to count me worthy to be a pastor in His church a little longer, let Him give me strength, and I will willingly obey Him. But if He will call me out of this life, which is what I desire, I am also ready to obey His will; for nothing can be more welcome to me than to leave this wretched and sinful world, and go unto my Savior Christ."[2]

He said good-bye to his friends and to the pastors and professors in the city, urging them to be strong in the faith and to avoid sin. He exhorted them to promote unity among themselves and to defend one another. He also wrote several farewell letters to friends who lived farther away. In his pain, he often quoted the Psalms or the Lord's Prayer. At last, he died peacefully, on September 18, 1575, at the age of seventy-one.

Bullinger may well be the most underrated of all the Reformation heroes. Recent scholarship has shown that he was far more influential than is generally recognized. John Calvin often turned to him for advice, as did many of the Reformers. Bullinger's extant (still in existence) letters, which help reveal that he was indeed a major influence in the Reformation, outnumber those of Luther, Zwingli, and Calvin combined.

---

2. Thomas Fuller, *Abel Redevivus; or, The Dead Yet Speaking. The Lives and Deaths of the Modern Divines* (London: William Tegg, 1867), 2:34.

~ 11 ~

William Tyndale

(c. 1494–1536)

Tyndale began to understand the need for the people to have the Bible in their own language so that they could see the truth for themselves, directly from the Word of God.

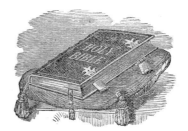

In recent chapters, we learned much about Luther, Melanchthon, and the work of the Reformation in Germany. Now we will look at what happened at around the same time in England.

Tyndale's birth and education

William Tyndale (Tĭn'-dayl) was most likely born in a small village near Dursley, in Gloucestershire, England, around 1494, about ten years after Luther was born. His family descended from prosperous landowners, wool merchants, and administrators. When he was quite young, he went to Magdalen College, Oxford University.[1] He received his B.A. degree on July 4, 1512, and his M.A. degree on July 2, 1515. Then he went on to Cambridge University.

The Lord blessed Tyndale with a special ability to learn languages. He could speak eight languages fluently: Hebrew, Greek, Latin, Spanish, French, Italian, English, and German.

His conversion

Tyndale had been a diligent student of the New Testament in the Greek language while he was in college. In those days, men studying to become priests needed to ask the bishop for permission to read or translate any part of the Bible. Rarely was permission granted. Tyndale was one of the few who

---

1. Both Oxford and Cambridge universities have several different colleges and buildings with different names. See Appendices C and D for more information about these universities.

dared to study the Scriptures in secret, without permission. At first he only studied it as he did other books. He thought of it as a kind of religious textbook. Soon, however, he began to see that the Bible was different. The Holy Spirit began to work in his heart, and he came to believe that the Bible is God's Word. In this way, he learned to know and love the Lord Jesus Christ.

While at Cambridge University, he met Thomas Bilney[2] and John Frith,[3] Protestants who became his good friends. His new friends were glad about his new faith. They understood how important the knowledge of the truth is and desired to bring the gospel to others. They told their fellow students that priests could not forgive sins; only the blood of the Lamb of God can take away the sin of the world.

One day, when Tyndale was talking with a priest, the priest remarked, "I believe it would be better to be without God's law than to be without the pope's law."

This made Tyndale angry. "I defy the pope and all his laws!" he exclaimed. "If God spares my life, I will make it so in England that ploughboys[4] will know more of the Bible than many of the priests do now."

God enabled Tyndale to keep this promise.

---

2. Thomas Bilney (1495–1531) preached in London and East Anglia. He was tried in 1527 as a heretic and yielded when the council forced him to recant. Upon this, he was released, but he renounced his recantation and resumed preaching. He was arrested and burned at the stake.

3. John Frith (1503–1533) assisted Tyndale in translating the New Testament. He was also burned at the stake.

4. Ploughboys worked on farms and did not receive an education.

His preaching

In 1521, Tyndale left Cambridge to become a tutor and private chaplain for the family of John Walsh, one of Henry VIII's knights. The Walsh family lived in a big house, which they called Little Sodbury. It was located on the Severn River, near Tyndale's birthplace. During the week he taught the Walsh children, but on Sundays Tyndale preached in the little chapel located behind the mansion. He spoke clearly and with authority, boldly pointing out the errors of the Roman Catholic Church against the truth of Scripture. He was a lively preacher and was not ashamed or timid about what he believed. He was invited to preach in other towns, too. People began to talk about this priest who spoke against the Roman Catholic Church. Other priests began to preach in the churches where he had preached, attempting to "undo" what Tyndale had stirred up. They called him a heretic and threatened to excommunicate anyone who took his doctrines to heart. They told lies about him. It was clear that they wanted to arrest and condemn him.

Sir John and Lady Walsh often invited well-educated and important guests to dinner. One of the main topics of discussion was Tyndale's preaching. The distinguished guests usually did not appreciate Tyndale's doctrines. They only wanted to believe what the Roman Catholic Church taught them. After one of these visits, Lady Walsh asked Tyndale, "Why should we believe you and your teachings, when these men are so much more educated than you are?"

Tyndale began to understand the need for the people to have the Bible in their own language so that they could see the truth for themselves, directly from the Word of God. It was not *him* the people needed to believe, but *God*. At the same time, other people besides Tyndale were beginning to feel that changes should be made within the Roman Catholic Church. People had strong opinions on the matter of religion. Tyndale felt it was no longer safe nor fair to his host family to remain with them, so in the summer of 1523, he left Little Sodbury and set out, not knowing exactly what he should do next.

His translation

All this time, his mind was full of the idea of translating the New Testament into English. During the last two hundred years, the English language had changed quite a bit, so Wycliffe's translation was not understood very well anymore. Tyndale wanted a translation that people could understand. The Roman Catholic Church, however, had written a law in 1408 forbidding anyone to translate the Bible into another language. The only authorized (accepted) version of the Bible was Jerome's Latin translation, known as the Vulgate.

Tyndale saw the people around him living and dying without knowledge of the Word of God, deceived by the false doctrines of the Roman Catholic Church. He had heard that the bishop of London, Cuthbert Tunstall, was a wealthy man. "Surely," he thought to himself, "the bishop would love to help me with such a wonderful task." But he soon found, as he later said, that "there was no room in the palace of the bishop of London for translating the New Testament."

Instead, Tyndale found a home with a godly merchant named Humphrey Monmouth. Monmouth was a kind, wealthy, Christ-like man who had heard Tyndale preach. He gladly welcomed Tyndale as his guest and supported him while he began working on his translation of the Bible. During his stay with his new friend, Tyndale preached at

William Tyndale

St. Dunstan's in London. Many people came to listen and enjoyed the fact that he preached so that everyone could understand his message.

Tyndale immediately began to translate the New Testament into English. It was dangerous work. Increasingly, persecutions broke out throughout England against those who dared to read Scripture or any of the works of the Reformers. Tyndale concluded sadly, "Not only is the bishop's house closed against the Bible, but all of England." It was no longer safe for Tyndale to remain in England.

Tyndale found a boat in the Thames River that was headed to Hamburg, Germany. Generously, Monmouth gave Tyndale money for his voyage. Arriving in Hamburg in 1524, Tyndale found someone who was willing to help him continue his work of translation. William Roy had left the Franciscan order because he was frustrated with the injustices and errors in the Roman Catholic Church, but he did not go so far as to embrace Protestantism. Some historians believe Tyndale visited Luther at Wittenberg, but there is no evidence for this.

It was too dangerous to stay in one place for long, so Tyndale moved to Cologne. He lived in remote buildings and kept himself hidden as much as possible. Here he found a printer named Peter Quentell who was willing to use the new printing press to print his English New Testament.

When Wycliffe translated the Bible into English, the art of printing was not known. Just before the Reformation, the printing press had been invented by John Gutenberg. The first major work he did was the Latin Vulgate, which was finished in 1456 in Mainz, Germany. This Bible was called the Gutenberg Bible. The benefits of this new invention were obvious, and printing presses were much in demand. Clearly, it was also a blessing in the work of translating the Scriptures into English and other languages, so that the gospel could reach many more people. Without the printing press, it would have been impossible to produce copies of the Bible fast enough to meet the needs and demands of the people, and the great work of the Reformation could never have spread as quickly as it did.

Printing began in Cologne in the summer of 1525, but after completing only the first twenty-two chapters of Matthew, Peter Quentell was discovered. A man named Johann Dobneck, or John Cochlæus as he called himself, a forceful enemy of the Reformation, was in Cologne at the same time as Tyndale. He soon discovered that someone had translated the New Testament into English and was printing it. He was determined to find the printer who was helping Tyndale and to destroy all Tyndale's work. Acting very pious and friendly, he talked to supporters of Tyndale's efforts and discovered the truth about the plan to print Bibles. The next morning, the house was surrounded by enemies, and the press was seized. Thankfully, Tyndale was warned of Dobneck's plans. Before the soldiers came, he and William Roy quickly gathered up as many of the translated pages of the Bible as they could and escaped. They fled by way of ship, going up the Rhine River to Worms, where Lutheranism thrived.

In Worms, Tyndale found a new printer to help him, named Peter Schoeffer. By the end of 1526, thousands of Tyndale's English New Testaments were ready to be sold. Here is the same passage that we showed you from Wycliffe's translation, now in Tyndale's translation. In our Bible it can be found in John 5:2–9.

There is at Jerusalem, by the slaughterhousse a pole called in the ebrue tonge, bethesda, havynge five porches, in them laye a greate multitude off sicke folke, off blynde, halt, and wyddered, waytynge for the movynge off the water. For an angell went doune at a certayne ceason into the pole an stered the water. Whosoever then fyrst after the sterynge off the water stepped doune was made whoale off whatsoever disease he had. And a certayne man was there, which had bene diseased xxxviii yeares. When Jesus sawe hym lye, and knewe that he nowe longe tyme had bene diseased, he sayde unto hym: Wilt thou be whoale? The syke answered hym: Syr, i have no man when the water is moved, to put me into the pole. Butt in the meane tyme, whill i am about to come, another steppeth doune before me. Jesus sayde unto hym, ryse, take up thy beed and walke. And immediatly that man was whoale, and toke up his beed, and went. And the same daye was the saboth daye.

The people had to be very careful, however. It was dangerous to read the Bible, for the Roman Catholic Church did not want people to read it. They passed a law forbidding anyone to buy or read the Book, and they burned the Bibles they found. People caught with Bibles were persecuted. This opposition did not stop the spread of the knowledge and love of God's Word, however. Secretly, cautiously, people distributed the Bibles. In spite of the determination of the Roman Catholic Church to stop the circulation of the New Testament, copies made their way into England and Scotland, often hidden amid the merchandise of merchants traveling into England from Germany. "The people that walked in darkness have seen a great light: they that dwell in the land of the shadow of death, upon them hath the light shined" (Isaiah 9:2). Many were blessed by the new translation of the New Testament into English, and they rejoiced at the good news of the gospel.

Enemies' plans ruined

Not everyone welcomed the translation of the New Testament. The Roman Catholic Church condemned Tyndale as a heretic. Their intent was to arrest him and bring him to trial. Bishop Tunstall determined to stop the spread of this English Bible. He thought the best way to do this was to buy as many copies as he could find and then burn them. He believed God would be pleased that he was ridding his country of the Scriptures in the common language of the people.

Though some scholars now question the accuracy of the following story, a sixteenth century source reports that Bishop Tunstall hired a man named Augustine Packington, a merchant who knew Tyndale, to buy all the copies of the New Testament he had to sell. The bishop had plenty of money, so he told Packington not to worry about the price. Packington found the house where Tyndale lived. "William," began the merchant, "I know you are a poor man, and that you have many New Testaments for sale. You have endangered yourself and your friends for these, and have given all your money to this cause. I have found a merchant who is willing to buy all your New Testaments. That way you will get rid of all your Testaments and earn some money as well."

"Who is the merchant?" asked Tyndale.

"The Bishop of London," answered Packington.

"But he will burn them!" exclaimed Tyndale.

"True," admitted the visitor.

Amazingly, Tyndale agreed. "It is good. That way I will get money to get myself out of debt, and the whole world will cry out against the burning of God's Word. With the money I will receive, I will make a better edition of the New Testament."

The bargain was made. The Bibles were bought. They were carried over to London, and Bishop Tunstall ordered his servants to make a huge bonfire with the Bibles near St. Paul's Cross. The bishop himself preached a sermon on this occasion, claiming to have found 2,000 errors in Tyndale's work, but in his ignorance he was comparing the New Testament to the Latin Vulgate rather than the original Greek.

The bishop thought he had stopped the circulation of the Scriptures, but it was not so. Tyndale took the money he had received for the Bibles and printed a larger and better edition than before! The bishop discovered that instead of stopping the circulation of the Bibles, he had helped it. It seemed that for every Bible burned, many more Bibles appeared. Though it was forbidden to bring the Bible into England, people smuggled them in anyway. They hid them in cargoes of wheat or in bundles of merchandise. The attention given to the Bible aroused the curiosity of even irreligious people; those who could afford it bought a New Testament simply to see for themselves what all the fuss was about.

Bishop Tunstall summoned Packington. "I thought you bought all the Bibles. Why are there still so many around?"

Packington replied, "I certainly did buy all that were available, but I believe they have printed more of them. What you need to do is buy the printing presses too, or they will continue printing more and more Bibles."

A man in London who had worked hard to sell many of the Bibles was arrested and put on trial. During the trial, the judge asked him if he knew who was helping Tyndale print so many Bibles. The man answered, "The bishop of London is doing more to help him than anyone else, for the money he paid to buy the Bibles he ordered to be burned has been used to print new ones." God was bringing good out of evil.

His writing

One of the most influential books Tyndale wrote is called *Obedience of a Christian Man*. In this book, he explains why it is important to have the Bible in the language of the people. He tells his readers what their duties are and condemns the Roman Catholic practices of penance, confession, absolution, and the worship of saints. He also points out the false power of the pope. A lady named Anne Boleyn owned a copy of this book. Anne was the second wife of King Henry VIII. She loved to read the Scriptures and any books written about them. The Lord used this particular copy of Tyndale's book in a special way.

Anne Boleyn lent this book to one of her servants, who enjoyed it very much. This lady had a friend who also read it with great interest. The Lord used it for his conversion. This man, named George Zouch, loved this book so much that he even dared to read it during a Roman Catholic mass. He was caught reading it by the dean of the chapel, who gave it to the cardinal. When the cardinal heard that the book actually belonged to the queen, he decided he had better consult King Henry about it. When Anne heard about it, she was angry and said, "It is the dearest book that ever the dean or the cardinal took away!" She then went straight to King Henry and asked him to get it back for her. She even asked him to read it for himself.

When the cardinal appeared with the book in his hand and told the king what a terrible book it was, the king asked to see it. He scanned some of the pages and said it seemed like a very good book. King Henry kept the book and read

Arrest of Tyndale

it carefully later on. He was impressed with it, although its truths never penetrated his heart. He commented to Anne after reading it, "This is a book for me and all kings to read!"

Because Tyndale knew his life was in danger, he moved to Marburg, where he stayed for four years. Tyndale did not rest after finishing his New Testament translation. He revised his New Testament and began to translate the Old Testament from Hebrew into English. In December 1528, his college friend John Frith came from England and joined Tyndale in Antwerp to help him with this monumental task. In 1529, having completed the translation of the Pentateuch, or the first five books of the Bible, Tyndale wanted to have it printed. He boarded a ship for Hamburg but was shipwrecked on the coast of Holland. He located another ship which took him to Hamburg. A short time later he moved to Antwerp. Finally, in 1530–1531, the Pentateuch was published by Johan Hoochstraten of Antwerp. In 1531, he also completed translating the book of Jonah, which was printed that same year.

In addition to translating much of the Bible, Tyndale wrote commentaries on several books of the Bible as well as some books describing the errors of the Roman Catholic Church.

His imprisonment

Tyndale was not able to finish translating the Old Testament. Thinking he was safe, he moved to Antwerp in 1534 and lived there openly. He was mistaken. The enemies of God's Word asked the pope for permission to have Tyndale arrested. Even Henry VIII was in agreement, accusing Tyndale of stirring up the people against the church. The Roman Catholic clergy hired Henry Phillips, a wicked, young

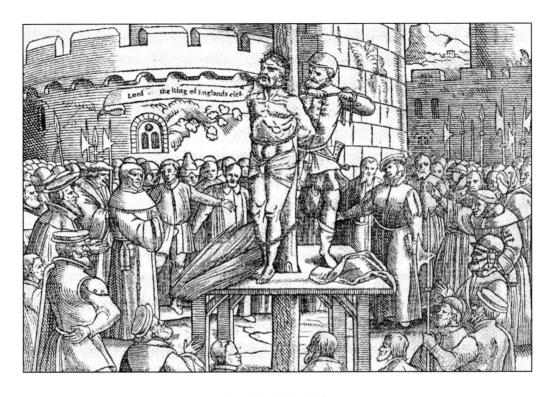

Death of Tyndale

Englishman who wanted money, to pretend to be Tyndale's friend by showing interest in his translation work. The plan was successful; Phillips betrayed Tyndale for cash. Phillips tricked Tyndale into leaving the safety of his Antwerp home, only to be met by waiting officers. On May 21, 1535, Tyndale was arrested, the Antwerp home was raided, and Tyndale was imprisoned in the castle of Vilvoorden near Brussels under horrible conditions. His prison cell was small, damp, and gloomy, but his faith in Christ and the love and comfort of God upheld him in these difficult months. The other prisoners were impressed with his godliness and said to one another, "If this man is not a good Christian, we don't know what is good anymore."

Even while in prison, Tyndale tried to continue his work. Some historians believe that he completed translating the books Joshua through 2 Chronicles while in prison, but there is no proof of that. In a surviving letter written by Tyndale to the governor of the prison, he begs for warmer clothing and that he might be allowed the use of his Hebrew Bible, Hebrew grammar, and Hebrew dictionary.[5]

His death

While he was in prison, the priests often came to persuade him to return to the Roman Catholic Church. When they realized they could not change his mind, Tyndale was sentenced to death by seventeen commissioners on August 12, 1536. Tyndale was summoned from his cell to the castle courtyard on October 6, 1536, after five hundred days of imprisonment. He was tried on a charge of heresy in 1536 and condemned to the stake. The executioners bound him to the stake, strangled him with the chain tied around his neck, and then burned his body to ashes. His last words were, "Lord, open the king of England's eyes!" Tyndale was approximately forty-two years old.

King Henry VIII had opposed the circulation of the Scriptures through his kingdom, but the prayer of the dying martyr was answered to some degree, at least outwardly.

---

5. Gertrude L. Woodward, *The History of the Transmission of the Bible* (Chicago: The Newberry Library, 1935), 44.

Several years after Tyndale's death, John Roger assembled all of Tyndale's biblical translations, which included half of the Old Testament published for the first time, and all of the New Testament. To this he added Miles Coverdale's work on the remaining Bible books and published this Bible in 1537 as Matthew's Bible. Two years later, after Roger made a few additional revisions, a new Bible was published that became known as the Great Bible of 1539. King Henry made a law that a copy of this Bible was to be placed in every church in England, so that all the people might read it or hear it read. Thus, within a few years after Tyndale's death, several editions of the Great Bible, which was seventy percent Tyndale's work, were circulated through England by royal permission.

The Lord greatly blessed the work of this faithful servant of God. Later on, the translators of the King James Version of the Bible (1611) leaned heavily on Tyndale's translation. Scholars estimate that more than seventy-five percent of the King James Version is taken from Tyndale's work. The Reformation continued to grow because of God's blessing on the efforts of William Tyndale.

~ 12 ~

King Edward VI

❖◆❖

(1537–1553)

God called this young prince to know and serve Him when he was still young. Like Samuel, Edward obeyed the call of the Lord.

His birth and education

King Edward VI, son of King Henry VIII, was born at the Hampton Court Palace on October 12, 1537. His mother, Jane Seymour, died only twelve days after his birth. His father believed education was important, and when Edward was only six years old, King Henry selected two well-educated men to be Edward's teachers. One was a godly nobleman and the other, a faithful minister of the gospel. They found that Edward was eager to learn. He made such good progress in his studies that, by the age of nine, he could speak, read, and write in four different languages, including Greek. Some of his letters and compositions, written in Latin and French, are on display in a British museum.

His love for God's Word

Prince Edward was privileged to hear godly court preachers. Some of these were Hugh Latimer, Nicholas Ridley, and John Knox. Archbishop Thomas Cranmer was also one of the instructors of the young prince. Better than these distinguished instructors, however, the Lord Himself taught Edward. The Holy Spirit blessed their preaching to the young prince's heart. Just as the Lord called Samuel when he was just a child, God called this young prince to know and serve Him when he was still young. Like Samuel, Edward obeyed the call of the Lord.

Edward loved the Bible and desired to understand it better. He tried to live the way the Bible taught him to live. One day, the young prince was in the library. He was trying to get something from a high shelf, but he couldn't reach it. A large book was lying on the table. One of his servants picked it up and laid it on the floor for him to stand on. Edward saw that it was the Bible. Lifting it up from the floor, he placed it reverently on the table again. Laying his hand on it, he said, "This is God's blessed Book. It is not right that we should trample under our feet that which He has given us to treasure in our heads and hearts."

He becomes king

King Henry VIII died when Edward was only ten years old. At that young age, Edward became king of England. A grand ceremony was held to celebrate this special occasion on February 28, 1547. Three swords were to be carried before him in the procession, representing his three kingdoms: England, Ireland, and France. Edward stated he wanted one more sword: the sword of the Spirit, which is the Bible. He insisted on having a Bible carried with those three swords, to show that he received his authority as king from the Word of God.

His fruitful reign

In a letter to his friend, Thomas Cranmer, Edward wrote, "I believe that I must desire and practice godliness above all things, since St. Paul has said, 'Godliness is profitable to all things.'"

Cranmer replied, "From your letters I perceive that in your love of learning, heavenly truths are the things you care most for, and whoever cares about those things, shall not be overcome by any worries. Go on, therefore, in the way upon which you have entered, and adorn your native land,

that the light of virtue which I behold in you may hereafter enlighten all your England."[1]

King Edward resisted the attempts of Roman Catholics at court to influence him. He did not give in, and the Reformation proceeded. In a letter to Bullinger from a man named John ab Ulmis, we learn of the happy changes in England:

> England is adorned and enlightened by the Word of God and the number of the faithful increases largely every day. The mass, so dear to papists, begins to give way—in many places it is already dismissed and condemned by divine authority.... Peter Martyr has proven, from the Scriptures and the writings of orthodox divines, that purgatory is only a burden which we have been forced to bear. He has proven that Eucharist, or the holy Supper of the Lord, is a commemoration of Christ, and a solemn showing forth of His death, not a sacrifice.[2]

King Edward did much good in his short reign. He had the Scriptures circulated all through the country. Thirty-six different editions of the whole Bible or of the New Testament were printed and sold during his reign. Besides these, portions of the Bible and other good books were printed in great numbers. He had a new *Book of Common Prayer* published, as well as a new catechism and the Forty-Two Articles of Faith. Images were removed from the churches. Candles and processions were no longer permitted. Priests were allowed to marry. He removed the restrictions King

---

1. *Lives of the British Reformers, From Wickliff to Foxe* (London: The Religious Tract Society, 1884), 236.
2. Ibid., 237.

Henry had made against preaching, so that the gospel was freely preached.

When King Edward was near the end of his life, already weak and ill, Bishop Ridley preached to him. The subject of the sermon was kindness to the poor. Much affected by this sermon, the king asked the mayor and aldermen of London to visit him. He wanted to think of more ways to help the poor. In a few days, the men returned with a plan.

A monastery was turned into a school for poor children. Another monastery became a home for handicapped people. A sanctuary was established for people with mental disorders. He established hospitals and gave money to support them. A way was found to help widows and poor women. In this way, King Edward helped thousands of people. He cared very much for the spiritual needs of the people, but he also realized the need for physical help for his subjects.

King Edward VI

His early death

Sadly, Edward reigned only six years. In the year 1552, he contracted the measles and the smallpox, and he never quite recovered. In the spring, he moved to the country to get fresh air and sunshine, but during the following winter he developed a cough, and symptoms of tuberculosis appeared.

John Foxe writes: "About three hours before his death, this godly child, his eyes being closed, and thinking that none heard him, made this prayer: 'Lord God, deliver me out of this miserable and wretched life, and take me among Thy chosen. However, not my will, but Thy will be done. Lord, I commit my spirit to Thee. O Lord! Thou knowest how happy I would be to live in heaven with Thee, yet for Thy chosen's sake, send me life and health, that I may truly serve Thee. O my Lord God, bless Thy people, and save Thine inheritance. O Lord God, save Thy chosen people of England. O my Lord God, defend this realm from papistry, and maintain the true religion, that I and my people may praise Thy holy name, for Thy Son Jesus Christ's sake.' A little later he said, 'I am faint, Lord, have mercy upon me, and take my spirit.'"

He died when he was sixteen on July 6, 1553, and was buried in Westminster Abbey on August 8. Thomas Cranmer led the funeral, insisting on a Protestant service even though the new Queen Mary wanted a Roman Catholic one. The sorrow of the English people was great, for they knew how much he had cared for them and grieved over how much the Protestant Reformation would suffer in England because of his death.

~ 13 ~

Thomas Cranmer

---◆◆◆---

(1489–1556)

*Stretching forth his hand
into the flame, he exclaimed,
"This hand hath offended;
oh, this unworthy right hand!"*

His education

Thomas Cranmer was born on July 2, 1489, in the town of Aslockton, Nottinghamshire, England. His father died while Thomas was just a child, but his mother did her best to raise him well. At age fourteen, she sent him to Jesus College, Cambridge. He graduated with a bachelor's degree in 1511 and a master's degree in 1515.

Soon afterwards, Cranmer married a young woman named Joan, but she died in childbirth a short time later. After being licensed to preach in 1520, Cranmer continued on at Jesus College, earning his doctorate in divinity in 1526. After graduating, he remained there, studying, lecturing, and serving as an examiner of young men studying for the ministry. Cranmer studied the Bible extensively. He began to see that the teachings of the Roman Catholic Church were in error, but he did not yet break away from the church.

He becomes the king's chaplain

When the plague[1] struck Cambridge, Cranmer and some of his students moved to Waltham Abbey. There he met some of King Henry VIII's advisers. One of the main topics of discussion at that time was that King Henry wanted to divorce his wife, Catherine. These men asked Cranmer what he thought would be the best way to help the king attain this divorce. Cranmer replied

---

1. Plagues struck England several times over the centuries, each time claiming thousands of victims.

that they should ask the universities for their opinion. The men told the king what Cranmer had said. King Henry was so pleased with his advice that he appointed Cranmer to be his chaplain, a position he held until the end of his life. A few years later, the king appointed him to be archbishop of Canterbury; he was officially ordained on March 30, 1533. This was the highest position in the Church of England.

One of the first services the new archbishop performed for King Henry was to grant him a divorce from Catherine. He then validated Henry's marriage to Anne Boleyn. She was a Protestant, and this made life a little easier for the Reformers and their followers.

He becomes a friend of the Reformation

Cranmer's position sometimes included travel. During these travels, he met some of the Reformers in Germany and read Luther's books. Cranmer also carried on correspondence with other Reformers such as Martin Bucer and Heinrich Bullinger. This led to a firmer embracing of the Reformed doctrines and teachings.

Cranmer was a humble, gentle man. He had learned to repay evil with good. It was said of him, "If you want to make this archbishop your friend, the surest way is to wrong him." But this same gentle character was also a flaw. He was not as firm as some of the other Reformers, yet the Lord used Thomas Cranmer to bring about much good in England. Cranmer agreed with King Henry that the pope should no longer rule over the Church of England. He also was instrumental in getting Tyndale's English translation of the Bible placed in every church. A lovely edition of the entire Scriptures, completed on August 4, 1537, and dedicated to King Henry VIII, was presented to Archbishop Cranmer.

Reading the chained Bible

Cranmer had someone show it to the king, and he asked the king for a royal "license that the same may be sold, and read of every person, without danger of any act, proclamation, or ordinance, heretofore granted to the contrary." The king granted his permission, and the people of England could now read the whole Word of God in their own language. The churches were open at all times so that anyone could go in to pray or read the Bible for himself whenever he wanted to do so.

From 1537 to 1547, Cranmer became very involved in the politics of England, which would help him during the reign of Edward VI. He was able to accomplish much for the Reformation because of his political friendships. Throughout these years, Cranmer began to change his view on two important doctrines of the Reformation: the Lord's Supper and justification by faith through the righteousness of Jesus Christ alone. Henry VIII did not support these doctrines, choosing rather to follow the Roman Catholic doctrines of justification by faith and works, and the bodily presence of Christ in the bread and wine of the Lord's Supper. Cranmer spoke about this issue in Parliament and made clear his position on these issues in 1548. He argued for the spiritual presence of the Lord Jesus Christ in the Lord's Supper and taught the Reformation doctrine of justification by faith alone.

After Henry died in 1547, Cranmer, together with the new king, Edward VI, helped bring about many changes in the Church of England. The Latin prayers were translated into English. The altars were changed into communion

Thomas Cranmer

tables. Images were removed from the churches. The use of candles and incense and other similar practices were stopped. Cranmer also had a book of homilies (sermons) printed, and the ministers were ordered to read them in their churches. In this way, the people were taught the nature of true religion.

A new prayer book was published, as well as a primer and catechism. In 1550, Cranmer published his major work, *A Defense of the True and Catholic* (universal) *Doctrine of the Sacrament of the Body and Blood of our Savior Christ*. This book was a confirmation of his view of the Lord's Supper as he had argued for it in 1548. During the reign of Edward VI, Cranmer was able to make gains for the Reformation, but he constantly dealt with enemies who were undermining his work.

Before Edward died, Cranmer signed a document that gave the crown to Lady Jane Grey rather than to King Henry's two daughters, Mary and Elizabeth. This action was contrary to the promise that Cranmer had made to Henry to uphold the princesses' rights to the throne. In a way, it was understandable that he would prefer Lady Jane Grey since she was a Protestant, and next in line was Mary, a rigid Roman Catholic. Still, he broke his promise to King Henry VIII, revealing his wavering character.

He is condemned

When the Roman Catholic Mary was crowned queen in 1553 after Edward died, a time of persecution ensued. Queen Mary hated the Protestants and the Reformation. It became a law that Protestants had to change their religion to Roman Catholicism. Those who did not were imprisoned or put to death. Archbishop Cranmer was among those who refused to change to Roman Catholicism.

Queen Mary condemned Cranmer for treason because of his role in helping Jane Grey to the throne.[2] Mary also hated Cranmer for the part he had taken in helping Henry divorce her mother, Catherine. She had him arrested and sent to the Tower prison, where Latimer and Ridley were also imprisoned. The three of them were transferred to Oxford, where they were called upon to give a legal defense of themselves. Their defense was not heeded, and they were pronounced heretics and sentenced to death.

Cranmer was convicted of treason on November 13, 1553. He was publicly degraded as he was stripped of the office of archbishop. Cranmer was stripped of his lovely garments and dressed in old rags. His accusers delighted in degrading the man who had held such a high position. He was examined in Oxford in April 1554, tried for heresy in September 1555, and condemned by Rome in December 1555.

His enemies tried to make him give up his Protestant faith and profess himself a Roman Catholic. He refused to do this. Mary knew his weakness and believed that if Cranmer would fall, great damage would be done to the spread of the Reformation. At her request, Cranmer's enemies suddenly changed their tactics and treated him kindly, working on his fears. They allowed him to stay in the home of the dean of Christ Church, where he was treated well. They talked about the danger of being killed for his beliefs and told him how much better it would be if he were to become a Roman Catholic. Happily, Cranmer stood firm and would not recant.

Mary was angry when she heard that Cranmer had not recanted. She ordered him to be sent to the worst part of the prison, where he was treated harshly. He was isolated from his friends. No one was allowed to give him anything that would alleviate his suffering. He was kept in prison for three long years.

He recants

Cranmer's friends, Ridley and Latimer, were burned at the stake before his eyes, and Cranmer felt sad and discouraged. Finally, his enemies succeeded in getting him to sign a paper stating that he had given up his Protestant faith and become a Roman Catholic. His enemies rejoiced at his sad fall. He signed not one, but several recantations, stating his agreement with Roman Catholic doctrine and authority.

Recanting didn't help Cranmer, however, since Queen Mary was still determined to have him killed. Signing a paper did not save his life after all. Instead, the Roman Catholics decided that Cranmer should read his recantation in front of all the people before he was burned at the stake.

His bold profession of faith before his death

On the day of his death, a huge crowd gathered to watch. Cranmer was forced to stand on a platform that had

---

2. Jane reigned only nine days before Mary's friends deposed Jane and crowned Mary queen of England.

been constructed near the pulpit in St. Mary's Cathedral. A priest had been selected to preach against Cranmer and the sin of heresy. Then the condemned man was asked to read his recantation.

"I will do so," said Cranmer. "Good people, my dearly beloved brethren and sisters in Christ, I beseech you most heartily to pray for me to Almighty God, that He will forgive all my sins and offences, which are many, without number, and great above measure. But one thing grieves my conscience more than all the rest, whereof, God willing, I intend to speak more later. But how great and how many my sins may be, I beseech you to pray to God for His mercy to pardon and forgive them all."

Then he kneeled down and prayed. After this, he rose and said,

> I am come to the end of my life on earth, and am near to beginning the life to come. First, I believe in God the Father Almighty, maker of heaven and earth. And I believe every article of the Christian faith, every word and sentence taught by our Savior Christ, His apostles, and the prophets, in the New and Old Testament.
>
> And now I come to the great thing that troubles my conscience more than any other thing that I ever did in my life, and that is that I wrote things against the truth, because I was afraid I would be killed. I now here renounce and refuse these things as things written with my hand contrary to the truth which I believed in my heart. All such things which I have written and signed with my own hand I now proclaim untrue. My hand has offended in

writing contrary to my heart; therefore, my hand shall first be punished, for when I come into the fire, it shall be burned first. As for the pope, I refuse him as Christ's enemy and as antichrist, with all his false doctrines.

This filled Cranmer's enemies with astonishment and rage. They had expected to triumph over the Reformers by having such a well-known man as Cranmer publicly recant. However, God triumphed over evil and over Cranmer's fear.

They rushed Cranmer to the stake, the same place where Latimer and Ridley had died. Dressed in an ankle-length robe, he was chained to the stake. He presented a lamentable picture: an old man with a long white beard, a bald head, and bare feet. As the flames rose around him, he looked up toward heaven, and stretching forth his hand into the flame, he exclaimed, "This hand hath offended; oh, this unworthy right hand!" Then, using the words of Stephen, the first martyr, he said, "Lord Jesus, receive my spirit."

On March 21, 1556, at the age of sixty-seven, Thomas Cranmer died for his faith. He was timid and had been so afraid to suffer; he did not always stand up for the truth; he had sins and faults like any other man. But God used him to extend the truths of the Reformation in England and enabled him to die as a heroic martyr for the faith.

~ 14 ~

Hugh Latimer

◆◆◆

(c. 1485–1555)

Nicholas Ridley

◆◆◆

(1500–1555)

In the last chapter, we mentioned Queen Mary, who became queen of England after her half-brother, Edward VI, died. Queen Mary tried to undo all the good that King Edward had done. She restored papal authority and Roman Catholic doctrine in England. These two aspects had been abolished during the reigns of Henry VIII and Edward VI under the influence of Archbishop Cranmer. The laws against heretics were now carried out and many Protestants were burned at the stake. Hundreds were martyred and thousands fled the country. Queen Mary became known as Bloody Mary because of her terrible persecution of the Protestants.

Part One: Hugh Latimer

His education

Hugh Latimer was born around the year 1485 at Thurcaston, Leicestershire, England. His family heritage was humble; his father and mother were farmers and earned their living from the land. Early in his life, Hugh's parents recognized his amazing mental ability and made sure that he would receive a good education. He attended Peterhouse College at Cambridge University at the age of fourteen, was elected a Fellow of Clare College in 1510, and graduated with several degrees in the 1520s.

At Cambridge, the writings of Wycliffe and Luther were read by some of the students with great interest. Hugh was raised a devout Catholic and did all in his power to oppose the influence of the Reformation. He attended the meetings of those studying the Reformers and debated with them, begging them to stay true to the Roman Catholic Church. He even defended his divinity degree in 1524 by attacking the theology of Philip Melanchthon.

His conversion

Latimer's conversion was brought about by means of Thomas Bilney. [1] Bilney noticed that Latimer was intelligent and a good orator. He began to pray that God would convert Latimer and use him to promote the Reformation. God answered Bilney's prayers in a remarkable way by helping him think of a way to share the gospel with Latimer. Bilney went to Latimer and asked to make confession. Kneeling before Latimer, Bilney shared "the anguish he had once felt in his soul," "the efforts he had made to remove it," and "lastly, the peace he had felt when he believed that Jesus Christ is the Lamb of God that taketh away the sins of the world."

Latimer no doubt knew this anguish as he tried to live by the rules of the church which could never satisfy a guilty conscience. And so, Latimer listened, trying to chase away his thoughts. But Bilney continued. When Bilney finally arose from his knees, Latimer remained seated, weeping. The gracious Bilney consoled him, "Brother, though your sins be as scarlet, they shall be as white as snow" (Isaiah 1:18). [2]

---

1. Thomas Bilney (1495–1531) did not believe many of the doctrines of the Roman Catholic Church. He influenced many students when he studied at Cambridge University. In 1527, he was tried as a heretic but recanted and was set free. He was later arrested again and burned at the stake.

2. J.H. Merle D'Aubigne, *History of the Reformation of the Sixteenth Century*, Book 18, Chapter 9.

Hugh Latimer

Latimer was convicted about the errors of the Roman Catholic Church and began to speak against them. The change to Protestantism came slowly for Latimer as the Word of God began to shed light on the errors of Roman Catholicism. He began to be convinced that the only way to salvation was through faith by hearing the preached Word of God (Romans 10:8–17).

God had done what no one thought possible: Latimer became a Protestant and a child of God. His attacks against the Reformers stopped, and he began to point out the errors of the Roman Catholic Church with as much zeal as he had criticized the Reformation before his conversion. He was even so bold as to write a letter to King Henry protesting a new law which forbade people to read the Bible as they pleased.

From the time his eyes were opened to see and understand the gospel of Jesus Christ, Latimer was untiring in his efforts to make it known to others. He, like the apostle Paul, determined to know nothing else among men "save Jesus Christ and him crucified" (1 Corinthians 2:2). He was an earnest, eloquent preacher. It was unusual in those days to hear such preaching, and great numbers of people followed him wherever he went, hungering for the truth. The clergy of the Roman Catholic Church was not pleased. They tried to make things difficult for him.

Latimer did not immediately leave the church, however, but remained a member of the Roman Catholic Church for quite some time. When his education was finished, Latimer became a Greek professor at Cambridge. Then he was ordained a priest. He was appointed rector, or pastor, of the church at West Kington in Wiltshire in 1531.

Summoned to London

Latimer did not hesitate to do what he believed was right. The Roman Catholic priests tried to stop him from preaching the doctrines of the Reformation, but he was not afraid of them. He continued boldly and did the work which he felt sure God had sent him to do. The bishops tried to stop him by telling him not to put the Bible into the hands of the people, but Latimer believed that the more people who could read the Bible for themselves, the better. They threatened him with a trial and imprisonment. He did not heed their threats, however, but went on bravely with his work.

At last they succeeded in having him summoned to London in 1532 to be examined by Bishop Gardiner, who was bishop of Winchester and a powerful enemy of the Reformation. Gardiner accused Latimer of preaching against the Roman Catholic Church. Latimer was actually ill when this summons came, but he obediently set out for London, ready to defend the truth. The bishops, however, only wanted him to sign a paper stating that he believed the Roman Catholic teachings were the truth and that any other doctrines were false. Latimer refused. Several times a week they questioned him, but he steadfastly refused to agree with them. Finally, he was excommunicated and condemned.

Later on, as J.H. Merle D'Aubigne writes, "Latimer was restored to favor by appealing to the king. He was released only after he agreed to fourteen points of Roman Catholic practice and worship which included approval of Lent and the lawfulness of crucifixes and images in the churches. This moment of weakness was, by his own admission, the low point in Hugh's life, a black day indeed, a sin which he confessed before his God, but a crucial point in his life: he resolved that, come what may, he would never do such foolishness again. It was a resolution which would be sorely tested."[3]

During King Henry VIII's reign, Latimer was twice imprisoned in the Tower of London (1539 and 1546). On one occasion, King Henry VIII asked Latimer what he answered

---

3. Ibid.

to these charges of heresy. Humbly yet boldly, Latimer answered, "I never counted myself worthy, nor did I ever ask to be a preacher before your grace, but I was summoned to court against my will, and am ready, if you dislike my sermons, to give place to those better than I; for I believe there may be many people better fitted for the position than I am. If it be your grace's pleasure to have them for preachers, I shall be content to walk behind them carrying their books. But if your grace should choose me for a preacher, I would desire you to give me permission to free my conscience and to teach my doctrine according to my audience. I would be very unwise indeed, to preach the same sermons at court as I do in the country."[4]

The king was pleased with this wise answer and gave him liberty to go on preaching the gospel. King Henry did not live according to all the laws of the Bible, and Latimer was not afraid to speak the truth to him. Normally, chaplains were very careful to avoid saying anything that might offend King Henry, but Latimer was different. While speaking before the king of England, he never forgot that he was also speaking before the King of heaven, and his first desire was to say what he knew would be pleasing to the Lord. This gave him courage to say some things before the king that no one else dared to say. Latimer was not afraid to speak about sin and repentance. Despite his pointed messages, the king had so much respect for Latimer that he was never angry with him.

His influence in government

In 1535, through the influence of Thomas Cranmer and Anne Boleyn,[5] wife of Henry VIII, Latimer was appointed to be the new Bishop of Worcester. Now Latimer had an even larger congregation to serve. He worked enthusiastically, preaching, visiting people, and refuting wrong teaching.

Latimer was chosen to preach at the opening of Parliament in 1536 and in the same year at a convocation called to confirm Henry VIII as head of the church in England. In both sermons, Latimer stressed the need for reform and urged his listeners to do what they could to bring about this much-needed change.

Imprisonment

Latimer gave up his position as bishop in 1539, however, when he realized he could not agree with a church that had corrupt doctrines, rules, and practices. His desire was to live quietly in the country studying the Scriptures. This was not God's will for him, however. During a storm, a tree fell on him and hurt him badly. He needed the expertise of a London doctor, so he set out at once to go there. His enemies soon discovered that Latimer was in London, and they quickly brought exaggerated charges against him. This resulted in his imprisonment in the Tower of London. He remained there for six years until King Henry's death. He was released in 1547, when Edward VI became king. King Edward offered him his former position as bishop, but Latimer refused, saying he was too old. He then accepted an invitation from Cranmer to help him in his work as archbishop, so he moved

---

4. *Foxe's Book of Martyrs* (Springdale, Penn.: Whitaker House, 1981), 475.

5. Anne Boleyn (c. 1507–1536), second wife of Henry VIII, was beheaded after being convicted of adultery.

to Lambeth and began his new work. For the next six years of his life he assisted his dear friend, Thomas Cranmer. People came to tell him their troubles, and Latimer tried to help as best he could. He became so well-known for his kindness and ability to help the poor that people came from all over England to seek his help.

As a preacher, Latimer also preached Lenten sermons at the court of Edward VI, but rarely did he write out his sermons before or after preaching them. His scribe, Augustine Bernher, recorded Latimer's sermons for other preachers to use. Latimer received funds from Katherine Brandon, a godly duchess of Suffolk, to write and publish these sermons.

His death

Edward VI died after reigning only six years, and Mary ascended the throne in his place. When Queen Mary began her persecution of the Protestants, Latimer knew he was in danger. She sent a message to summon Bishop Latimer to London, having decided that he should be burned at the stake. Latimer heard of this some time before the messenger arrived. Some of his friends urged him to flee, but Latimer would not take their advice. He preferred to seal the great truths of the gospel, which he had preached all his life, with his blood, rather than to flee England. He was thrown into the Tower of London with Cranmer, Nicholas Ridley, and John Bradford. There he became so frail and spent so much of his time praying that at times he could not get up without help.

Part Two: Nicholas Ridley

Nicholas Ridley, the second son of Christopher Ridley of Willimoteswick, was burned at the stake with Hugh Latimer. His early years were spent as a Roman Catholic, but like Latimer, his views began to change while at university. God greatly blessed Ridley with a sharp mind, and he became a student at Pembroke College, Cambridge. He earned his Bachelor of Arts degree in 1522, his Master of Arts degree in 1525, his Bachelor of Theology degree in 1537, and his Doctor of Theology degree in 1541.

In 1538, Archbishop Cranmer appointed Ridley to be one of his chaplains and vicar of Herne in Kent. During his years under Cranmer, Ridley slowly began to change his views about Roman Catholic doctrine and practice. His first concerns were to preach Christ and to get the Bible in the hands of the English people. He also changed his views on the Lord's Supper, moving from the Roman Catholic view

Ridley preaching at St. Paul's Cross

Nicholas Ridley

of Christ's body and blood being literally present during the Lord's Supper, to the Protestant position of Christ as spiritually present in the Lord's Supper. Ridley faced opposition for his views, but the Lord sustained him and he was able to influence Archbishop Cranmer for further reforms about the Lord's Supper.

The reign of King Edward VI (1547–1553) allowed Ridley to preach the doctrines of the Reformation more boldly. In 1547, King Edward appointed Ridley the bishop of London. In this position, Ridley was able to do much good for the cause of the Reformation in England. He changed the altars into communion tables, preaching the true meaning of the spiritual presence of Christ in the Lord's Supper. He ex-

amined the men who were under his charge for doctrinal soundness, dismissing those who did not reach his standards. He also worked very closely with Archbishop Cranmer, bringing in changes to reform the English Church.

The people loved Ridley because of his care for the sick and the poor. He had several hospitals built in London. When King Edward VI died, Ridley was part of a plot to put Lady Jane Grey on the throne rather than Queen Mary, because Lady Jane Grey was a Protestant while Mary was a Roman Catholic. This plot failed and Lady Jane Grey only reigned for nine days, after which Mary became queen. Queen Mary had Bishop Ridley thrown into prison because of his participation in the plot. He was also accused of heresy for spreading the truth of God's Word and arguing against the errors of the Roman Catholic Church.

Ridley and Latimer condemned

Imprisoned in the Tower of London, Latimer and Ridley were deprived of any basic comforts. They were tormented and questioned, threatened and mocked, while every effort was made to get them to recant. On September 30, 1555, Latimer, Ridley, and Cranmer who was imprisoned with them, were transferred to Oxford for trial and sentencing.

Ridley was questioned first. He was reprimanded because he did not remove his hat when the pope was mentioned. He was not afraid and boldly stated his beliefs. He admitted that he had tried to help Lady Jane become queen rather than Mary.

Latimer was questioned next. He remembered the shame of his earlier weakness, but now he steadfastly maintained his faith in his Savior Jesus Christ. His response to the taunts and ridicule of his tormentors was: "I thank God most heartily that He hath prolonged my life to this end, that I may in this case glorify God with this kind of death."

He also was not afraid to state the errors of the Roman Catholic Church. Both men were ordered to appear before the council the following day. Again, they were questioned, but they stood firm. Neither would recant, so they were sentenced to death.

The evening before his death, Ridley had supper in his guard's house. He was not frightened or gloomy. God filled his heart with joy. He invited the guard and his wife, as well as all who were at the table with him, to his "marriage" the next day, for this is what he considered his death to be. He would soon be married forever with the Lord Jesus Christ. He said he hoped that his sister would be there too, and asked his brother, who was sitting at the table, whether he thought she would be able to come.

"Yes, I believe she will be present," answered Ridley's brother.

"I am glad," replied Ridley.

This made the keeper's wife weep, but Ridley comforted her, saying, "My friend, quiet yourself. My breakfast tomorrow morning will be somewhat painful, but I am sure my supper will be more pleasant and sweet." Ridley knew he would be present at the great feast in heaven.

When supper was finished, Ridley's brother offered to stay the night with him. But Ridley answered, "That is not necessary. I intend to go to bed and sleep as quietly tonight as I ever did."[6]

---

6. Foxe's *Book of Martyrs*, 305.

Their deaths

On October 16, 1555, Ridley and Latimer were led from their place of confinement to a site near Balliol College. They passed by the prison where Cranmer sat, but they did not see him. Ridley looked back and saw Latimer lagging a bit because of his feebleness.

"Are you there?" asked Ridley.

"Yes," answered Latimer, "I'm coming as fast as I can."

When they reached the site, Ridley embraced Latimer. "Be of good cheer, brother Latimer, for God will either lessen the fury of the flames, or else strengthen us to bear them."

Many of the citizens of Oxford came to watch. Then they knelt down and prayed. Someone preached a sermon on 1 Corinthians 13:3b: "Though I give my body to be burned, and have not charity, it profiteth me nothing." The preacher urged the prisoners to repent and return to the holy church, thus saving their lives and their souls.

Ridley said to Latimer, "Will you answer the sermon, or shall I?"

Latimer replied, "You begin first."

Ridley asked for permission to speak, but some of the men ran toward him and covered his mouth with their hands. "You only have liberty to speak if you recant."

"So long as the breath is in my body, I will never deny the Lord and His known truth. God's will be done to me," stated Ridley. With a loud voice, he added, "I commit our cause to Almighty God, who shall impartially judge all."

Latimer then requested permission to speak, but was also denied.

When the men were stripped of almost all their clothing, Ridley prayed, "I beseech thee, Lord, have mercy upon this realm of England, and deliver the land from all her enemies."

An iron chain was fastened around their waists. Ridley's brother tied a bag of gunpowder to both of their necks. Gunpowder was a way of hurrying the death process, shortening the terrible pain.

When a lighted torch was laid on the wood, Latimer said to his friend, "Be of good comfort, Master Ridley, and play the man. We shall this day light such a candle, by God's grace, in England, as I trust shall never be put out."

As the flames reached Latimer, he cried, "'Father of heaven, receive my soul!' He received the flame as if embracing it. After he had stroked his face with his hands, and as it were bathed them a little in the fire, he soon died, as it appeared, with very little pain."[7]

But the case was not so with Ridley. The wood was wet and burned only around his legs. His agony was great and all but unbearable. His legs were

Latimer and Ridley being burned at the stake

completely burned while his upper body was still untouched. Finally, an onlooker moved some of the wood to permit the flames to rise higher and explode the gunpowder, which ended his life as well. Ridley's suffering had been horrific, but at last he entered eternal glory. Foxe wrote, "And as hundreds of bystanders looked on at these two motionless bodies, all that could be heard was weeping."

At the time of their deaths, Bishop Latimer was about seventy years old and Bishop Ridley was fifty-five. They were heroes of the faith. Their lives and words speak of great faith in a great God. Latimer's words of encouragement to Ridley proved to be true. The candle of the Reformation had indeed been lit. By God's grace, the work of the Reformers was blessed and directed by God. Many people were converted in spite of the persecutions that continued, and the Roman Catholic Church was unable to stop God's work.

7. Ibid., 307.

~ 15 ~

John Foxe

◆━◆━◆

(1517–1587)

Perhaps no other book had such a great impact on the Reformation as Foxe's Acts and Monuments.

His education and conversion

John Foxe was born at Boston, Lincolnshire, England, in 1517, the same year in which Luther began the work of the Reformation in Germany. When he was seventeen years old, he entered Brasenose College, Oxford, where he studied hard. He graduated with a bachelor's degree in 1537, and then he studied further at Magdalen College, earning a master's degree in 1543. Afterward, he became a fellow at the college. When he became a student, he was a devout Roman Catholic and believed his soul was safe due to his diligent obedience of the church's rules. He lived a strict and moral life, confessed his sins to the priest, and did penance. He gave to the poor and reverenced God and the saints.

The Lord, however, is stronger than the most religious sinner. Foxe began to study the Bible because he was curious. Why did these Protestants feel it was so important to oppose much of the church's teachings? To his surprise, he discovered that it was not the Protestants, but the Roman Catholics who were in error! He did not reach this decision without much inner turmoil. Often he walked alone in the garden in the middle of the night, thinking and praying.

This aroused the suspicion of some clergy of the Roman Catholic Church, and he was questioned. By this time, he was converted and was convinced that Scripture and not the Roman Catholic Church was correct. In 1545, Foxe resigned his fellowship at Magdalen College, feeling that he and his few God-fearing friends were a real minority. He could not agree with a college rule that every graduate had to enter holy orders within one year of graduating.

John Foxe

Foxe returned home. His father had died while he was at school, and his mother had remarried. His stepfather wanted nothing to do with a "heretic," so Foxe was forced to continue his wandering journey. For several years, he worked as a private tutor in the home of Sir Thomas Lucy of Charlecote, Warwickshire. During these years, he married Agnes Randall, the daughter of a citizen of Coventry.[1]

When King Henry VIII died, and his son Edward VI ascended the throne, Foxe moved to London, since it was

1. A city in central England.

now safe to do so. He had no job, however, and was soon out of money. While Foxe sat in church one day, thin and haggard from hunger and grief, someone approached him. Foxe had never seen the man before. The man handed him a considerable sum of money and said, "Be of good comfort, Mr. Foxe. Take care of yourself, and use all means to preserve your life. Depend on it, and in a few days, God will give you a better job and a better income." Foxe never found out who the man was, but it was clear that God had sent him to relieve the needs of His servant.

A few days later, he was invited to become a tutor to the children of Sir William Lucy, the Duke of Norfolk. So Foxe and his family lived at Rygate, the home of the Duchess of Richmond. Some time later, he was ordained on June 24, 1550, by Bishop Ridley. There is evidence that Foxe preached in the neighborhood where he lived.

But the young King Edward soon died, and the bloody reign of Queen Mary began. Foxe was constantly in danger, but the Duke of Norfolk believed it was his duty to protect his children's tutor, though he himself was not a staunch Protestant. One day, Bishop Gardiner visited the duke. Foxe happened to enter the room where they were visiting. Realizing his mistake, he left quickly. The bishop was suspicious.

"Who is that?" he asked.

"He's our physician," the duke replied. "He's just out of medical school and doesn't know proper manners yet."

"He looks intelligent," stated Bishop Gardiner cunningly. "I'll have to make use of him."

Both the Duke of Norfolk and Foxe understood the danger Foxe was in. The duke sent a servant to Ipswich to prepare a ship. Another servant made sure a trustworthy farmer would shelter Foxe and his pregnant wife until the ship was ready to sail. Everything went as planned until the ship headed out to sea. A sudden storm arose, and the captain turned back. It took them a day to return the ship safely to shore. In the meantime, Foxe's enemies had searched the farmer's house. Not finding him, they hurried to the harbor. Realizing the ship had already left, they gave up in defeat. The ship left a second time and, although the seas were rough, it made its way safely to Nieuwport in Flanders. God took care of his servant once again.

From Nieuwport, Foxe went to Antwerp in 1554, then Frankfurt, and from there to Basel, Switzerland, where it was safer. There were many other English refugees sheltered in Basel. The city was famous for its printing. Foxe earned a living working as a proofreader for the printer Johann Oporinus. This job helped him stay informed of religious and political events and also made it easier for him to get his own books published later on.

His work

While living in Basel, Foxe wrote his famous book, *Acts and Monuments*, later known as his *Book of Martyrs*. Martyrs are Christians who were killed because of their faith, and Foxe told many of their stories in his book. The first edition was written in Latin and was published in 1563.

Foxe lived in poverty while in Basel, eating little and working late into the night. He grieved about the troubles in Frankfurt and other places where theological debates raged. He urged people to live peaceably, in love. In a letter to Peter Martyr, he wrote that he would not have believed how much bitterness is to be found among those who are acquainted with the sacred Scriptures, which ought to make people loving and kind.[2]

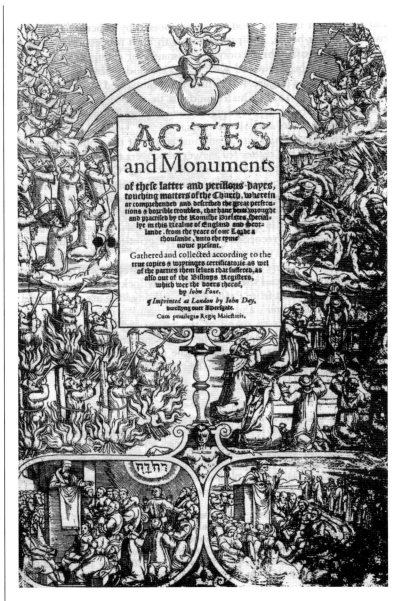

Title page of Acts and Monuments *(1563)*

---

2. *Lives of British Reformers, from Wickliff to Foxe,* 473.

Foxe returned to England after Queen Mary's death in October 1559. By then he had two children. He returned to his friend, the duke of Norfolk, who kindly received him. The Foxe family lived in the duke's home for about a year. The duke was involved in political secrets that, when brought to light, produced the death sentence for the duke. Foxe and another man went with him to the place of execution. Some people had also accused the duke of being a Roman Catholic, which he vehemently denied on the day of his death. "For myself, God is my witness, I have always been a Protestant, and never did agree with their blind and fond ceremonies. And now, before God and you all, I utterly renounce the pope and his popedom, which I have always done, and will do to my life's end. And as to that which is the chiefest point of our belief—I believe and trust to be saved by faith in Jesus Christ only, and by none other means, for if I did, I should be greatly deceived at this instant."[3]

In 1563, Foxe accepted a ministerial call to Salisbury Cathedral, Shipton. Throughout his ministry, he continued working on his *Book of Martyrs*. Four editions of this work were published in his lifetime. This set of books helped support and spread the Protestant faith; it had a powerful impact on tens of thousands of people.

Foxe's *Book of Martyrs* consisted of eight volumes. It was a detailed account of the martyrs and Christians who lived from the tenth until the fifteenth centuries. It took Foxe eleven years to complete this task. He wanted to be sure that he was accurate and had all the facts correct, so he examined all the records of the martyrs carefully. Over the years,

scholars have concluded that though Foxe did exaggerate at points in his work, for the most part it is accurate.

Foxe wrote other books as well, including a large Latin commentary on the book of Revelation. He also translated Luther's famous commentary on Galatians into English.

Foxe did his best to be helpful to those in need. He was known for his compassion to the poor and those in sorrow and trouble. His home was constantly visited by rich and poor who came to him for advice and comfort. He never failed to lead them to the God of comfort, using these opportunities to point people to the Lord Jesus Christ.

One story is told of his care for the poor. He had just left the palace of Bishop Aylmer in London when some poor people begged him for money. Feeling bad that he had none to give, he returned to the palace and asked the bishop for a loan. Thanking him, Foxe left and distributed all the money to the poor. Some months later, the bishop asked Foxe about the loan.

"I have taken care of it," replied Foxe, "I paid those you owed—the poor people who beg at your gate."

Instead of being angry at this bold statement, the bishop thanked him for being such a good steward. He was ashamed that Foxe was more willing to care for others than he was himself.

Although Foxe gave generously to those in need, the Lord took care of him and his family. His wife was a great help to him, caring for the family with the little they had.

John Foxe died on April 18, 1587 and was buried at St. Giles's Church. He left behind a legacy of being one of the most famous authors and prominent members of the Elizabethan church. Perhaps no other book had such a great impact on the Reformation as Foxe's *Acts and Monuments*.

_____
3. Ibid., 478.

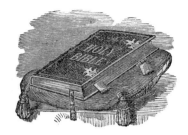

~ 16 ~

John Knox

(c. 1514–1572)

Knox had great piety as well as insight and courage.... He served his Lord and Master, Jesus Christ, and was not ashamed of the gospel.

His education

John Knox was born about 1514, at Gifford Gate, Haddington, Scotland. He went to a school near his home when he was a young boy, then moved to St. Andrews, Fife (also in Scotland) to attend the University of St. Andrews. While at the university, he became a very good speaker and debater. This talent proved useful later when he preached the gospel and persuaded others of its truth.

His conversion

Around the year 1540, John Knox was ordained priest in the Roman Catholic Church. As he studied the Bible and such early Christians as Augustine, Knox became convinced of the errors of the Roman Catholic Church and joined the Reformers. In 1543, he publicly stated that he was no longer a Roman Catholic but a Protestant. Not many details are known about Knox's conversion, but upon his deathbed, Knox requested that John 17 be read. He then said that this was the text upon which "I cast my first anchor."

After his conversion, Knox could no longer be a priest. Instead, he found employment tutoring the children of several Protestant families in St. Andrews.

George Wishart

Knox's friend, George Wishart, was a Protestant. Because of the persecution of Protestants in Scotland, Wishart moved to England for a time. There he became discouraged and doubted the doctrines of the Protestant faith. After some time, he traveled to Germany and Switzerland. While he was there, he learned more about God's Word. Meeting other Protestants strengthened his faith. The Lord used this time to prepare Wishart for his return to Scotland.

When he returned to Scotland, he began to preach passionately. Many people came to listen eagerly. He preached the truth, not as the Roman Catholics taught, but as God teaches in His Word. He told the people that all preaching and teaching must be tested by Scripture. One of the Roman Catholic doctrines he preached against was purgatory. Roman Catholics believed that purgatory was a kind of waiting place where a believer's soul went after he died. If people prayed for that soul, burned candles, and had masses said often enough, the soul eventually would go to heaven. Wishart taught the people what the Bible said about this false doctrine and other errors promoted by the Roman Catholic Church.

John Knox accompanied Wishart on many of his travels throughout Scotland. The Holy Spirit used this time to nurture Knox in the faith and to help him form scriptural conclusions about the doctrines of God's Word.

The Roman Catholic clergy had Wishart arrested on January 16, 1546. They brought him to trial in St. Andrews, and condemned him to death. John Knox was devastated at this news. He wanted to die alongside his beloved friend, but Wishart said, "Return to your pupils, and God bless you; one is sufficient for a sacrifice."[1] Knox experienced that "to live is Christ, and to die is gain" (Philippians 1:21). On March 1, Wishart was burned at the stake, leaving Knox to take up the leadership of the Reformation in Scotland.

Captured by the French

As the persecution continued, Knox concluded he would be safer in Europe, but his friends in Glasgow persuaded him to take refuge in the castle of St. Andrews, along with other Protestants. At the castle, Knox continued to teach some children and young people who were staying there for safety. His time in the castle lasted from April through July of 1547.

A preacher in a parish church near the castle, John Rough, who was a converted monk, wanted Knox to help him in the ministry. Knox hesitated, feeling the heavy weight of such a calling. He did not think he was qualified to do such work. One day, as Rough finished his sermon, he looked at Knox sitting in the pew and said, "Brother, you must not be offended.... In the name of God and of His Son, Jesus Christ, and in the name of these people gathered with us, I charge you that you refuse not this holy calling. We know that you treasure the glory of God, the increase of Christ's kingdom, the edification of your brethren, and the comfort of men. Take upon you the public office and charge of preaching. Do not turn away from this calling, or you will bring down God's heavy displeasure. We desire that He should multiply His graces with you."[2] Knox was startled, burst into tears,

1. William Brown, *The Life-Story of John Knox* (Edinburgh: W.P. Nimmo, Hay, & Mitchell, 1905), 12.

2. Erasmus Middleton, *Evangelical Biography; or, An Historical Account*

John Knox

and left. He begged the Lord for direction, and when God showed him that he must preach, Knox obeyed.

People flocked to hear the new preacher. He was firm and clear in his explanations of Scripture. He was not afraid to point out the errors of the Roman Catholic Church. He made some blunt statements which angered the Roman Catholic clergy but made the Protestants rejoice. People were happy to hear Knox explain Scripture because he gave them a correct view of biblical doctrines in contrast to the errors of Rome.

Before long, however, Knox's work was interrupted. In 1547, because of hostilities between Scotland and France, the French sailed to St. Andrews and captured it, taking Knox prisoner along with other Scottish Protestant men. For almost two years, Knox had to work as a galley slave. A galley was a low, flat, one-decked vessel, propelled by long, heavy oars. The slaves who worked these oars were chained to their seats. They had to work for hours on end and were not treated well. Sometimes Knox was whipped. On one occasion, the French tried to make him pray to an idol of Mary, but Knox refused to do this. He grabbed the image and flung it into the river in disgust. "Let our lady now save herself," he scoffed, "she is light enough: let her learn to swim!"[3]

Knox patiently bore his imprisonment. Many times his thoughts became prayers for deliverance.

of the Lives and Deaths of the Most Eminent and Evangelical Authors or Preachers, Both British and Foreign, in the Several Denominations of Protestants, from the Beginning of the Reformation to the Present Time (London: W. Baynes, 1816), 2:135–36.

3. Brown, *The Life-Story of John Knox*, 19.

Once, when the galley ship sailed along the shoreline near St. Andrews, someone asked him if he recognized the place. "Yes," answered Knox, "I know it very well, for I see the steeple of the place where God first publicly opened my mouth to His glory. Although I am very weak right now, I am fully persuaded that I shall not die until my tongue shall glorify Him again in that same place."[4]

In England

In February 1549, after nineteen months of imprisonment, Knox was released from the galleys, in large part through the influence of the young King Edward VI. After this, he went to England and continued his labors for the Reformation. The Protestants were being persecuted in Scotland, and it would have been too dangerous for Knox to remain there. He took refuge in England, where Protestants were safe under King Edward VI. Knox became the minister at Berwick and at Newcastle, later becoming a royal chaplain.

Knox was a great help to the English Reformers. He joined them in speaking against the errors of the Roman Catholic Church in England and in establishing a Protestant Church there. The English Protestants wanted to make him a bishop, but Knox declined the offer because he preferred the government and worship of the Presbyterian Church in Scotland. He also said that the Church of England needed much reform, since they still clung to some unbiblical traditions of the Roman Catholic Church.

John Knox's house

4. Ibid., 20.

Escape to Germany and Geneva

When Edward VI died and Queen Mary came to the throne, Knox was not safe anymore, so he fled to Germany. For a time he pastored the English refugees in Frankfurt am Main. When that church divided, Knox went to Geneva with a heavy heart. There he became a student under John Calvin and pastored the English congregation. It was in God's providence that these two men met, since through them the Genevan and Scottish Churches established close ties. Calvin and Knox shared a friendship that grew over the years.

In 1556, Knox married Margery Bowes. Though not much is known about her, she was a loving wife and provided much support for Knox in his preaching and pastoral duties. God blessed them with two sons, Nathanael and Eleazer, who were born in Geneva. Knox was plunged into mourning when Margery died after only four years of marriage.

In 1564, Knox married Margaret Stewart, the daughter of Andrew Stewart, Lord Ochiltree. This marriage was also a happy one, and together they had three daughters, Martha, Margaret, and Elizabeth.

Although he was happy in Geneva, Knox longed for his beloved Scotland. He believed the Lord had called him to bring the gospel to his fellow countrymen. He knew he would be in constant danger in Scotland, but he was willing to suffer for Christ's sake.

Back to Scotland

In carrying on the work of the Reformation in Scotland, one of the greatest difficulties that Knox encountered was Mary, Queen of Scots. (This was not Mary, Queen of England, who was also called Bloody Mary.[5]) When King James V of Scotland died in 1542, he had only one daughter, named Mary Stuart. Since she was only one week old when her father died, her mother, Mary of Guise, the widow of James V, became queen in her place. She was beautiful and capable, but wicked. Born and brought up in the Roman Catholic Church, she tried everything in her power to have that church preserved in Scotland, with all its errors and false doctrines.

As soon as Knox arrived in Scotland, he began to preach the gospel. He spoke openly about the truth of Scripture and was not afraid to point out the errors of the Roman Catholic Church. He called the mass "idolatry" and condemned the worship of images. Some of the people misunderstood and began to break images in the Roman Catholic churches and monasteries. Knox condemned this destructive behavior and explained that they could not ruin other people's possessions, no matter how much they disliked them.

Tensions mounted. Roman Catholics and Protestants argued; the queen ordered the persecution of the Protestants. It seemed war would be the result, but this was averted by the efforts of the Duke of Argyle and the prior of St. Andrews, who were friends of the Reformation.

Many Protestants went to live at St. Andrews because they felt safe there. The archbishop of St. Andrews heard that Knox was planning to preach there. He gathered some soldiers and warned Knox that if he dared to preach, he would do so at the risk of his life. Some of his friends were afraid and pleaded with Knox to be silent. Knox refused,

---

5. Because many of the names of the kings and queens of Scotland and England are the same, it can be confusing. See the family tree charts in Appendix B for help.

The town church, St. Andrews, where John Knox preached

trusting his life to God. On the appointed day, he preached fearlessly, not shying away from the truth. Despite the soldiers' presence, the preaching was blessed, and the Reformation spread. Knox's prophecy, uttered on the galley ship many years ago, was fulfilled.

After Mary of Guise died, her daughter, Mary Stuart, became queen. Though she was still a teen, she was just as wicked as her mother. Knox compared her to Queen Jezebel. Sometimes Queen Mary sent for Knox to see him and hear what he had to say, or to reprimand him for what he had said. He talked to her, explained the Bible, and preached to her. What he said seemed, on occasion, to have an effect on her. Sometimes it moved her to tears, but her heart was not changed.

If Queen Mary was a problem for Knox, Knox was also a problem for her. He stood in the way of her plans. She could usually make those around her do just what she wanted, but not so with Knox. He was just as unmoved by all she did and said as a solid rock is unmoved by the waters of the sea that swirl around it. Mary said that she was more afraid of Knox and his prayers than of an army of men.

As a preacher in Edinburgh, Scotland's capital, Knox was at the center of the politics and government of the country. He was a fiery preacher and often spoke against the queen and the other rulers. This combination of being in the center of politics and his fiery style of preaching forced him to flee the city several times because of the opposition of the government. Despite this opposition, large crowds of people came to listen to him, sometimes as many as three thousand people.

Knox was summoned several times to appear before the queen. Finally, she had him tried for treason because she said he spoke against her in a disrespectful way. Knox explained that he was not being disrespectful to her, but that he was being true to God, his country, and his conscience when he spoke against wrongs while promoting the right. Mary desired Knox's death, but his defense was so clear and powerful that no one could find fault with him. Even the strongest supporters of the queen and the Roman Catholic Church had to acknowledge Knox's honest manner, and they proclaimed him innocent and set him free.

Queen Mary lived an unhappy life. If only she had listened to the wise, life-giving words of John Knox! Her power weakened until at last she was taken captive and, after a long imprisonment, was beheaded.

His character

Thomas Randolph wrote of John Knox, "He thunders out of the pulpit; he rules the roost, and all men stand in fear of him." Knox's preaching style was rough and blunt. He spoke sharply against the errors of the Roman Catholic Church. He courageously declared that the pope and the whole Roman Catholic system was the antichrist. Though at times he appears to have acted and spoken too harshly, we must remember that he had rough people to deal with and difficult work to do. If he had not been a stern, brave man himself, he would not have been fit to do the work he had been called to do.

Knox had other characteristics that were helpful to him in his work. He had good insight. He knew the right thing to do and the right time to do it. He also understood people. Queen Mary tried to deceive him, but she could not. He seemed to read and understand her like a book. That was very helpful to him in the work he had to do, and it was an important part of his character.

He also had great courage. He was not afraid to state his beliefs. He clearly told the people what the errors of the Roman Catholic Church were. He did go back to Geneva a second time because of the danger in Scotland, but he returned, determined to continue preaching the gospel to his countrymen.

Knox had great piety as well as insight and courage. Love to the Lord Jesus is the root out of which all true piety springs. Paul said, "The love of Christ constraineth us" (2 Corinthians 5:14). This was the secret of Paul's greatness, and so it was with John Knox. He served his Lord and Master, Jesus Christ wholeheartedly, and was not ashamed of the gospel.

John Knox's study in his house in Edinburgh

His work

John Knox did much to help the Reformation in Scotland. The General Assembly of the Church of Scotland met for the first time on December 20, 1560. They had already adopted a confession of faith, but they wanted to discuss the system of church government that would be best for the church in Scotland. The result was the establishment of the

Presbyterian Church in Scotland, despite the opposition of the queen, the priests, and the pope.

They decided that the church should have a minister, elders, and deacons. Since ministers were few in number, they chose some serious-minded men to read Scripture and pray on the Sabbath. After a time, these men would be examined, and if they had progressed sufficiently, they would become "exhorters." Also, ministers were appointed to oversee large districts. These ministers were called "superintendents." They especially cared for vacant churches.

His writings

John Knox wrote several books and tracts. He is well known for his book, *The First Blast of the Trumpet Against the Monstrous Regiment of Women*, which he wrote in 1558. This book was aimed at the female rulers of his day, in particular, the three Marys: Bloody Mary, Mary of Guise, and Mary Stuart. These Roman Catholic female rulers were known for their opposition to the Reformation, which is why Knox wrote against them.

During the winter of 1558, when Knox was in Geneva, he wrote another major book, *An Answer to a Great Number of Blasphemous Cavillations*.[6] This book was written against those who disagreed with the doctrine of predestination. This scriptural doctrine says that God graciously elects some people to salvation and others are justly rejected to damnation. Knox passionately defended this doctrine of predestination in his book.

Another important book that Knox wrote is *History of the Reformation in Scotland*, published in 1587. This book is

an important work on church history; it emphasizes the struggles he faced with Mary of Guise. His books *Orders of Fasting*, published in 1566, and *Excommunication*, published in 1569, were written to help the Scottish Presbyterian Church form its church practices.

His death

At the age of fifty-seven, Knox's work was done. He became weaker and weaker, suffering a slight stroke, until he was no longer able to preach. He had much pain, but he did not complain. Rather, he confessed, "To Thee, Lord, do I commit myself. Thou knowest how intense my pains are; but I do not complain. Yes, Lord, if such be Thy will concerning me, I could be content to bear these pains for many years yet, which in Thy just judgment Thou hast laid upon me. Only do Thou continue to enlighten my mind through Christ Jesus." He prayed much for God's church and for the work of the Lord to continue. Just before he died, he said to a friend, "These two last nights I have been in meditation on the troubled state of the kirk [the church of God], the spouse of Jesus Christ, despised of the world, but precious in the sight of God. I have called to God for her, and have committed her to her Head, Jesus Christ."

God called His faithful servant home on November 24, 1572. At Knox's funeral, the Earl of Morton, one of the noblemen of Scotland, pointed to his coffin and said, "There lies a man who never feared the face of man. He has often been threatened with the sword, yet he ended his days in peace and honor, for God's providence watched over him in a special manner when his very life was sought."

---

6. Cavillations are unimportant objections.

~ 17 ~

Guido de Brès

(1522–1567)

Guido de Brès's Confession of Faith… now known as the Belgic Confession of Faith, remains one of the most influential confessional documents of Reformed churches around the world.

His youth

In 1522, Guido de Brès's mother was listening to the preaching of an Augustinian monk. Impressed with the monk's preaching, she asked God to give her a son who would be a good preacher. Several months later, Guido was born to the de Brès family in Mons, Belgium. He was the fifth child born into a strict Roman Catholic family. His mother's wish would be realized, but Guido would be a Protestant preacher, not a Roman Catholic one.

After several years of schooling in his hometown, de Brès became an apprentice to a glass painter. He did his work well, but he kept his eyes and ears open, showing an interest in the stories about the Protestants. These "heretics" were imprisoned, beheaded, or burned when they were caught. He heard the stories of the Reformation and the men who were used by the Lord to do His work. De Brès heard about Luther and Calvin and many of the others who lived and worked during his lifetime.

His conversion and studies

During his teen years, de Brès obtained a Bible and read it. He also read the writings of Reformers. The Lord used these means to convert him and call him to the ministry.

In 1548, at the age of twenty-six, he left home to study in England. King Edward VI was on the throne, and England was a safe place for Protestants. De Brès had excellent training under men like Jan Łaski, Martin Bucer, Petrus Dathenus, and other Reformers. He learned not only from their lectures, but also from hearing their preaching and observing them establishing congregations. There were many refugees in England at the time because of the persecutions going on in other countries. Several congregations were established for the people to hear the Word preached in their own language.

He becomes a minister

In 1552, de Brès returned to Mons from England. He wanted to minister to the people of his own country. He became a traveling preacher, which was a dangerous calling, since the teachings of Luther and Calvin were not accepted by the church.

De Brès was careful, however, and did not use his real name. Instead, he used the name Augustine of Mons.

Eventually, de Brès established a congregation in the town of Lille, about forty-five miles from Mons. He did not preach in a church building, but he met with people in their homes to avoid detection. The young pastor taught people the Scriptures. He called the new church the Church of the Rose.

He also continued to study the Scriptures for himself, as well as the writings of the Reformers. His first book was published in 1555. It was titled *La Baston de la Foy Chrestienne*, [The Staff of the Christian Faith]. Many of the topics discussed in his book are found in de Brès's later Confession of Faith. This book was very popular among many Christians because it was written against the errors of Rome.

Persecution

In 1555, Philip II of Spain became king in the place of his father, Charles V. People said that the new king promised more freedom for his subjects. Charles had persecuted the Protestants, but Philip seemed to be more tolerant, they said. Perhaps things would be better in Belgium now. The rumors proved to be false, however, and his subjects found that rather than being more tolerant of the Protestants than his father had been, Philip was fiercely determined to root out these heretics. He sent his soldiers into each country under his power to find and destroy the Protestants.

Philip was a cruel king, and his soldiers tortured Protestants in terrible ways. Sometimes people were stretched out on a rack, or put upside down in stocks. They were imprisoned in damp, dark dungeons where they kept company with rats and other vermin. Sometimes they were beaten. At times, the torture was so intense that some people gave in and renounced their Protestant faith. Usually, however, the tortured Protestants remained steadfast, bravely suffering for the name of the Lord Jesus Christ whom they loved.

After one family in de Brès's congregation was arrested and burned at the stake, many people fled from Lille to Frankfurt am Main, where it was safer. Three refugee churches were established there: an English, a French, and a Flemish church. Flemish was the language of the Lowlands, which is now the Netherlands, Belgium, and northern France. De Brès remained in Frankfurt for only a few months, and then he decided to go to Switzerland to study in Lausanne and Geneva. There he studied under Theodore Beza and sat under the preaching of John Calvin.

De Brès's heart was in his homeland, however, with his own people. After two years of study, at the age of thirty-seven, he returned to the Lowlands, this time to Doornik, a short distance from Lille, where he became pastor of the

Church of the Palm. In this church he met Catherine Ramon. When he asked her to marry him, he told her plainly that he could not promise a life of ease. She would most likely have a life of worries about his safety and much time away from him, since he had to be very careful in his work. Nevertheless, she agreed to marry him.

The Confession of Faith

During his first year in Doornik, de Brès began working on a confession of faith. The Roman Catholic authorities accused the Protestants of being disobedient and the cause of unrest. De Brès wanted to prove to them that the Protestants were peace-loving citizens who believed the Scriptures.

De Brès was being noticed by the Protestants as a gifted minister, valuable to the work of the Reformation. To protect himself and his family, he disguised himself when he went out and used the name Jerome. Even the people of his own congregation did not know that Jerome was really Guido de Brès. Again, there was no church building for him to preach in, but he met secretly with people in their homes. The church began to grow as the Lord blessed his hard work and preaching.

Trouble in Doornik

Satan did not want God's work to prosper, so he stirred up trouble in the church at Doornik. Some of the people of the congregation were tired of the secrecy. Two men became their leaders. Their names were Mr. du Four and Mr. du Mortier. They wanted the people to come into the open and not be afraid to let people know what they believed. De Brès asked them not to do this, since it would be dangerous and destructive. Many people, however, followed du Four and du Mortier.

One evening in September 1561, a few hundred people walked down the streets of Doornik singing psalms. Psalm-singing was forbidden by the authorities. When the governor heard what was happening, he ordered his soldiers to shoot at the people. Du Four and du Mortier and their followers were determined not to give up. The following evening they did the same thing. When Philip II heard about it, he ordered his troops to go to Doornik. The city rulers were reprimanded for not putting a stop to these occurrences sooner and not trying harder to root out the Protestants. People were imprisoned and punished. A special search was made for the leaders of the psalm-singing and for Jerome, but du Four and du Mortier had escaped.

De Brès hid in his home alongside the city wall. He was very sad. Matters had turned out just as he feared. Trouble had come to the Church of the Palm. De Brès thought it would be helpful to write a letter to the governor. He included a copy of his Confession of Faith to explain the doctrines the Protestants believed. He wanted the king of Spain and the authorities to know that Protestants were not troublemakers. He asked the king to stop persecuting the Christians. He then wrapped up the letter and a copy of the Confession of Faith in a package, disguised himself, and managed to throw it over the wall of the governor's castle without being noticed.

The next morning, November 2, 1561, the package was found and, if read by the authorities, did not make a difference. Instead, the search for Jerome was intensified. The Lord protected his servant, however, and he escaped from Doornik into France. Margaret, the king's half sister, who was in charge of the Lowlands, was furious when she found out de Brès had escaped. She ordered his effigy (likeness) burned along with all the papers and books they had found in his abandoned house.

His work

The Protestants in France were glad to have de Brès and welcomed him eagerly. De Brès lived in France for five years. During this time, he was briefly imprisoned and then set free through the help of the Duke of Bouillon, a friend of the Reformation. This duke ruled over the city of Sedan, France, and in 1563 announced that people living in Sedan were free to worship as they wished. The Protestants, of course, were delighted, and many moved to Sedan, including de Brès and his family. Here they stayed for three happy years. De Brès ministered to the people of Sedan and continued to write.

One of his books was written to denounce the heresies of the Anabaptists. It was called *La Racine, Source, et Fondamente des Anabaptistes,* [The Root, Origin, and Basis of the Anabaptists]. His purpose, as always, was to make people aware of error and point them to the truths of Scripture.

Even though de Brès had his freedom, his heart was still with his countrymen. He traveled several times, in disguise, to visit Doornik and several other cities in the area. The Lord protected this brave servant from his enemies on his many long journeys.

The first synod meeting

In May 1566, a very important meeting was held in Antwerp, Belgium. It was the first synodical meeting of the Reformed Church in the Lowlands. One of the decisions made at this meeting, held in secret, was to adopt de Brès's Confession of Faith as one of the official documents of the church. Today, this document, now known as the Belgic Confession of Faith, remains one of the most influential confessional documents of Reformed churches around the world.

Later that year, the church in Antwerp asked de Brès to preach for them, since their own pastor was attending a conference. Once again, de Brès made the dangerous trip to Antwerp. From there, he answered another call for help, this time from Valenciennes, near the French border. The church there was called the Church of the Eagle, and her pastor, Peregrine de la Grange, needed help.

Around this time, Protestants became more daring. Traveling preachers had audiences of several thousand. The women and children stood in the center of the gathering, and armed men stood guard around them. De Brès also preached in the fields around Valenciennes.

As the Protestant movement grew, trouble accompanied it. Some people began to smash statues and break things in the churches. Once again, Philip II heard about the commotion and sent his troops to subdue the rebels. The city was declared guilty of open rebellion. Pastor de la Grange wanted to stop the army and declared that he and his followers would not meekly yield. In spite of de Brès's admonitions, the people barred the city gates against Philip's troops. They were counting on help from William, Prince of Orange, but William did not come to help them.

Although the Huguenots (French Protestants) living in villages around Valenciennes tried to fight the enemy, they were easily overpowered. There was a short battle on Sunday,

March 23. It began while de Brès was preaching and was over in a matter of a few hours. Margaret, who controlled the Lowlands, ordered the death of the two preachers of Valenciennes, but once again, they had escaped.

Imprisoned

Sadly, however, someone recognized de Brès and de la Grange, and they were turned in to the authorities. For two weeks, they were prisoners at the castle at Doornik. It was ordered that they stand trial in Valenciennes, so they were transported back to that city and put in a foul, dark dungeon called the Black Hole. They were shackled with very heavy chains that produced sores on their wrists and ankles. The only time they could leave their cells was for questioning and torture.

Amazingly, while in prison, de Brès was able to write several farewell letters to family and friends, as well as a long paper on the Lord's Supper. It was 233 pages long and written in semi-darkness! In the midst of awful circumstances and facing death, de Brès never gave up working for his people and for his God.

His death

On May 31, 1567, de Brès and de la Grange were awakened early. They were to be hanged that morning at six o'clock. De la Grange was hanged first. De Brès stopped to pray before he climbed the ladder to the platform, but the guards pushed him forward. Speaking to the people even with the noose around his neck, he testified of God's love and faithfulness. He died while he was still speaking. After his hanging, his body was burned and his ashes were scattered in the Scheldt River.[1] Another faithful servant of Jesus Christ was martyred for His name and entered triumphantly into heaven.

---

1. The Scheldt River begins in France and flows through Belgium and the Netherlands into the North Sea.

~ 18 ~

The Heidelberg Catechism

1. Caspar Olevianus

2. Zacharias Ursinus

3. Frederick III

4. The Heidelberg Catechism

The Lord protected this precious document, the Heidelberg Catechism, so that we may still enjoy it today.

Part One: Caspar Olevianus

His education and conversion

Caspar Olevianus was born on August 10, 1536, in Treves, Germany, which is located on the Mosel River.[1] His grandfather paid for Olevianus to study law in France. In the French cities of Paris, Bourges, and Orléans, Olevianus met many Protestant believers. He was impressed with the firmness of their faith and was amazed that they were willing to suffer and die for it. Through the influence of these Protestant friends, Olevianus was introduced to the Scriptures. The Holy Spirit worked in his heart, and he was converted when he was around sixteen years old.

Tries to save the prince

In 1556, something happened that changed his plans for the future. Some students got together for a good time. Some of them got drunk. They thought it would be fun to go boating. Several of them got into a rowboat that was tied up on the shore. Among them was Herman Louis, the son of Frederick III. The young men were rough-housing when suddenly, in the middle of the Eure river, the boat overturned and the students were thrown into the river.

---

1. The Mosel River is a tributary of the Rhine River and runs south into France, where it is called the Moselle River. It is a winding river about 200 miles long.

The young men on the shore dove in to try to rescue the frantic young men. Some were rescued, but not Herman Louis. He drowned. The young man who tried to save the prince was Caspar Olevianus. The tragedy made such an impression on Olevianus that he vowed to become a minister of the gospel instead of a lawyer, though he completed his doctorate in law in 1557.

Studies in Geneva and Lausanne

After this, Olevianus went to Geneva, where he studied theology under Calvin. In nearby Lausanne, he met Theodore Beza, who became his lifelong friend. Firmly convinced that the Reformation was God's work and that the message of salvation through Christ alone must be spread to all people, Olevianus asked God to use him in this great work. When he spoke to William Farel about this, Farel, in his firm, confident manner, said to Olevianus, "Go back to Treves and bring the Reformation there."

Back to Treves

In May 1559, Olevianus went back to his hometown. During the year 1559, many important things were happening all over Europe. In Paris, the French Protestants held their first synod. John Knox founded

Caspar Olevianus

the Presbyterian Church in his beloved country, Scotland. John Calvin opened a school called the Genevan Academy for young men to learn about the Bible and be trained for the ministry. He also published his final edition of the *Institutes*. In the Netherlands, William of Orange, tired of the Spanish persecution, determined to drive the Spaniards out of his country. And in the Palatinate (Germany), Otto Henry died, leaving the crown to Frederick III. The Reformation was well under way, but there was still much work to be done.

Olevianus was hired in Treves to teach philosophy and to lecture in Latin at the local university, but it was his preaching that made the greatest impression on the people of Treves. Fully and clearly, he explained the doctrines of Scripture, pointing out the errors of the Roman Catholic Church. Many people were glad to hear the gospel and believed on the Lord Jesus Christ, but others were upset. The leaders of the city were angry, and they ordered Olevianus to leave the city. However, Olevianus did not leave. He believed God had placed him in Treves, and he wanted to obey God rather than men.

Imprisoned

In response, the archbishop sent his soldiers to Treves and arrested Olevianus along with other leaders of the church. God, however, had other plans for his faithful servant. When Frederick III heard of the imprisonment of Olevianus, he paid the city leaders of Treves a sum of money to have him released. The city leaders agreed to release Olevianus only if he promised never to return to the city.

What should he do now? He wanted to be used by the Lord in His service, so he asked God where he should go. God answered him in the form of a message: Frederick invited him to come with him to Heidelberg to teach in the College of Wisdom, which was converted into a theological seminary. This is how Caspar Olevianus was led to Heidelberg, where he became both professor of theology and pastor in the Holy Ghost Church. Ultimately, Olevianus would prove to be one of the most humble Christians and one of the most capable Reformed theologians of his generation.

——◆◆◆——

Part Two: Zacharias Ursinus

His education

Zacharias Ursinus was born into a Protestant family in the town of Breslau[2] in the year 1534. His father was a tutor. When Ursinus went to school, he worked hard. The people of his hometown noticed that Ursinus was a gifted boy, and, knowing that his family could not afford higher education, offered to pay for his education and his travels. In 1550, when he was sixteen years old, he went to Wittenberg to study at the university there. Very quiet and not outgoing, Ursinus enjoyed his studies. In God's providence, Philip Melanchthon, a professor at the university, took notice of this promising student. They soon became close friends and frequently traveled together.

---

2. Breslau is in modern-day Poland, about eighty to ninety miles from the German border.

His travels and teachings

Ursinus accompanied Melanchthon to Worms and then to Heidelberg. From there, Ursinus continued alone to Strasbourg, Basel, Lausanne, Geneva, Paris, Zurich, Wittenberg, and then back to Breslau. In his hometown, he took a job as a school principal. When people understood his views on religion, however, they began saying hateful things against him. Many of the people in the German states were Lutherans, and they opposed Calvin and Zwingli. Instead of focusing on their similarities, the people of Breslau emphasized their differences. Once again, the matter of the Lord's Supper was discussed. Tempers flared and angry words were spoken.

Ursinus was very unhappy about this. He liked peace and quiet; he hated controversy and arguments. Seeking peace, he wrote a paper about his beliefs, but the people were still angry with him. In his unhappiness, Ursinus asked God to help and direct him.

At the end of April 1560, Ursinus received a message with some very sad news. His dear friend, Melanchthon, had died in Wittenberg. Ursinus decided to leave Breslau. His friend was dead, and the people of Breslau did not appreciate him. He wanted to go somewhere to

Zacharius Ursinus

work among fellow believers. He decided to go to Zurich. There, Ursinus studied under Peter Martyr, who was a great comfort to him after Melanchthon's death.

When Frederick requested Peter Martyr to become the principal of the College of Wisdom in Heidelberg, he declined. He said he was too old (sixty), but he knew a young man who would be perfect for the job. That young man was Zacharias Ursinus.

But Ursinus was afraid. He did not like to be in the limelight. "Oh, that I could remain hidden in a corner!" he complained. "I would give anything for the shelter of a quiet village." However, he was more afraid of disobeying God, so he yielded to Frederick's invitation and moved to Heidelberg.

———◆◆◆———

Part Three: Frederick III

His family

Frederick was one of seven children. They were not a wealthy family, although Frederick's uncle, Otto Henry, was the Elector of Heidelberg. When Frederick was a young teen, he spent some time in the court of Emperor Charles V in Brussels. Frederick saw the princes and rulers of the church drinking, dancing, and living ungodly lives. This bothered Frederick. How could such people rule the land and the church? When he got the opportunity, he spoke to Jan Łaski, the Polish Reformer, about it. The Lord was preparing Frederick for the work He had planned for him.

Soon after this, Frederick met Maria, princess of Brandenburg-Kulmbach. The seventeen-year-old princess would not marry Frederick, however, unless he promised to study the Bible and read Luther's writings. Because he loved Maria, Frederick promised to do this. This was God's way of introducing Frederick to His Word.

Soon they were married. Maria and Frederick lived in a castle in Treves for twenty years. They had seven children. They were not wealthy by any means, but they were happy together. Their lives were not without sorrow, however. One of their daughters died just before she turned fifteen. Wanting the best for his sons, Frederick sent Herman Louis and Casimir to study in France where there were many Protestants. There Herman Louis drowned in the Eure River.

He becomes Elector of the German Palatinate

Otto Henry died in February 1559. Because he had no children and his brother had died two years earlier, his nephew Frederick became elector in Otto Henry's place at the age of forty-four. Although Otto Henry had welcomed the Lutheran doctrines into his land, all was not peaceful. When Frederick became elector, there were arguments and troubles among the people. So many questions! So much debate and arguing! Who was right? Praying for wisdom and light, Frederick searched the Scriptures for hours at a time for an answer.

He also wrote to Philip Melanchthon for advice. This was Melanchthon's answer: "In all things seek peace and moderation. This is done best by holding carefully to a fixed doctrinal position as regards the Lord's Supper and all other matters of faith. Meanwhile, summon to your land from churches of various countries such learned and pious men as can advise you best when controversy does arise."[3]

The more Frederick studied the Scriptures, the more he was convinced that the Calvinist view of the Lord's Supper was correct. His wife, Maria, feared that Frederick was straying from the truth, but Frederick believed he had come to the correct conclusion about the Scriptures. Following Melanchthon's advice, he invited two godly men to come to Heidelberg, Zacharias Ursinus and Caspar Olevianus. He asked them to write a catechism that clearly stated the doctrines of Scripture. Perhaps this would help the people reach an agreement.

—————◆◆◆—————

Part Four: The Heidelberg Catechism

The work begins

Ursinus immediately began working on the catechism for Frederick. This was not his first catechism; he had already written two catechisms in Latin. At this time, Ursinus was only twenty-eight years old. Olevianus, who was to help him, was twenty-six. As they worked, they showed their drafts to Frederick, who wrote his comments and suggestions.

The year was 1562, and the idea of a statement of beliefs was not new. That same year, the church in England accepted the Thirty-Nine Articles of Faith. Switzerland accepted the

Frederick the Wise

3. Thea B. Van Halsema, *Three Men Came to Heidelberg* (Grand Rapids: Baker Book House, 1963), 37–38.

Second Helvetic Confession written by Bullinger. In the Lowlands, Guido de Brès had written the Belgic Confession the previous year. Frederick was anxious for the catechism to be done as soon as possible.

The catechism printed

In January 1563, Frederick held a meeting with many godly teachers and ministers in order to examine the new catechism. The men were very pleased with it. After the meetings, Frederick wrote an introduction, and the catechism was ready for printing.

The German people eagerly read the new catechism. A Latin translation was made for use by scholars. Frederick sent a copy of the German catechism to the princes, teachers, and ministers in his country. But not everyone was pleased. Emperor Ferdinand in Vienna sent a letter to Frederick informing him that not all the doctrines in this catechism were correct, and that people were suspecting Frederick of heresy.

In the summer of the same year, a second edition was printed. Frederick made a change to this edition. Since the main point of controversy at that time was about the Lord's Supper, Frederick added a question and answer—probably at Calvin's request—that would make it very plain. This is Question and Answer 80:

Q. *What difference is there between the Lord's Supper and the popish mass?*

A. The Lord's Supper testifies to us that we have a full pardon of all sin by the only sacrifice of Jesus Christ, which He himself has once accomplished on the cross; and that we by the Holy Ghost are ingrafted into Christ, who, according to His human nature is now not on earth, but in heaven, at the right hand of God the Father, and will there be worshiped by us—but the mass teaches that the living and dead have not the pardon of sins through the sufferings of Christ, unless Christ is also daily offered for them by the priests; and further, that Christ is bodily under the form of bread and wine, and therefore is to be worshiped in them; so that the mass, at bottom, is nothing else than a denial of the one sacrifice and sufferings of Jesus Christ.

This is where the answer ended in the second edition.

So many people requested a copy of the catechism that the printers had a lot of work to do. In December 1563, a third edition was printed in German. This time Frederick added a phrase to the end of Q&A 80, so that it ended with the words we have placed in italics: "so that the mass, at bottom, is nothing else than a denial of the one sacrifice and sufferings of Jesus Christ, *and an accursed idolatry.*" Strong words for a biblical truth!

The fourth edition of the Heidelberg Catechism grouped the questions into fifty-two Lord's Days. Petrus Dathenus translated the third edition into Dutch. In July 1563, Calvin dedicated his commentary on Jeremiah to Frederick III, commending him for his piety and sound doctrine. Many people were very happy with the new catechism, but others were not.

The town and castle of Heidelberg

Opposition

Some people began spreading false rumors about Frederick III. They said that the devil wouldn't let him sleep at night. The Catholics and even many Lutherans began writing things against the catechism, saying it was not according to Scripture. Ursinus was appointed by Frederick to write against these objections, pointing out the scriptural accuracy of the Heidelberg Catechism.

Even the emperor, Maximillian, became involved. He was interested in this debate. Was Frederick really troubled by the devil? Why was there so much conflict over a catechism? Frederick himself had written a few letters to the emperor stating the facts, and Maximillian had been impressed by

the quiet confidence of the elector. He did not use harsh language or call people names. What sort of man was this, the emperor wondered.

The Diet of Augsburg

Finally, March 23, 1566 was set as the date for the Augsburg Diet. Many people attended this important meeting, and many issues were discussed. Frederick did not attend the meeting until the following month. His friends feared for his life, but he was determined to go, trusting that the Lord would take care of him.

Frederick had only one friend at this meeting. No one else wanted to defend him. Either they disagreed with him, or they did not dare to stand with him for fear of their own lives. When Frederick was questioned, the Lord gave him the words to speak and the quiet confidence he needed. Everyone was impressed. The emperor sensed that people liked this kind, principled man. They did not ask him any more questions at that time, but they asked him to attend a meeting on May 23 and 24.

In this meeting, Emperor Maximillian told Elector Frederick III that he must give up all his Calvinist errors and rid his country of Calvinist preachers and teachers. He also asked him to give up his new catechism. Again, the Lord guided Frederick, and he spoke so convincingly that the emperor decided not to pursue the matter. Later, in a letter to a friend, Maximillian called Frederick "the Pious," a name that suited him.

Throughout this upheaval, Frederick gained the respect of his friends and enemies alike. He behaved himself wisely and trusted the Lord in these difficult times. He did not have to fight, for the Lord fought for him. The Lord protected this precious document, the Heidelberg Catechism, so that we may still enjoy it today.

The three men at Heidelberg

There is much to tell about the three men at Heidelberg, but we will only tell you briefly about the rest of their lives.

Zacharias Ursinus married a widow in the year 1572. They had one son in their nine years of marriage. These years were quite difficult, as Ursinus was repeatedly called to defend the truths of the Heidelberg Catechism against the attacks of both Lutherans and Roman Catholics.

Although Frederick lived a godly life, he also did not have an easy life. Trouble and debates about various issues continued. Frederick wanted the best for his beloved country and did his best to bring God's Word to all the people and every church.

In 1568, Maria, Frederick's wife, died. He was very lonely without her, especially because she had finally agreed with her husband about the Catechism and the truths of Scripture. After a year and a half, he married Amalie, countess of Neunar, widow of a Dutch count.

Two of Frederick's sons, Casimir and Christopher, fought in the Huguenot wars. Casimir returned home victorious, but Christopher was killed. Elector Frederick III died on October 26, 1576. At his funeral two of his favorite passages were read: Psalm 31 and John 17.

Frederick's eldest son, Louis, succeeded him. Being Lutheran, he was not in agreement with his father, and he absolutely would not tolerate the "heresy" of Calvinism. Less than a month after Frederick's death, Louis deposed Olevianus from his offices. Olevianus left Heidelberg for Berleburg to tutor the sons of Count Ludwig of Wittgenstein. From there, Olevianus eventually accepted a call in 1584 as pastor and teacher in the new academy at Herborn. He died triumphantly on March 15, 1587, declaring that belonging to Jesus Christ in life and death was his only and certain comfort.

Ursinus was also forced to leave Heidelberg after Frederick III's death. On October 3, 1577, he closed the College of Wisdom, since none of the sixty-three students would accept the Lutheran Smaller Catechism. Ursinus accepted a teaching position at Neustadt-on-Hardt, where he lectured faithfully for a few years before passing on to glory in 1582.

People may come and go; they may die for their faith, or be removed from their homes. Some may think that Satan has won the victory or destroyed what they worked so hard to do, but the truth of the Lord stands forever. Thanks be to God, it is because of His faithful care that we may enjoy the riches of the Heidelberg Catechism until this day.

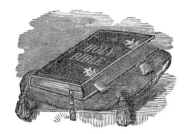

~ 19 ~

Peter Martyr Vermigli

◆◆

(1499–1562)

This Italian Reformer was willing to leave his country for the sake of the gospel.... His main goal in life was to become more and more like the Lord Jesus.

Birth and early life

Peter Martyr was born in Florence, Italy, on September 8, 1499. His father's name was Stefano Vermigli and his mother's name was Maria Fumantina. His parents consecrated him to a saint named Peter Martyr, so his baptismal name was Pietro Martire Vermilius (*Vermilius* means "son of Vermigli"). Sometimes he is called Peter Martyr, while other times he is called Peter Vermigli. His mother was an educated woman and taught him Latin. Together they also studied various literary works. He was only twelve when she died. There were many other children born to the Vermiglis, but they all died in infancy except one girl.

At the age of sixteen, Vermigli joined the order of St. Augustine at the college of Fiscoli, which was only a few miles away from his hometown. He studied at this college for several years before moving to Padua, where he entered the monastery of St. John de Verdera. He stayed there for eight years. He studied philosophy, Greek, Hebrew, and literature. In 1527, he graduated with a Doctor of Divinity degree.

His teachers noticed that he had a gift for speaking, so they appointed him to preach, beginning in 1526. He preached in some large Italian cities such as Brescia, Pisa, Venice, and Rome. He became well-known as a speaker and a scholar. He was appointed abbot of Spoleto, where he remained for three years. Then he took the position of abbot of the monastery of St. Peter ad Aram in Naples.

Vermigli first discovered the writings of Bucer and Zwingli in Naples. He began to read Bucer's commentaries on the Gospels and Psalms, and Zwingli's *Concerning True and False Religion*. As he read the works of these Reformers, Vermigli began to read Scripture in a new light. His change of heart began to show itself as he came face to face with the errors of the Roman Catholic Church.

Once, on a visit to Rome, he preached to some high-ranking members of the Roman Catholic Church about the error of the doctrine of purgatory. His audience was angry and forbade him to preach anymore; in fact, he was banned from preaching altogether! Friends in the Roman Catholic Church had the ban removed, but from then on he was no longer trusted.

People noticed the difference in his preaching, and he faced opposition from the Roman Catholic clergy. Rather than being discouraged, Vermigli kept searching and studying the Scriptures. It was not until 1542, however, twelve years after his arrival in Naples, that he renounced the Roman Catholic Church and embraced the Protestant faith as truth.

After three years in Naples, he became ill and quit his position as abbot of the monastery. When he recovered, he took on the position of prior of St. Fridian in Lucca in Tuscany. His teachings, becoming more and more scriptural, made the monks angry. They rejected him and his "heresy." Knowing this, Vermigli decided to leave. The words of Matthew 10:23 were his guide: "But when they persecute you in this city, flee ye into another."

Fleeing for the truth

Not all the monks disagreed with Vermigli, however; eighteen of them followed him out of the monastery in Lucca.

Together with his friend, Bernardo Ochino, a preacher and Reformer, Vermigli fled to Zurich, where he stayed for several months. In December 1542, he traveled to Strasbourg, where Martin Bucer was a pastor. Vermigli was useful in the church there, teaching the people of the congregation as well as the students at the university there. He remained in Strasbourg for five years and lectured on the Old Testament and Romans; he also published a commentary on the Apostles' Creed that denied the Roman Catholic doctrines on the Lord's Supper and the papacy.

At Strasbourg, he married Catherine Dampmartin, a former nun. She died eight years later and was buried in the cathedral church of Oxford. Four years after her death, her body was dug up and buried in a waste heap. Queen Mary said it was because she had been a nun who had scorned her vows. Later, when Queen Elizabeth came to the throne, she ordered the body to be reburied honorably.

Invitation to England

In 1547, Vermigli and his friend, Ochino, were invited by Edward Seymour, Lord Protector, and Archbishop Cranmer to assist in the great work of the Reformation in England. A year later, Vermigli was appointed to be the King's Professor of Theology at Oxford University, the highest theological office in England. At Oxford, Vermigli participated in many debates. For example, in a 1549 debate about the nature of the Lord's Supper, he explained the doctrine of the sacrament so well that no one could convincingly speak against it. Some people were glad and thankful, but others were angry. His opponents stirred up the people against him. People threw rocks through his windows and shouted threats and insults at him.

During his time in England, Peter Martyr helped the Reformation there. He influenced Archbishop Cranmer's views on the Lord's Supper and he helped write the 1552 *Book of Common Prayer*.

After his wife's death in 1551 and Queen Mary's accession to the throne, he moved to Strasbourg, where he lectured once again at the university. Bucer, his beloved friend, had also died in the year 1551, and the Strasbourg church leaned more and more toward Luther's teachings on the Lord's Supper. The debate about this sacrament continued to rage.

Move to Zurich

In 1556, Vermigli moved to Zurich, where he found peace. He married for the second time. Catherina Merenda was a loving wife. They had two children, both of whom died very young. When Vermigli died, Catherina was expecting her third child.

In Zurich, Vermigli wrote his greatest work, written against the Lutheran views of the Lord's Supper. Vermigli loved the Lutherans, but he could not agree with their view on the Lord's Supper. He did not write angry, bitter words, but he tried to explain from Scripture the doctrine of this wonderful sacrament. Vermigli was also invited twice by John Calvin to come to Geneva and pastor the Italian congregation there and lecture for Calvin.

Peter Martyr Vermigli

His death and influence

This Italian Reformer was willing to leave his country for the sake of the gospel. He wanted to bring the truth to his countrymen, but because of the efforts of the Inquisition, he had to leave. His main goal in life was to become more and more like the Lord Jesus. He died on November 12, 1562. He was mourned by many, including Elizabeth, Queen of England.

Peter Martyr was not afraid of opposition, but he bravely brought the message of the gospel wherever he went. His influence on the Reformation was great; today more and more research is being done on Vermigli, since not much was known about him. He corresponded with many of the great Reformers, such as Calvin, Bucer, and John Jewel. Many scholars say Peter Martyr is nearly as important to the Reformation as John Calvin was, especially in defining Reformed doctrines.

~ 20 ~

John Calvin

(1509–1564)

"Almost all scholars of Reformation history would agree that the greatest Reformer of all was John Calvin. He was a scholar, a theologian, a teacher, a preacher, an evangelist, an administrator, and a leader of men."

His education

John Calvin was born in Noyon, France, on July 10, 1509. In French, his name is Jean Cauvin; in Latin, it is Johannes Calvinus. His mother died when he was only three. His father, Gérard Cauvin, soon remarried. He was able to provide a good education for his son, and Calvin studied diligently. In 1523, he went to a college in Paris named the Collège des Capettes, which means "college of the little hooded capes." His father wanted John to study for the priesthood.

Young Calvin also studied theology at the Collège de Montaigu. It was a solemn, depressing place with strict rules. The students were required to speak Latin at all times. They were given very little food and were to obey strict schedules. Calvin was a gifted student, and in 1528, at the age of eighteen, he received his Master of Arts degree.

In 1528, Calvin moved to Paris and studied at the famous law schools in Orléans and then Bourges, where he completed a law degree in 1532. Calvin decided to go into law because his father was in dispute with the Roman Catholic Church and didn't want his son to become a priest. Instead, his father urged him to become a lawyer. After his father died, however, Calvin returned to Paris to study theology.

During his years at school, Calvin heard about the famous Dutch scholar, Desiderius Erasmus, who had published a Greek New Testament with a modern, more easily understood Latin translation. Erasmus realized the need for change and reform in the Roman Catholic Church, but he never went as far as the Reformers who actually left the church. His Latin translation, the Vulgate, was a great help to many scholars, but the Roman Catholic Church authorities were not pleased. They wanted to keep the people ignorant. Calvin, however, was intrigued. He also heard about Martin Luther, who was teaching that salvation was God's gift and could not be earned. He was interested but cautious.

Although Calvin had been raised to be a devout Roman Catholic, he attended meetings with other students. At these meetings, the Bible was studied and discussed. Secretly, they also read and studied the writings of Martin Luther. This was dangerous because the Protestants were being persecuted. Some of the discussions were about the faith of the martyrs. Calvin also heard Protestant ideas from relatives and his Greek teacher, Melchior Wolmar.[1] Eventually, Calvin realized that the Roman Catholic Church was mistaken. He could not find peace in absolutions, penances, and the intercessions of the church.

His conversion

In 1533, when Calvin was twenty-four years old, God suddenly converted him through private study. Although Calvin wrote more than one hundred books, he only speaks of his conversion twice in all those books. In his *Commentary on the Psalms,* Calvin says, "God subdued me and made me teachable." Elsewhere he writes, "Like a flash of light, I realized in what an abyss of errors, in what chaos I was." God saved Calvin, and he came to see the errors of the Roman Catholic Church. For Calvin, the pope had invented

John Calvin in his study

---

1. Melchior Wolmar had a positive influence on Calvin. In 1546, Calvin dedicated his commentary on the Corinthian Epistles to Wolmar.

doctrines that were against Scripture, ignoring the authority of the Bible. So he became a Protestant.

Flees from France

After his conversion, Calvin saw much suffering and pain brought on God's people by the Roman Catholic authorities in France. This troubled Calvin and he wanted to help them. Soon, however, Calvin became the target of persecution as well, and he was forced to flee for his life.

In 1533, a good friend of Calvin's named Nicholas Cop made a speech about Jesus and the Beatitudes (Matthew 5:1–11). In this speech, Cop explained that justification was by faith alone in Christ alone, not by the works of the law. The authorities said the speech was full of heresy. Because Calvin had helped Cop write it, the authorities wanted to arrest both men. Cop fled the city. The officers were at the front door asking for Calvin. Calvin's friends spoke with the officers while Calvin escaped through a back window. The next morning, Calvin left the city dressed up as a wine farmer, a hoe on his shoulder. He was never recognized. The Lord had work for Calvin to do.

Calvin found safety with his friend, Louis du Tillet. It was quiet and peaceful there, and Calvin studied, prayed, and asked many questions of his host. After a few months, Calvin went to visit another friend, whose influence left a deep impression him.

For a final time, Calvin returned to Noyon to inform the church that he could no longer serve the Roman Catholic Church. They were angry and disappointed. They called him a traitor and a heretic. He knew now, without a doubt, that France was no longer a safe place for him.

John Calvin

After this, Calvin went from city to city. He could not use his own name, for his life was in danger. He used assumed names to protect himself. Everywhere he went, he secretly taught people the truth of God's Word. The Word was spread just as it was when the apostles had to flee because of persecution. The Lord is never perplexed or dismayed because of sin and Satan. His work goes on, regardless of the wrath of men.

The Institutes

In 1535, Calvin finally settled in Basel, Switzerland. Here, he had time to organize his thoughts on the truths of the Bible. In the spring of 1536, at the age of 26, he published the first edition of his famous *Institutes of the Christian Religion*. This work, describing what Reformed Christians believe, became one of the greatest works of the Reformation. Calvin was the first to give a systematic presentation of the evangelical, Reformed faith. This book caused fear and consternation in the Roman Church and was a powerful unifying force among Protestants.

In 1559, the final edition of the *Institutes* was published. Calvin revised the *Institutes* several times during his life in order to present a clearer meaning of the Christian faith, but he never wavered from any of the doctrines he explained in the first edition. Already in the sixteenth century, the *Institutes* were translated into nearly all of the languages of Western Europe.[2]

William Farel

When he finished the first edition of the *Institutes*, Calvin decided to go to Strasbourg, Germany. He wanted to live quietly as a scholar. He was frail and tired and wanted some rest. God, however, had other plans for Calvin. These plans were made clear when Calvin met William Farel in Geneva in 1536.

William Farel

William (or Guillaume) Farel was born in 1489, in Gap, France. He studied in Paris and became professor in the Collège du Cardinal Lemoine. Afterward, he became involved with the work of the Reformation. He moved to Basel in 1523, where he met and disputed with Erasmus. Erasmus persuaded the city government to expel Farel because of his strong Protestant beliefs and fiery character. After this, Farel preached in different parts of Switzerland,

---

2. Jack L. Arnold, "John Calvin: From Birth to Strassburg (1509–1541) Reformation Men and Theology, Lesson 7 of 11," *IIIM Magazine Online* 1, no. 7, April 12–18, 1999, http://www.thirdmill.org/files/english/html/ch/CH.Arnold.RMT.7.HTML.

sowing the seeds of the Reformation as he went. Finally, he settled in Geneva in 1532.

Farel was a bold, brave man. He preached the doctrines of God's Word and was not afraid of the anger of the Roman Catholic Church. It is not easy to stand up and fight for something that may get one killed! But Farel loved the Lord Jesus and was willing to suffer and die for Him if he was called to do so.

Yet Farel had his faults. He was a hot-tempered man. One day, he saw a Roman Catholic procession in the street. He went up to the priest who was carrying a statue of St. Anthony, snatched the image out of his hands and threw it into the river. This made the people very angry, of course, and Farel almost lost his life in the uproar that followed. One of his friends, Johannes Œcolampadius, reminded him that people are led by gentleness, not violence, and that he was sent to preach to people, not to shout at them.

CALVIN PRESIDING AT THE COUNCIL OF GENEVA

Farel and Calvin

On a summer night in 1536, God arranged for Farel and Calvin to meet. Farel heard that Calvin was staying at an inn in Geneva while on his way to Strasbourg, so he visited him there. Farel explained to Calvin the situation in Geneva and asked for his help because of the constant struggle between the Protestants and the Roman Catholics.

Calvin did not want to help. He wanted to go to Strasbourg to study and rest. Calvin was not only frail and tired, but he was also quiet and reserved. He did not like the idea of getting involved in debates, arguments, and struggles. He wanted peace and quiet. For a long time, the two men argued back and forth. Farel pleaded with Calvin to assist in the great work that needed to be done in Geneva. Calvin, however, wanted to rest and continue his studies to promote the Reformation.

At last, Farel stood up and looked piercingly at John Calvin. "May God curse your studies if now, in her time of need, you refuse to help His church," he said in a powerful voice. Then he turned and left with a heavy heart.

John Calvin sat rooted to his chair. He was terrified. Was he really being selfish? Through Farel's powerful voice, Calvin heard God speaking. He knew he had to stay in Geneva. God had work for him to do there, and God would give him the strength to do it.

Just as the Lord put Luther and Melanchthon together, so He put Calvin and Farel together. Both Luther and Farel were firm, bold, strong workers for the Lord's cause, while Melanchthon and Calvin were more quiet and meek. They needed their partners to encourage and support them in their efforts. The Lord was wise to put these men together in this great work.

Calvin and Farel worked very hard. They tried to persuade the government of Geneva of the errors of the Roman Catholic Church. They had several debates with the city government. Life was very difficult for Calvin and the Protestants in Geneva during this time. Once, some armed people stormed into the church, determined to force their way to the communion table. Calvin firmly resisted them. There were many fierce arguments between the Protestants and the Roman Catholics.

Calvin endured much persecution in Geneva because he boldly preached the doctrines of grace. His home was often riddled with bullets. People named their dogs after him to ridicule him. Pope Pius IV said, "The strength of that heretic consisted in this, that money never had the slightest charm for him. If I had such servants, my kingdom would extend from sea to sea." Calvin fearlessly bore the derision and scorn, looking to his Master, becoming a living testimony of Acts 20:24, "None of these things move me, neither count I my life dear unto myself, so that I might...testify the gospel of the grace of God."

Finally, two years later, in 1538, Calvin and Farel were banished from Geneva. Had all their work been in vain? They had tried to fight against error, but it seemed they had

Farel preaching at Neuchâtel

Geneva

lost the battle. The people of Geneva did not want to listen to the Reformers. They did not want to part with their sins and become thoroughly Reformed.

Farel made his home in Neuchâtel, where he remained a preacher until his death. He made many trips to various towns and villages in Switzerland, Germany, and France to encourage those who had become Protestants. In this way, he did much work for the Reformation. The Lord blessed his efforts and helped him in his labors. On one of his trips, Farel became sick. He was seventy-six years old and traveling in northern France in the winter. He died not long afterward.

Strasbourg

While Farel went to Neuchâtel, John Calvin went to Basel, thinking that perhaps now he could rest and study. From there, however, he moved to Strasbourg because the people there pleaded with him to become their pastor. At first, Calvin refused. He felt the bitter pain of failure in Geneva, but Martin Bucer and others urged him to come, assuring him he was needed. Many of the members of the church in Strasbourg were people who had fled from France to escape persecution. Calvin enjoyed being pastor of this church. He had time to study and write, and he added to his great work, *The Institutes*. He also published a psalm book as well as a commentary on the book of Romans.

Marriage and family life

After the difficult time in Geneva, Calvin enjoyed a peaceful four years in Strasbourg. While there, he married a widow named Idelette de Bure. She had two children from her first marriage, Jacques and Judith. Calvin's dear friend, William Farel, came to perform the ceremony in August 1540.

Calvin and his wife loved each other and the Lord. Idelette was a wonderful help to Calvin. E.M. Johnson writes that she "was good in the home and cared greatly for his well-being. She visited the sick and comforted the dying. She went with him on some of his journeys and entertained his friends. A woman of some force and individuality, Calvin himself said that she was the best companion of his life."[3] On July 28, 1542, a baby boy named Jacques was born, but he only lived a few days. Calvin wrote to one of his friends, "'The Lord has certainly inflicted a severe and bitter wound, in the death of our baby son, but he is himself a Father and knows best what is good for his children.'"[4] Idelette died after only nine years of marriage to John Calvin. He missed her terribly after her early death.

Geneva Again

In 1541, Calvin heard that things were not going well in Geneva. The Roman Catholic Church was trying very hard to win the Protestants in Geneva back to the Roman Catholic Church. The Council of Geneva decided that they needed Calvin to preach and teach in their city. They sent him a letter by way of messengers asking him to return, promising to treat him better.

"The tears ran down [Calvin's] cheeks, and he buried his face in his hands. The Strasbourg friends who were with him…did not know what to say or do to help him. Never before had they seen their pastor in such distress. When he recovered a little and was able to speak, he told them, 'The very thought of Geneva is agony to me. Geneva was my cross, and every day I suffered a thousand deaths. Of course I want to assist them, but how can I return?'"[5]

It was not an easy decision to go back to the city that had banished him earlier, but, in September 1541, Calvin returned to Geneva after several months of thought and prayer. "'I am not my own,' he said, 'I offer up my heart as a sacrifice to the Lord. I submit my will and my affections to the obedience of God.'"[6] The people who had been in power when Calvin was banished had been replaced by others, and he was welcomed back with joy. He joined these people in their attempt to stop the errors in the city of Geneva.

Again Calvin worked unceasingly in Geneva. He preached and wrote. One important work he wrote is called *Ecclesiastical Ordinances*. In this book, he described the tasks of pastors, elders, deacons, and teachers and professors. Another important work was titled *On the Christian Life*. It included spiritual and practical advice for Christian living. He even took time to urge the council to pass laws that benefited the health and safety of the citizens of Geneva. He supported good hospitals, a proper sewage system, adding railings to upper stories to keep children from falling, special

3. E. M. Johnson, *Man of Geneva: The Story of John Calvin*, (Edinburgh: The Banner of Truth Trust, 1977), 94–95.

4. Ibid., 104.

5. Johnson, *Man of Geneva*, 100.

6. Ibid., 103.

care for the poor and infirm, and the introduction of new industries. He encouraged the use of French in churches so that the people could benefit from hearing the service in their own language.

One sad occurrence was the death of a man named Michael Servetus.[7] This man was a heretic, despising the truth of Scripture. Many letters had been written back and forth between him and Calvin, debating various doctrines —especially predestination. Servetus persisted boldly in his heresy. He arrived in Geneva in the summer of 1553 and was quickly arrested. A lengthy trial followed. "Calvin felt that the honor of Christ was at stake, and he believed that it would be a service to God and the church, if the man was removed from Geneva as soon as possible, not by banishment, but by death."[8] The council asked the advice of other cities. They agreed that he was guilty of heresy and blasphemy and that he deserved to die. He was sentenced to be burned at the stake. Calvin asked for a less painful death for him, but this request was denied. Servetus was burned to death on October 27, 1553.

Calvin's enemies often used against him the fact that he was part of the government that condemned and sentenced Servetus to such a cruel death. Burning heretics at the stake was not an uncommon practice then, but it was a sad thing that the Protestants did the same as the Roman Catholics in this case.

"Those who really knew Calvin, however, found him to be a gentle man with real love in his heart for others. He grieved in their sorrows and rejoiced in their joys. He had a heart for people and would write beautiful notes of sympathy when tragedy would strike a home. When a wedding occurred or a baby came to grace a home, he took a warm, personal interest in the event. It was not unusual for him to stop on the street in the midst of weighty matters to give a schoolboy a friendly pat and an encouraging word. His enemies might call him pope or king or caliph [ruler]; his friends thought of him only as their brother and beloved leader."[9]

Time went on, and as more and more Protestants heard about Calvin's efforts in this city, they fled to Geneva from their persecutors in other countries. Soon there were more Protestants than Roman Catholics in Geneva. By 1555, John Calvin's supporters became predominant in the city of Geneva. Many good laws were passed that brought about positive changes. Calvin established schools for young children as well as a Protestant university called the Geneva Academy. The Geneva Academy was set up by Calvin especially to train young men to become pastors. Many of these pastors returned to France to spread the gospel there. Theodore Beza was one of the professors at this new university. Students loved to listen to Calvin and Beza lecture. The Lord blessed them with great intelligence and insight. They brought the doctrines and teachings of Scripture into sharp focus. Their work and teachings still benefit us today.

---

7. Servetus (1511–1553) did not believe in the Trinity or original sin, so he did not agree with either the Roman Catholics or the Protestants. He was convicted of heresy by the Roman Catholic Church, but he escaped from prison and went to Geneva.

8. Johnson, *Man of Geneva*, 110.

9. Jack L. Arnold, "John Calvin: From Birth to Strassburg (1509–1541) Reformation Men and Theology, Lesson 7 of 11," *IIIM Magazine Online* 1, no. 7, April 12–18, 1999, http://www.thirdmill.org/files/english/html/ch/CH.Arnold.RMT.7.HTML.

In his later years, Calvin was afflicted with fever, asthma, and gout, among other ailments. In the midst of his sufferings, however, he continued his work for the Lord, saying, "Would you wish that the Lord should find me idle when He comes?" Although he was weak and in pain, Calvin continued to preach until the end of his life. Friends carried him from his home to the church so that he could address his beloved congregation. On February 6, 1564, John Calvin preached his last sermon, having only with great difficulty found breath enough to carry him through it. Several times after this he was carried to church, but never again was he able to take any part in the service. On May 27, 1564, John Calvin died quietly and peacefully in the arms of Beza. Calvin found the rest for which he had been longing—to be with Christ in heaven forever. He was buried quietly in the Genevan cemetery the following day.[10] He did not want his grave to be marked, for he wanted all glory ascribed to God alone.

As Jack Arnold has observed, "Almost all scholars of Reformation history would agree that the greatest Reformer of all was John Calvin. He was a scholar, a theologian, a teacher, a preacher, an evangelist, an administrator, and a leader of men. Few men have suffered like Calvin from the attacks of unbelievers and believers alike. Many who attack John Calvin simply are ignorant of church history. It would be well for some of those who condemn him to spend some time studying his works. Without Calvin, the Reformation would not have succeeded as it did. Probably no servant of Christ since the days of the apostles has been at the same time so loved and so hated, admired and abhorred, praised and blamed, blessed and cursed, as the faithful and fearless Calvin. He did much good for the cause of the Reformation."[11]

10. The Bible Museum, Inc., "John Calvin," The Bible Museum, Inc., 2003, http://www.greatsite.com/timeline-english-bible-history/john-calvin.html

11. Jack L. Arnold, "John Calvin: From Birth to Strassburg (1509–1541) Reformation Men and Theology, Lesson 7 of 11," *IIIM Magazine Online* 1, no. 7, April 12–18, 1999, http://www.thirdmill.org/files/english/html/ch/CH.Arnold.RMT.7.HTML.

~ 21 ~

Theodore Beza

(1519–1605)

His zeal for the cause of the Lord and the Reformation never failed. He faithfully led the Reformation in Geneva after Calvin died.

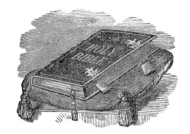

His education and marriages

Theodore Beza (Théodore de Bèze) was born on June 24, 1519 in Vézelay, France. He was the youngest of seven children born to Pierre Beza, royal governor of Vézelay, and Marie Bordelot. When Theodore was only three, his mother passed away. His uncle, Nicholas Beza, was so impressed with the mental abilities of the young Theodore that he took him to Paris to be educated. In 1528, Nicholas sent Theodore to Orléans to study under Melchior Wolmar. Even though Wolmar was not a Christian, he taught Beza many useful subjects, including Greek and Latin. God blessed Beza with a bright mind and equipped him for His service through these studies.

In 1530, Beza went with Wolmar to Bourges, another city in France. Five years later, Pierre Beza ordered his son back to Orléans because he wanted him to become a lawyer. Though Beza obeyed his father and returned to Orléans, he continued to spend time with people who liked to study Greek and Latin. During this time, Beza enjoyed writing poetry. He was a good writer and some of his poetry can still be read today.

Around 1544, Beza became engaged to a young girl of humble descent, Claudine Denosse. They had a long and happy marriage of forty years. In 1588, Claudine died childless. Beza married for the second time to Catharina del Piano, upon the advice of his friends, so that he had a loving helpmeet as he became older and weaker. "Esteemed friend and very dear brother," he wrote to Johann Piscator of Basel on August 20, 1588, "here again, by the advice of friends, and led by the very many inevitable ills of old age to seek for the help of another, I have returned to matrimony. I have taken to wife a widow approaching her fiftieth year, so adorned, according to the testimony of all good people, with piety and every female virtue, that I could not have found a more suitable companion. Regarding this blessing of God toward me, I wish you to render thanks to Him with me, and to join your prayers to mine."[1]

His conversion

By 1539, Beza had acquired his degree in civil law and moved to Paris to begin his career. The Lord, however, had other plans for Beza. In God's providence, Beza found some literature written by the Reformers, and he read it with great interest. Finally, he was convinced the Reformers were right and their doctrines were true.

This decision did not come without a struggle, however. It was not easy for him to discard his old beliefs. It is not pleasant to think that we are totally depraved and need a Savior because we cannot save ourselves. Beza went back and forth in his mind, becoming so distressed that he became very sick. Beza knew he was not ready to meet God and began to think about eternity. The Holy Spirit showed him his sin, and he was overwhelmed by it. He knew he had offended a just and holy God. When he confessed his sin and prayed for forgiveness, however, God heard and answered him. Peace replaced the turmoil and grief in his heart. Joyfully, he fully consecrated his life to the service of his Savior.

In those days, social standing was very important. Marrying someone of a lower social class would lower one's own status as well. Because Claudine Denosse came from a lower class of society, Beza had married her secretly, though he promised her he would marry her publicly when circumstances were more favorable. Beza was afraid that his benefactors would look down on him and would not want to associate with him or financially support someone of such a humble social status. After his conversion, however, his conscience troubled him for this. He had been receiving financial support from the Roman Catholic Church as if he were a faithful member, while in his heart he was actually a Protestant, though he hid his real opinions and beliefs. He also felt guilty for not keeping the promise he had made to Claudine. Beza was convinced that he had to be honest and dedicate himself wholly to the Lord, without worrying about the consequences. When he was not yet fully recovered from his illness, he and his wife packed what they could carry and made their way to Switzerland. Later, Beza wrote, "From the moment that I could leave my bed, I broke all the bonds that until then had enchained me. I gathered all my belongings and left my country, my family, and friends in order to follow Christ, willingly retiring to Geneva with my wife." On October 23, 1548, Beza and his wife reached the city of Geneva. One of the first things Beza did in his new hometown was to marry his wife in a church.[2]

---

1. E.S. Cyprian, *Catalogus Codicum Manuscriptorum Bibliotheca Gothanae* (Leipzig, 1714), 51–52, cited in Scott Michael Manetsch, *Theodore Beza and the Quest for Peace in France, 1572–1598* (Leiden: Brill, 2000), 185.

---

2. http://www.ccel.org/s/schaff/history/8_ch19.htm. (cf. Manetsch, *Beza and the Quest for Peace in France*, 11–12).

Geneva

Because Beza had embraced the Protestant religion, he was accused of heresy and officially banished from France by its rulers. The government took all the belongings he had left in France and condemned him to be burned at the stake. Beza was safely in Geneva, however, so they burned an effigy (likeness) of him instead.

In Geneva, Beza studied diligently under Calvin, joyfully soaking in the blessed truths of God's Word. He wanted to learn as much as he could from the great Reformer. By 1559, he had become a professor of theology and a rector at the Genevan Academy which Calvin founded. He also accepted a call to become the pastor of St. Pierre, one of several churches in Geneva.

Beza preached many sermons each week. It was the custom in Geneva to have two services on Sundays, as well as services every day of the week. It was a heavy workload for Beza and the other ministers to preach so many sermons. The format of the Genevan church service was much like traditional worship in Reformed churches today. There was singing before and after the sermon, a pastoral prayer, the reading of Scripture, and a sermon of about forty-five minutes in length.

After Calvin's death, Beza became Calvin's successor at Geneva and labored tirelessly in preaching and in caring for the thousands of destitute, persecuted saints who fled to Geneva for refuge. He remained at Geneva for many years until his death in 1605.

Theodore Beza

His work

Besides his many sermons, Beza wrote other things, most of them Christian, some of them not. He wrote Latin poems and plays, biographies, and political papers. He also edited a Greek New Testament that had notes in the margin. Called *Codex Bezae*, this was his most important work.

Beza followed Calvin in his teachings. Together they talked about doctrines such as justification, sanctification, predestination, and the Lord's Supper. Through his previous studies, Beza had learned about the teachings of men who had lived before him. He knew how to debate against the wrong doctrines taught by others, and he upheld the correct teachings of Scripture.

After Calvin died, Beza was asked to provide leadership for a group of Geneva's ministers called the Company of Pastors. Beza was also a counselor to the French Reformed churches, which meant that he frequently traveled to France for meetings. In France, Beza sometimes spoke before kings and nobles, trying to win them over to the cause of the Reformation. He spoke boldly, defending the truths of the Bible, but he was not heeded in his calls for reformation in France.

Because of his kindness to them, the Huguenots loved Beza. When persecutions against them grew fierce, many Huguenots fled to Geneva, where they were lovingly welcomed. They gladly attended the worship services in Geneva, where they could listen without fear of punishment. Beza took time to write letters to various government authorities, pleading the cause of the Huguenots. In times of confusion and unrest, they knew they could ask Beza for help and advice. Even the rulers of Navarre, Jeanne d'Albret and Henry of Navarre, sought the wise advice of this Reformer during the wars that threatened their country. After Geneva learned of the cruel massacre of the Huguenots on St. Bartholomew's Day 1572, Beza preached a comforting sermon to the mourning Christians.

Beza also helped write the French Psalter, or Psalmbook. He built upon the work of Clement Marot, who had already translated many of the psalms into French. These psalms became so dear to the Huguenots that they sang them everywhere and became identified by them.[3]

He also carried on extensive correspondence. In those days, people depended heavily on mail for communication. He wrote letters to many of the Reformed churches throughout Europe and Britain. He also wrote letters to friends, especially his friend Heinrich Bullinger of Zurich. In his letters, Beza spoke of the Lord and of the truths of His Word, encouraging his fellow Reformers. Sometimes people wrote him to ask questions, and Beza helped them find biblical answers.

He led the last French Reformed synod in La Rochelle; after the horrible massacre of Protestants by the Roman Catholics on the eve of St. Bartholomew's Day 1572, other French Reformed synods became impossible. While they were worshiping in a barn, these Protestants were attacked by the Duke of Guise, who butchered hundreds of them. Once, in a confrontation with this same Duke of Guise, Beza made this memorable statement: "Sir, it belongs, in truth, to the church of God, in the name of which I address you, to *suffer* blows, not to *strike* them. But at the same time let it be

---

3. Henry Martyn Baird: *Theodore Beza, The Counsellor of the French Reformation* (Eugene, Oregon: Wipf & Stock, 2004), 243–44, 288

your pleasure to remember that the church is an anvil which has worn out many a hammer."[4]

His enemies did their best to stop Beza's work. They accused him of the worst kinds of sins. The Roman Catholic Church tried to convince him to return to them, but Beza stood firm. In 1597, when Beza was an old man, a certain French Roman Catholic came to Geneva to try to persuade Beza to give up his Protestant faith. The man was only thirty, zealous, skillful in debate; he was confident that he could win Beza back to the Roman Catholic Church. But all his skill failed to move Beza. When argumentation failed, he tried bribery and, in the name of the pope, offered Beza a large sum of money. This Beza could not tolerate. Politely but emphatically Beza told him, "Go, sir! I am too old and too deaf to be able to hear such words!"[5]

The Lord's Supper

The doctrine that Protestants disagreed about most vehemently was the doctrine of the Lord's Supper. When Jesus gave the bread to His disciples, He said, "Take, eat; this is my body." Then He gave them the cup, saying, "Drink ye all of it; for this is my blood of the new testament, which is shed for many for the remission of sins" (Matthew 26:26b–28). Some people followed Luther's teaching that the body and blood of the Lord Jesus was actually in, with, and under the elements of bread and wine, because they reasoned that Jesus said, "This is my body," and, "This is my blood."

Calvin and Beza, however, taught that when Jesus said this, He did not mean that He was *literally* feeding His disciples His body and blood. Rather, Jesus meant the Lord's Supper to be a feast of *remembrance*, in which He was spiritually but not bodily present. They taught that believers feast on Christ *spiritually* in the Lord's Supper. In 1 Corinthians 11, Paul says that Jesus commanded the disciples, "This do in remembrance of me. For as often as ye eat this bread, and drink this cup, ye do shew [remember] the Lord's death till he come" (verses 24b and 26).

Sadly, the Lutherans and the Calvinists could not agree, and they argued bitterly at times. In 1581, Beza helped put together a book that tried to clear up this debate. It was called *Harmonia Confessionum Fidei* (The Harmony of the Confessions). Beza met a Lutheran named Jakob Andrae in 1586. They had a debate in which they tried to come to an agreement about the teaching of the Lord's Supper. Regrettably, they could not agree. In 1593, Beza made a final attempt to explain the doctrine of the Lord's Supper in a book called *De Conciliatione*.

Beza worked diligently for the cause of the Reformation. He taught actively until 1597. His zeal for the cause of the Lord and the Reformation never failed. He faithfully led the Reformation in Geneva after Calvin died. He lived to be eighty-six years old and died peacefully on October 13, 1605. Of him the Lord surely said, "Well done, good and faithful servant;... enter thou into the joy of thy lord" (Matthew 25:23).

---

4. http://www.prca.org/books/portraits/beza.htm: (cf. Baird, *Theodore Beza*, 28).

5. Ibid.

~ 22 ~

Jan Łaski

❖◆❖

(1499–1560)

He was an outstanding church organizer, a practical theologian, and a good defender of truth.

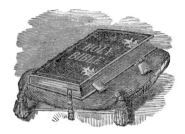

When we hear about the Reformation, we think of Luther, Calvin, Zwingli, Knox, and perhaps a few others. Some men who worked for the Reformation, however, are not as well known, even though they made significant contributions to it. Jan Łaski is one of these little-known heroes, and that is one reason that he is included in this book.

His education

Łaski, sometimes called John Alasco, or Jan à Lasco, was born in 1499. He belonged to a rich and honorable family in Poland. One of his uncles, also named Jan Łaski, was an archbishop, the leading priest connected with the Roman Catholic Church in Poland. Łaski's family and friends wished him to enter the church and become a priest. His parents made sure that he received the best education possible.

After studying for several years in his own country, Łaski was sent to other countries to continue his education. First he went to France and after that to Switzerland. There he met Ulrich Zwingli, the famous Swiss Reformer. From conversations with Zwingli, Łaski became acquainted with the cause of the Reformation. When his friends and family—especially the archbishop—heard that Łaski was becoming friends with Zwingli, they called him back home. They were afraid that the Reformer would be a bad influence on him.

His conversion

What Jan Łaski's family considered to be a "bad influence," however, had already penetrated the young man's heart. He had been studying the Scriptures to find out what the truth was. David said in Psalm 119:130, "The entrance of thy words giveth light." So it was in Łaski's case. God's Word had entered his mind and heart, and its entrance gave him light. As that light shone in his heart, he began to see the difference between the doctrines taught by the Roman Catholic Church and those that the Bible taught.

Łaski did not leave the church immediately, however. Though he saw the truth, it was hard for him to leave the church to which all his friends and family belonged. Also, he had been trained for the office of priest. He saw that there were many things wrong in the Roman Catholic Church, but he hoped that these errors might be reformed one day. And so, in 1521, he became a priest and carried out his duties faithfully and diligently.

After some time, Łaski was offered the position of bishop. If he were to take this position, he could become the archbishop of Poland after his uncle died. It was a splendid opportunity for such a young man, his friends and family told him. He decided not to accept this tempting offer, however. After he became a priest, he began to discover how wicked most of the clergy was. Their doctrines were false, and they lived lives full of sin. Łaski saw that it would be impossible

Jan Łaski

to reform such a corrupt church by staying in it. He made up his mind to leave the church.

As soon as he made this decision, he went to the king of Poland, who was his friend, and bravely told him how he felt. He thanked the king for the offer he had made to him of becoming a bishop, but he told the king he felt it was his duty to leave the Roman Catholic Church and join the Reformed Church. This was not an easy thing to tell the king! Like Moses, Łaski chose "rather to suffer affliction with the people of God, than to enjoy the pleasures of sin for a season; esteeming the reproach of Christ greater riches than the treasures in Egypt: for he had respect unto the recompense of the reward. By faith he forsook Egypt, not fearing the wrath of the king; for he endured, as seeing him who is invisible" (Hebrews 11:25–27).

His work in the Netherlands, England, and Poland

In 1539, Łaski left Poland, desiring to serve the Lord wherever God would send him. First, he went to the Netherlands and worked there for some time. While in the Netherlands, he began to publish some of his writings. In Emden in 1542, he was appointed pastor and superintendent of the East Frisian churches. During this time, he debated with Roman Catholics and Anabaptists, and he corresponded with many of the leading Reformers.

In 1548, Archbishop Cranmer invited Łaski to come to England to help with the work of the Reformation there. In England, he was put in charge of all the congregations of people who had fled to England from persecution in their own countries. He was kind and helpful to these people, and he did much to organize these churches along Calvinistic lines. He probably would have spent the rest of his life there, if Bloody Mary had not become queen of England in 1553 and begun fiercely persecuting the Christians.

Łaski returned to Poland in 1556. While he was away, the cause of the Reformation had grown there. Łaski was appointed superintendent of the Reformed churches in Poland. His last years were spent in this work. By his preaching, advice, and writings, he helped the cause of the Reformation in his home country. He died on January 8, 1560. He was an outstanding church organizer, a practical theologian, and a good defender of truth. He enjoyed the personal friendship of many Reformation heroes, including John Calvin and Martin Bucer.

Despite the fact that Poland turned away from the Reformation, many Poles stayed faithful to the Reformed faith. Men like Bartłomiej Keckermann (1572–1609), Makołaj Rej (1584–1641), Jan Makowski (1588–1644), and Makołaj Arnoldi (1618–1680) were able to exercise significant influence in and outside Poland.

~ 23 ~

The Duke

of Alva

---◆◆◆---

(1507–1582)

&

William,

Prince of Orange

---◆◆◆---

(1533–1584)

Part One: The Duke of Alva

Fernando Alvarez de Toledo, Duke of Alva, was born in Piedrahita, Spain, on October 29, 1507, to a family of the Spanish nobility. During the reign of Emperor Charles V of the Holy Roman Empire, the Duke of Alva became famous for his skills as an army general. His father trained him from a young age, and he spent a long life as a famous and successful general in service to the Spanish king. It is sad, however, that much of his fame came because of his opposition to the Reformation in the Netherlands. He did much to harm the cause of the Reformation, killing many people for their faith. He was not one of the "heroes" of the Reformation, but he is important to understanding the Reformation in the Netherlands.

His persecution of the Dutch Protestants

The Duke of Alva entered Brussels, the capital of the Netherlands at that time, on August 22, 1567, with a well-trained army of twelve thousand men. The Netherlands during this time was under the rule of King Philip II of Spain. Philip, a strict Roman Catholic and a fierce persecutor of the Protestants, had given the duke full power to get rid of as many Protestants as he could. The Duke of Alva was determined to root out all opposition against Spanish rule in the Netherlands. On February 16, 1568, the entire population of the Netherlands was condemned to death, with only a few exceptions.

The first thing Alva did upon coming to the Netherlands was to set up a special court of law to punish the men who had stirred up rebellion. This became known as the Blood Council. His aims were to bring the Dutch towns into submission with terror. On one day alone, five hundred arrests were made, mostly noblemen and town rulers, and their deaths soon followed if they did not submit.

As if the Blood Council were not enough to frighten the Dutch people into submission, the Duke of Alva introduced a tax, called the Tenth Penny. This tax was put on everything that was sold in the Netherlands, much like a modern sales tax. The sad thing about this tax is that it was not used to benefit the Dutch, but it was used against them by Alva.

At first, the persecution by Alva seemed to be only political, that is, only with things dealing with the government and loyalty to Spain. However, the oppression changed for religious reasons. Reformed doctrine had begun to enter the Netherlands during Luther's lifetime. Zwingli also had influence in the Netherlands, but by the 1560s Calvinism was beginning to spread quickly. Many Calvinist churches began to appear, and they adopted the Belgic Confession of Faith, written by Guido de Brès, as their confession.

The Duke of Alva became known as the "Iron Duke" because of his cruel persecution of many of the nobles early in the revolt, but later Protestants were also persecuted. The Spanish army, under his leadership, forced the leaders of the towns to submit and promise not to support the Protestants in any way. They had to pledge this over the sign of the cross. Those who did not were arrested, tried by the Council of Blood, and often executed. During the six years of his rule, Alva cruelly executed thousands of people.

The Dutch people responded to the iron hand of Alva by burning Roman Catholic churches, destroying images, and, at times, even hurting the priests. The leaders of the revolt did not want this to happen, but the people were angry and bitter against the Duke of Alva. It seemed as though the Duke of Alva was successful in defeating the Protestant cause, but many Protestants who had fled began returning to the Netherlands. Among those who had fled was Prince William of Orange. He longed to return and help his fellow countrymen in getting rid of Spanish oppression.

On December 18, 1573, the Duke of Alva left the Netherlands, never to return. After his return to Spain, he got into trouble and was imprisoned. He died on December 12, 1582. It appears that he never repented of his sin and never regretted his cruelty.

Part Two: William of Orange

Birth and early life

William I of Orange-Nassau was born on April 24, 1533, in the castle of Dillenburg in Nassau, Germany. He was the eldest son of William, Count of Nassau, and Juliana of Stolberg-Werningerode. From his earliest years, William was raised a Lutheran by his mother. He had four younger brothers and seven younger sisters: John, Hermanna, Louis, Mary, Anna, Elisabeth, Katharine, Juliane, Magdalene, Adolf, and Henry.

In 1544, William's cousin, René Châlon, Prince of Orange, died without a son. William inherited his property and title, Prince of Orange. This inheritance included much property in the Netherlands. At age eleven, William was sent to Brussels to the court of Charles V, the emperor of the Holy Roman Empire and ruler of the Netherlands. At the court, William received a Roman Catholic education, but he also received military, diplomatic (dealing with other countries), and foreign language training. God was preparing him for the task of leading the Netherlands.

His marriages

In 1551, William married Anna, Countess of Egmond and Buren. Together they had three children. By marrying Anna, William inherited the lands of her father, as well as the titles of Lord of Egmond and Count of Buren. Anna died seven years later, on March 24, 1558, and in 1561, William married Anna of Saxony. The couple had five children. William had this marriage legally dissolved in 1571, claiming that Anna was insane. William was married for the third time on April 24, 1575, to Charlotte de Bourbon. Together, they had six daughters. After her death, William married Louise de Coligny (1555–1620) in 1583. She was the daughter of Admiral Coligny, the leader of the French Protestants, who was assassinated in 1572.

Leadership in the Dutch revolt

The Dutch revolt began in 1572, and it would start what is known today as the Eighty Years' War. William of Orange became the leader of this revolt, although he was not in the Netherlands all the time. William was a man of compassion and tolerance, showing much love for his countrymen. He was saddened and angered at the Duke of Alva's persecution of the Protestants. He did not want the Protestants to take

revenge, however, and at first he tried to keep the peace in the country. He wanted the noblemen of the Netherlands to be united against King Philip and the Duke of Alva. This became very difficult because the nobles were both Roman Catholic and Protestant. Soon, however, the nobility split and William lost much support.

In 1566, frustrated Protestants vandalized countless Roman Catholic churches throughout the Netherlands. Philip II decided to strike back with military force. But the revolt of the northern provinces continued, with varying degrees of success. When the Duke of Alva was sent to the Netherlands, William withdrew to Germany. During his exile in Germany, William visited many of his powerful friends, trying to raise money and soldiers to send back to the Netherlands to fight the Duke of Alva. He succeeded in raising an army, and he sent the soldiers to fight the Spaniards in the north of the Netherlands. This army was under the leadership of his brother Louis. At first this army was successful, but later it was destroyed when Alva visited the area with his own army. Three of William's brothers were killed in battle during the revolt.

Meanwhile, William had raised another army and led it into Brabant, the southern part of the country. The Duke of Alva did not fight with William there, so William was left waiting. Eventually the army fell apart because William was not able to pay them.

The war seemed discouraging for William. Though he lacked money and men to fight the Spanish threat, the Lord provided a way for William to win some victories. A group of rebels known as Sea Beggars joined William. These Sea Beggars would fight from their ships against the Spanish armies in the cities along the coast. They were quite

Assassination of the Prince of Orange

effective and captured some cities. At the siege of the city of Leiden, the Sea Beggars broke the dikes and flooded the Spanish army.

William longed for peace in the Netherlands. Although he was a Protestant, he wanted to see freedom of religion in his country. He tried to unite the provinces against Spain. In 1576, the provinces of the Netherlands united under William's leadership for the purpose of expelling the Spanish, but the provinces of the Netherlands were not united in matters of religion. The country remained divided because of religion.

The Union of Utrecht was signed in 1579 by seven provinces in the north. William's brother, Count Jan the Elder, Gelderland's stadtholder (that is, a viceroy or governor of a province who represents the king), was the driving force behind the Union of Utrecht. This Union was an agreement formed by seven northern provinces to fight against Philip II. These provinces were Protestant, and would be the home of the Synod of Dort and the Dutch Further Reformation, a movement that resembled Puritanism in England. The Treaty of Arras was signed by the southern provinces, declaring loyalty to the king of Spain and remaining Roman Catholic. Today, these northern and southern areas are roughly equivalent to the countries known as the Netherlands and Belgium, respectively.

His death

In 1582, a Spaniard named Juan de Jáuregui attempted to assassinate William in Antwerp. Although William suffered severe injuries, he survived, thanks to the care of his wife Charlotte and his sister Mary. While William slowly recovered, the intensive care given by Charlotte took its toll on her, and she died on May 5.

Prince William never lived to see peace in his time, since the war with Spain continued for some time. He wanted to recapture the Roman Catholic provinces from Spain, but this never happened.

In 1584, William was assassinated in Delft by a Catholic Frenchman named Balthasar Gérard. He was a supporter of Philip II, and in his opinion, William of Orange had betrayed the Spanish king and the Catholic religion. After Philip II promised a large reward of 25,000 crowns (golden coins) for Prince William's assassination, Gérard decided to travel to the Netherlands to kill William. After several failed attempts to get close to the prince, he made an appointment with William of Orange in his home in Delft, known today as the *Prinsenhof*. When William left the dining room and climbed down the stairs, Gérard fatally shot William in the chest from close range and then fled.

By the grace of God, Prince William was the leader of the Dutch during the revolt. Although the war was at first political, it soon became a religious war. Protestantism and Reformation teaching spread and thrived in the northern provinces of the Netherlands. The Reformation had taken hold in the Netherlands, and would be intensified in the seventeenth century through the Dutch Further Reformation.

~ 24 ~

Petrus Dathenus

(1531–1588)

Dathenus led a life full of travels and trials. He served the Lord from his youth, and although he strayed, he returned to the Lord, whom he loved with his whole heart.

In the monastery

Petrus Dathenus was born in 1531 in Cassel, a town in Flanders, which is now part of Belgium. He was still a boy when he entered a Carmelite monastery near Ypres, about twenty-five miles from Cassel. Monks were men who lived in monasteries, separated from society. They wanted to be as independent from their surroundings as possible. Although the main purpose of monasteries was for the monks to live completely in the service of the Lord, they had to take care of their physical needs too. For that reason, some of the monks studied medicine so they could help those among them who got sick. Some of them worked in the monastery's garden so they could provide their own fruit and vegetables. Some of them took care of the cows and sheep. Others spent their time copying the Scriptures in beautiful handwriting. Some monks used their talents by joining the monastery choir. Young Dathenus studied medicine under the teaching of learned monks.

Although monasteries were Roman Catholic in their religion, there were some monks in this monastery at Ypres who agreed with the Reformers. When this was discovered, three monks who embraced the Reformed doctrines were burned at the stake. Monasteries that were found to have monks agreeing with the Reformers were shut down by the Roman Catholic authorities. The Roman Catholic Church set up the Inquisition to search out and punish those monks who believed the Reformed doctrines. Instead of making people turn away from the Reformed doctrines, however, people became interested in them. They wondered what sort of religion would make men brave enough to die for

Petrus Dathenus

it, and they began asking questions. Many people believed the truth of God's Word and were converted.

His conversion

In the monastery at Ypres, there were discussions among the monks about the Reformed doctrines. Dathenus listened carefully as the monks debated among themselves. God used these discussions as the means for his salvation. Dathenus learned that salvation is based on Jesus Christ alone, and not on good works or penance.

Escape to London

Knowing that it was no longer safe in the monastery, Dathenus fled. He was only eighteen years old when he left Ypres. He decided to go to London, where he heard there were many other refugees. Since Edward VI was on the throne, England was a safe place for Protestants. Dathenus soon found work in a printing shop. He attended church with other refugees. The Polish Reformer, Jan Łaski, was one of the pastors of the large congregation, and Dathenus learned much from his teachings.

During this time, Łaski and others worked on material that was useful for the organization of the church service. They worked on the order of worship, wrote forms for the sacraments, and worked on a church order, which is a set of rules for churches. They even spent time putting the Psalms in poetry form so they could be sung. Young Dathenus was happy to help these men in their efforts.

It wasn't long before Dathenus felt a call to the ministry. He talked to some of his new friends about it. When he spoke to the church leaders, they agreed that he was called to the ministry. They recognized his talents, and they advised him to begin studying theology. From 1551 to 1553, Dathenus studied hard. It was a joy for him to study the Scriptures he loved so much. During this time, he married a former nun, Benedicta, and they had one daughter, Christina.

Frankfurt

In 1553, however, Edward VI died and Mary Tudor (often called Bloody Mary) ascended the throne. The church of refugees in London was in danger and quickly scattered. The work that Jan Łaski and his helpers had begun was not finished, but they carried their work with them as they fled to Frankfurt, Germany. Many people of the congregation followed the Polish Reformer, and a new church was quickly started.

In God's perfect timing, Dathenus completed his studies around this time, so the congregation of Frankfurt, under Łaski's guidance, called him to be their pastor. He was ordained as a minister of the gospel in Frankfurt in September 1555.

Satan is never happy when Christians worship God together, so he stirs up people to make trouble. This time, trouble came from the Lutherans. It is so sad when God's people argue among themselves. Jesus prayed, "That they all may be one; as thou, Father, art in me, and I in thee, that they also may be one in us: that the world may believe that thou hast sent me" (John 17:21). God is not honored when His children argue. God's work is hindered. Besides, the world notices and takes offense at seeing Christians at odds with each other when they should be one.

The Lutherans saw all the refugees moving into their city. Perhaps they were disappointed that the refugees did not join the Lutheran church. As more and more people sought refuge in Frankfurt, the Lutherans decided to make a law that the Calvinists must have their children baptized in the Lutheran church. Not wanting to cause trouble, Dathenus traveled to Geneva to ask Calvin's advice on this issue. Wisely, Calvin concluded that the Calvinists could agree to that law as long as they stated their beliefs regarding the Lord's Supper. Remember, the major disagreement between the Lutherans and the Calvinists was about the Lord's Supper. The Lutherans believed that Christ's bodily presence was in and with the bread and wine, whereas the Calvinists believed that Christ's body and blood were signified and sealed spiritually by the visible signs of the bread and wine.

Dathenus was satisfied with Calvin's advice and traveled back to Frankfurt. The Calvinists followed Calvin's suggestion. However, this solution was not successful for long. In 1561, a Lutheran pastor named Joachim Westphal proposed that the Calvinists be forbidden to worship in Frankfurt if they did not belong to the Lutheran church. How sad: Christians not welcomed by Christians!

Frankenthal

Many of the Calvinists left Frankfurt and returned to England. By this time, Elizabeth had succeeded Bloody Mary, and it was quite safe for them to be there. Other Calvinists returned to the Lowlands (present day Belgium and the Netherlands). About sixty families went with Dathenus to settle in Frankenthal, Germany. Frankenthal was in the Palatinate, an area of Germany ruled by Frederick III at the time. It was here that the Heidelberg Catechism was written. Frederick was a friend of the Reformation and had advised against the Lutherans' decision in Frankfurt, so his domain was a good place for Protestants to live. In Frankenthal, the Calvinists were happy.

Soon after Dathenus arrived in Frankenthal, Frederick III, also known as Frederick the Pious, asked him to be his court preacher. Dathenus agreed, taking on this position in addition to pastoring the church in Frankenthal.

During these peaceful years, Dathenus did much writing. He translated the Heidelberg Catechism into Dutch in 1563. His version of the Psalms for singing was also published. Although it was done rather quickly and contained many imperfections, it was used for many years. He also worked on compiling forms for the sacraments. The English version that is used in many Reformed churches today is mostly a translation of Dathenus's Dutch work.

The Lowlands and Germany

Dathenus left Frankenthal in 1566 and moved to the Lowlands. Having no church to pastor, he became a traveling preacher. Carrying his pulpit on his back, he preached as he traveled, and many people gladly heard him. Dathenus not only preached from the Bible, but he also talked about the political situation at that time. He condemned Spain for their stand against the Protestants and openly spoke against the Roman Catholic Church and its persecution of the Protestants.

Dathenus attended important church meetings, giving speeches about doctrine and politics. He disagreed with William of Orange. The Dutch prince wanted freedom for all religions, but Dathenus wanted to make it a law that everyone must be Protestant.

After a year, Dathenus went back to Germany, where he pastored a congregation for eleven years. He returned to the Lowlands after this to pastor a congregation in Ghent. While he was a minister, he traveled around the country preaching to the crowds who came to listen. All this time he continued making bold political statements in his sermons and writings. Finally, William of Orange had him imprisoned for eight months and then sent him into exile.

Since he was no longer welcome in the Lowlands, Dathenus returned to Frankenthal to pastor the congregation there. An epidemic disease broke out, and many people became ill and died. Dathenus became ill, too, and he nearly died. Weakened by sickness and tired from all his traveling, Dathenus did not have the strength to pastor well. The congregation decided to release him as their pastor.

Wandering

By this time, Dathenus was close to fifty years old. He felt rejected and sad. His imprisonment by William of Orange, a Protestant, and the dismissal by his congregation left him feeling alone and bitter. This was a difficult time for him. Since he was no longer a minister, he began practicing medicine to make the money he needed to support his family. He did not settle in one place, but instead he wandered throughout Germany.

During this time, he was joined by a group of people who agreed with neither the Roman Catholic nor the Protestant doctrines. Because of the heretical teachings of this group of people, Dathenus was barred from preaching in the Dutch Reformed Churches.

What a sad time this was for Dathenus! All God's people suffer trials on earth. Sometimes their own characters and personalities make things even more difficult for them. With all the unrest in the religious and political world, Dathenus added his voice to the clamor and suffered for it. Disappointed and bitter, he joined this group of people to whom he should not have listened. God's people are sinful creatures, and even great men sin against God and need to repent.

Restored

Happily, Dathenus realized his sin and confessed it to God. A group of men from the Dutch churches were sent to visit Dathenus; lovingly they pointed out to him the error into which he had fallen. These men soon rejoiced to hear him say that he had left the heretical group. He confessed his sin and was restored, but he was unable to preach in the Dutch churches because he remained exiled from the Netherlands by the prince of Orange. Although he longed to share the gospel with his fellow countrymen, he remained in Germany until his death on March 17, 1588.

The Lord used Petrus Dathenus in His service. He did much for the church through his writing and preaching. While he was away from his friends he wrote letters, some of which have been preserved to this day. Dathenus especially loved to write to Calvin, and he received comfort from his friendship with this Reformer. Dathenus also wrote letters to a Christian woman named Lady Elizabeth de Grave. These letters were written as a dialogue or conversation between two believers, one a mature child of God, the other a beginner in grace. Dathenus wrote about various spiritual matters, especially about the relationship of law and gospel. This material was put together in a book called *The Pearl of Christian Comfort*, which is available today in English. This book was written to comfort believers in spiritual distress. The pearl is assurance of salvation and the peace of conscience it brings in the believer's heart before God.

Dathenus led a life full of travels and trials. He served the Lord from his youth, and although he strayed, he returned to the Lord, whom he loved with his whole heart. We can learn much from Dathenus's life and still reap the benefits of his work today, particularly in the area of Dutch Reformed liturgy.

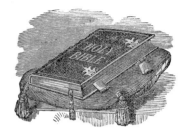

~ 25 ~

Queen Marguerite of Navarre

(1492–1548)

Marguerite brought the gospel into the royal court with remarkable effectiveness, and she influenced many of the nobility to become Reformed.

Marguerite possessed a remarkable combination of qualities. She was one of the most beautiful princesses of her day and very well educated. Some politicians of her time considered her the most intelligent person in Europe. Above her beauty and ability, however, shone her piety. Her beauty of soul was greater than her beauty of body. To her the Reformed people of France owe much, for had it not been for her influence and protection in God's providence, many of them would have been wiped out from the very beginning.

Marguerite was born April 11, 1492, at Angoulême. While she was still a child, there was a Frenchman preaching the gospel before the time of the Reformation. His name was Jacques Lefèvre d'Étaples,[1] and he preached as early as 1512. He taught that salvation is through Christ alone and not the church, for the church herself must be purified. His preaching and the letters of Bishop Guillaume Briçonnet[2] won Marguerite to the Protestant faith. She remained a member of the Roman Catholic Church, however, since the Protestants had not yet formally separated from the church.

She had one brother, who later became Francis I, King of France. He cared nothing for the Reformed faith, but he loved his sister. When an enemy complained to him that Marguerite was too favorable toward the Protestants,

---

1. Jacques Lefèvre d'Étaples (1455–1536), scholar, theologian, and forerunner of the Reformation, studied in Paris and then in Florence, Italy. He provided one of the earliest translations of the New Testament and the Psalms into French (1523–1530). He was frequently forced to flee for his life.

2. Guillaume Briçonnet (1470–1534), Bishop of Meaux, was sympathetic to the Reformation, but never broke with the Roman Catholic Church.

he replied, "If what you say is true, I love her too much to allow her to be confronted on that issue." Often he said in the presence of her enemies, "My sister Marguerite is the only woman I ever knew who had every virtue and grace without any mixture of vice."

Marguerite brought the gospel into the royal court with remarkable effectiveness, and she influenced many of the nobility to become Reformed. She used her influence over her brother to spread and protect Protestantism. She prayed that he would be converted and promote the gospel.

A German nobleman and good friend of Marguerite's, the Count of Hohenlohe, became a Protestant. Since he was a high dignitary in the Roman Catholic Church and spoke French fluently, he had great influence. He hoped to win France for the Reformation, and Queen Marguerite was the door through which he hoped the Reformation might enter. He wrote a book entitled *The Book of the Cross*, which he wished to distribute throughout the country. Marguerite asked her brother if this would be permitted. To her great surprise and sorrow, Francis forbade Protestant books and was careful never to invite Hohenlohe to court.

Disappointments such as these moved Marguerite to write poetry like this:

O Thou my Priest, my Advocate, my King,
On whom depends my life, my everything;
O Lord, who first didst drain the bitter cup of woe,
And knowest its poison (if man e'er did know),
These thorns, how sharp, these wounds, how deep—
Savior, Friend, King, oh, plead my cause, I pray;
Speak, help, and save me, lest I fall away.

In 1533, she published a book of religious poems titled *The Mirror of the Sinful Soul*. It was a commentary on the words, "Create in me a clean heart, O God" (Psalm 51:10a). In it, she focused on the great sacrifice of Christ for sin and never mentioned the Roman Catholic doctrines of the intercession of saints, indulgences, penance, or purgatory. This omission gave great offence to the Roman Catholics.

When Marguerite found she could no longer use her influence to introduce Protestantism, she tried to protect it, especially after the persecution of Protestants had begun. During the persecutions, her brother, out of respect for her, would not allow any Protestants to be put to death whenever she was in Paris. The Roman Catholics plotted against her, but the Lord protected her.

Repeatedly, Marguerite protected Reformed people, often saving their lives. For example, a friend of Marguerite's, a young man studying at the university in Paris, was arrested. He was dragged through the streets, followed by a shouting mob, and thrown into a foul, damp prison cell. The dirt floor was covered with water and had only one dry corner, just big enough to stand in. There was no light, no fresh air, and no communication with anyone. After three days, the poor man was exhausted. At last, unexpectedly, the cell door opened, and he was set free. He knew immediately that Marguerite must have arranged his release.

Dressed in his stinking, torn rags and staggering from weakness, he went through the streets of Paris. Not even his friends dared speak to him or give him food or clothes. He felt he had no choice but to go to the palace and appeal to Marguerite. Standing like a beggar at the gate which he had so often entered with honor, he wrote her a note stating his sad condition. Delighted to hear that her friend was safe, Marguerite immediately ordered him into her presence.

When he reached her elegant drawing room, he found her surrounded by splendidly dressed nobility, but that did not seem to matter to Marguerite. As soon as she saw him, she hurried to meet him, introduced him to her company as though he were a distinguished gentleman, and sent him to a guest room, where everything was done for his comfort.

Marguerite had been away from Paris, and when she returned and heard of her friend's imprisonment, she had gone to her brother and tearfully begged for his release. Francis had granted it, for he could never refuse her. The Roman Catholics only hated her all the more for this deed, and they made fun of her in a play by comparing her to a witch riding on a broomstick, an insult that Francis resented. He quickly put a stop to the play. So Marguerite was instrumental in freeing many imprisoned Protestants, and in inviting some of the Reformers to visit France.

In 1527, Marguerite's second marriage,[3] to King Henry of Navarre, made her Queen of Navarre.[4] The ceremony was splendid, but she soon found that her married life was not very pleasant. Her thoughts often turned to the Lord Jesus as she contemplated the spiritual marriage of Christ and His people. Another of her poems describes this union:

> *Would that the day were come, O Lord,*
> *So much desired by me,*
> *When by the cords of heavenly love*

I shall be drawn to Thee,
United in eternal life
The husband Thou, and I the wife.

That wedding day, O Lord,
My heart so longs to see,
That neither fame, nor wealth, nor rank
Can give to me;
To me the world no more
Can yield delight;
Unless Thou, Lord, be with me here,
Lo! all is dark as night.

The kingdom of her husband had never been penetrated by the doctrines of the Reformation. She at once began spreading them by her example and influence. As a Roman Catholic, Marguerite's husband was not pleased with this, but he said nothing to oppose her, except on one occasion.

Marguerite usually had a private worship service at her home in the palace, when Lefèvre or Gérard Roussel[5] would preach for her and her friends. Sometimes they would celebrate the Lord's Supper. In her palace at Nerac was an underground hall beneath the terrace of the castle. Here her servants placed a table, covered it with a white cloth, and set it with a plate of bread and cups of wine. Queen Marguerite went there and joined with Protestant-minded friends in their communion service.

---

3. Her first marriage was to Duke Charles of Alençon.

4. Navarre was a former kingdom in the Pyrenees in southwestern Europe, situated southwest of France. Today, much of it forms the Spanish province of Navarra.

---

5. Gérard Roussel (c. 1480–1550) was a close friend of John Calvin during their student days. Although he never broke with the Roman Catholic Church, he favored the Reformation. He died from injuries suffered when a mob attacked him while he was preaching.

Although it was done secretly, news of it reached the ears of Marguerite's husband, King Henry. He was not pleased and scorned the Holy Supper, calling it "the fastings in the cellar." One day, as he returned from hunting, he asked where she was. When he was told that she was in her suite, listening to a preacher, he went to investigate. The minister and the others were warned and escaped. Marguerite, trembling and fearful, was left alone to face him. The king was angry and struck her in the face as he shouted at her.

The flight of the Huguenots

This was too great an insult to be passed over lightly. She reported it to her brother. Francis was furious that anyone would hurt his sister, and he set out at once for Navarre, threatening war. When Henry heard that Francis was on his way, he was afraid. He begged his wife to forgive him. He not only promised to allow her to worship as she pleased, but he even promised to investigate the Protestant doctrines for himself. This actually led to King Henry's conversion, and so Navarre became a safe place for the Protestants fleeing persecution in France.

Marguerite died on December 21, 1548, rejoicing in the Lord Jesus Christ as her Savior. "I am certain that God will carry on the work He has permitted me to begin, and my place will be more than filled by my daughter, Jeanne, who has the energy and courage that I fear I have lacked," she declared.

~ 26 ~

Queen Jeanne d'Albret of Navarre

(1528–1572)

*Jeanne died as the champion
of the Reformed Church of France.
She had raised her banners
in the name of the Lord and
of her Reformed faith.*

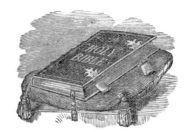

Jeanne d'Albret was born at the palace in Fontainebleau, forty miles southeast of Paris, on January 7, 1528. She was an open, frank, fearless girl who loved the truth. She was raised in France, away from her father and mother who lived in Navarre, because her uncle, Francis I, the king of France, wanted to have control over her. She was surrounded by Roman Catholic influences, but the king of France soon found that she had a will of her own.

When Jeanne was about fourteen years old, Francis determined to marry her to a German prince, the Duke of Cleves, in a political marriage. The king was very surprised when he heard that Jeanne absolutely refused to marry the duke. Francis had her father and mother help him, but their efforts were to no avail. Francis, however, refused to yield to this stubborn girl. So Jeanne did what she could. She wrote two protests against the marriage, stating that she was forced into it against her will. These were witnessed and filed. Still, she was forced to the wedding ceremony in 1546. She was so unwilling that they had to carry her to the altar! The duke then went off to war, and Jeanne was permitted to go home with her mother. The Duke of Cleves soon turned against the king of France, and Jeanne's marriage to him was annulled, or undone, by the pope because of the protests she had filed.

When Jeanne became twenty years old, her beauty again attracted suitors. She is described as fair, with a friendly, honest face, and violet eyes. Among her suitors was the Bourbon prince, Antoine, Duke of Vendôme. She accepted him for her husband.

At the death of her father, Henry of Navarre, the King of France wanted to acquire for himself the little mountain kingdom of Navarre, but Jeanne would not allow it. She raised troops and prepared for war. Just as she was in danger of being destroyed, the king of France died, and so her land was delivered from danger. Shortly after her first marriage with William, Duke of Cleves, Jeanne came into contact with the Reformed faith. She made an open profession of this faith before her people at Pau, the capitol of Navarre, on December 5, 1560.

Still, France and the Roman Catholics were not idle. Catherine de Medici,[1] the mother of Charles IX, of whom you will read in chapter 27, was a wicked woman. She favored either the Roman Catholics or the Huguenots (French Protestants) whenever it best suited her purposes, although her main purpose was to exterminate all Protestants. She helped plan the St. Bartholomew's Day massacre, but unlike her son, whose tortured conscience troubled him until the day of his death, Catherine remained callous and unmoved. She died in 1589, mourned by few.

---

1. Catherine de Medici (1519–1589) was the wife of Henry II of France. She ruled France (1560–1563) as regent before her son, Charles IX, reached adulthood and, unofficially, until Charles's death in 1574. Her plotting was largely responsible for the massacre of Protestants on St. Bartholomew's Day 1572.

Queen Jeanne d'Albret of Navarre

This Jezebel, as Catherine has been called, plotted against Jeanne. She came up with a plan to separate Jeanne and her husband, Antoine. She wanted to win him back to the Roman Catholic faith and thus gain the kingdom of Navarre for France. Since Antoine was then regent of France and had to be in France, away from Jeanne, a large part of his time, there was a very real danger that this plan would be successful.

Poor Jeanne! Her husband was caught in the net of the enemy and soon returned to the Roman Catholic faith. When Jeanne afterwards visited Paris, he treated her with disdain and tried to force her to go to mass. Jeanne, however, would not act against her conscience. When Catherine de Medici tried to help Antoine in forcing Jeanne to give up her Reformed faith, Jeanne nobly replied to her, "Madam, if I, at this moment, held my son and all the kingdoms of the world in my grasp, I would hurl them into the bottom of the sea, rather than risk the salvation of my soul." Her heart was breaking because of the change in her husband, but she remained true to the Lord. Jesus said, "So likewise, whosoever he be of you that forsaketh not all that he hath, he cannot be my disciple" (Luke 14:33). Jeanne was willing to give up everything, but not the Lord Jesus Christ, whom she loved.

Her enemies even plotted to kill her; one suggested that she be thrown over the wall into the Seine River. Knowing her danger, Jeanne asked to be permitted to leave France. Permission was granted, but it was given treacherously, for plans were laid to murder her on the way home.

The parting from her son, Henry, was heartrending. She trembled to leave him behind with the French, most of whom were Roman Catholic, but it could not be helped—they refused to allow her to take him with her. On leaving him, she made him promise never to go to mass.

To regain authority over her own land of Navarre, Jeanne bravely led her little company of two hundred through a land full of enemies, all the while receiving recruits from the people as she passed through the villages and towns. She did not know all the dangers that threatened her, but the Lord placed friends to help her in strategic places. The Reformed Duke of Condé fortified Vendôme, where she spent the night, thus preventing her enemies from murdering her.

The next day, Blaise Montluc, a marshall appointed by the French government to terrorize the Huguenots, was sent in pursuit of her, and followed her so closely that her flight was a race for her life. She sent ahead swift couriers to summon her soldiers to her aid. Her enemies were almost upon her. They were so close that the blast of their trumpets could be heard, when eight hundred of her brave soldiers from Navarre came rushing to her defense. It was the first of her many close escapes. She now realized her danger all the more, and with God's help, faced her enemies and dealt them a defeating blow.

Some time after this, Antoine lay on his death bed. His guilty conscience accused him of his cruel treatment of his wife, and he was filled with remorse. It is said that he again professed the Reformed faith before he died and vowed that if he were to live, he would introduce it everywhere in France, but he died.

Jeanne remained queen of Navarre, even though her husband was dead. She issued an order abolishing the Roman Catholic religion in Navarre. When the pope issued a papal bull against her, she compelled him to recall it by making her archenemy, Catherine de Medici, her intercessor with the pope. The pope also spoke of disinheriting her family by declaring her marriage to Antoine void because of her first marriage to the Duke of Cleves. Jeanne would not allow this to happen because it would disinherit her son Henry and prevent him from coming to the throne of France. This move by the pope would see the prince of Condé become king of France. Catherine de Medici hated the prince of Condé more than she did Henry, so Jeanne again used Catherine to prevent the pope from disinheriting her family. The Lord blessed Jeanne with unusual wisdom, so that she was able to use her enemies to her advantage.

Throughout her life, the Lord watched over Jeanne and protected her. Another example is when the king of Spain started a rebellion in Navarre, in an attempt to draw her to it and so capture her. However, the king's own wife warned Jeanne of this plot, and she was spared.

Jeanne's greatest desire was to see her thirteen-year-old son. Her plan was to get him out of France and under her control. She was afraid that he might become a Roman Catholic, or worse than that, live in the immoral French court. When she again visited France, she succeeded in gaining permission for her son to accompany her as far as Vendôme. Swiftly and secretly she planned his escape, sending a messenger to her own court, telling them to have an armed force meet her. Six hours after this courier left, she and her son slipped away and galloped at full speed for Pau, her capital city. They arrived safely. She now had her son under her loving control, and she had him carefully trained. He soon revealed remarkable abilities, especially in the art of war. He was being prepared by God for his part in the next great war between the Huguenots and the Roman Catholics. Although her mountain kingdom of Navarre was not involved in this war, Jeanne nevertheless foresaw that the defeat of Protestantism in France meant the downfall of her kingdom, too, because it was Reformed.

For this reason, she wanted to defend the Huguenots. She was afraid to tell her decision to her own counselors in Navarre, for fear they would prevent her from carrying it out. So she slipped away secretly from her own land and arrived at La Rochelle, where the Huguenots of France had gathered. Her arrival astonished the city. The Huguenots were beside themselves with joy at this new and unexpected reinforcement. The mayor of the city presented her with the keys to the city. She was greeted with thunderous applause as she first entered the council of the Huguenots. There, the prince of Condé, their leader, arose and resigned his command of the Huguenot army into the hands of Jeanne's son, Henry. The audience responded enthusiastically to this.

But Jeanne arose and with dignity declined the offer. "No, gentlemen," she said, "I and my children are here to promote the success of this great cause, or to share in its disaster. The cause of God is dearer to me than the promotion of my son."

After her speech, she compelled her son to decline the honor of commander-in-chief, although the people applauded, showing they would accept Henry as their leader even though he was only sixteen at the time. When the Huguenots found that she would not allow her son to lead their forces, they placed her at the head of the civil government, as the governess of La Rochelle.

Jeanne had many cares, yet in the midst of them all, she had the New Testament translated into the Basque language, which was spoken by some of her subjects. She published it at her own expense so that the gospel would reach these

Admiral Gaspard de Coligny

people, too. She was also in charge of all the correspondence with foreign princes, and it was her pleadings that secured Queen Elizabeth of England as an ally with the Huguenots. Elizabeth helped Jeanne save the Huguenots by aiding La Rochelle with her fleet. The war was terrible, the fighting fierce. While Jeanne was in La Rochelle, the king of Spain and the king of France thought they could seize Navarre, but her soldiers defended it and saved it.

On March 13, 1569, the beloved leader of the Huguenot army, the prince of Condé, died. The Huguenots were so sad that they did not want to fight anymore. Admiral Coligny could not rouse their courage, so he asked Jeanne to come and speak to the men. She came to the camp and viewed the flags draped in mourning. By her side rode her son, Henry. Then she made an encouraging speech:

> Soldiers, you weep. But does the memory of Condé demand nothing but profitless tears? No, let us unite and summon again our courage to defend a cause which can never perish, and to avenge him who was its firm support. Does despair overwhelm you—despair, that shameful feeling of weak natures? When I, the queen, hope still, is it for you to fear? Because Condé is dead, is all therefore lost? Does our cause cease to be just and holy? No! God, who has already rescued you from innumerable dangers, has raised up men to succeed Condé. To these leaders I add my son. Prove his valor. The blood of Bourbon and Valois flows in his veins, and he longs to fight for God's cause. Soldiers, I offer to you everything in my power to give—my dominions, my treasures, my life, and that which is dearer to me than all, my children. I make here a solemn oath before you all—and you know me too well to doubt my word—I swear to defend to my last sigh the holy cause which now unites us, which is that of honor and truth.

When she finished speaking there was silence for a moment, and then everywhere shouts went up among the soldiers, and the army hailed the young Prince Henry as their new leader. Jeanne stood there before her army, inspiring them not by the sword, but by her courage and her trust in God. Jeanne and Admiral Coligny conducted the war with wonderful skill. When the beloved admiral was defeated and badly wounded at Moncontour, she set off at once to see him, although there were many dangers in her way. She found him in his bed with his jaw so badly shattered that he could not speak, though he wept tears of thankfulness for her coming.

Putting that defeat behind her, she at once planned for victory. With God's blessing, the Huguenot army gained victory after victory, until they encamped under the very walls of Paris and forced the Roman Catholics to make peace. Then Jeanne returned, amid the applause of the people, to her kingdom of Navarre.

The Roman Catholics, however, did not easily give up. Where they could not conquer by war, they determined to conquer by deceit. Once again, Catherine de Medici hatched a plan. She proposed that young Henry of Bourbon, the new king of Navarre, should marry Princess Margaret, sister of Charles IX, who was then king of France. Jeanne objected; she did not want her son to marry a Roman Catholic. But all her counselors, with Admiral Coligny at the head, forced her to consent to the marriage. They thought that joining a Huguenot and a Roman Catholic would smooth the differences between them and end the bitter rivalry. The Roman Catholics were so eager to bring about this marriage that they agreed it should be according to the Reformed marriage form. The Huguenots had no idea that this was all a trap.

Jeanne traveled to Paris to make the necessary preparations and to see to it that the rights of her land and her religion were preserved. She opposed the French on many points, but they agreed to all she proposed, and she finally signed the proposal of marriage. Still, she was not satisfied; she felt there was deception somewhere. She did not know what was coming; she only felt it would be a blow for the Protestants.

Her anxieties proved to be too much for her. She became sick before the wedding, which took place on June 4, 1572. The Huguenots were dismayed by her sickness. If she died, who would look after them? Her faith was triumphant even until death. Lying on her deathbed, she said, "I have never feared death. I do not dare to murmur at the will of God, but I grieve deeply to leave my children exposed to so many dangers. Still, I trust it all to Him."

She died on June 9, 1572, with her beloved Bible at her side, relying on its promises and receiving Christ's crown. One of her last acts was to make her son promise to remain true to the Scriptures and the Reformed faith. She died not a moment too soon. She had seen great sorrows, but a greater one was to come after her death: the dreadful massacre of St. Bartholomew, which would have broken her heart.

Jeanne died as the champion of the Reformed Church of France. She had raised her banners in the name of the Lord and of her Reformed faith. When her generals were killed, captured, or wounded, she rallied her troops, inspired them with courage, and guided them to victory. In all her wars, she was never conquered. All this she did, not for herself, but for her Lord. She could sing with Deborah, "So let all thine enemies perish, O LORD: but let them that love him be as the sun when he goeth forth in his might" (Judges 5:31a).

~ 27 ~

Admiral Coligny

(1519–1572)

and the

Tragedy of St. Bartholomew's Day

(August 24, 1572)

A plot against the Huguenots

King Charles IX of France, his chief officers of state, and his mother, Catherine de Medici, met in solemn discussion in the council chamber of the old palace, the Louvre. On a table before them lay a roll of parchment that contained the names of all the noblemen in France who sided with the Reformation. A thorough search had been made in all the provinces of France to make sure all the names were recorded. The council was planning how and when the doom of these Reformed noblemen would be executed. This council was determined to root out the hated Huguenots from the kingdom.

Admiral Gaspard de Coligny

According to some, the word "Huguenot" means "united together," much like the word "brethren." The Huguenots were Protestants in France who believed the teachings of the Bible and of the Reformers. Their leader's name was Admiral Coligny. His full name was actually Gaspard de Coligny, but he became known as Admiral Coligny when he attained the rank of admiral.

Little is known about how Admiral Coligny became a believer. For two years, from 1557 to 1559, he was imprisoned after losing a battle. It is possible that the Christian books his brother sent him while he was imprisoned were used by the Holy Spirit for his salvation. Gradually, Admiral Coligny became convinced of the truths taught in the Bible, and he joined the Huguenot army in 1562.

Gaspard de Coligny

Catherine de Medici was especially concerned about the growing number of Huguenots and thought it would be best to destroy them. The ever-scheming mind of Catherine came up with a treacherous plan. On the evening of August 23, 1572, Catherine went to her son and told him that the Huguenots were planning to assassinate the royal family and all the leaders of the Roman Catholic Church. In order to prevent this, Catherine told Charles they had to act first. Resisting at first, the young King Charles finally signed his consent to what later became known as the St. Bartholomew's Day Massacre. He knew he was consenting to a horrible plan, but did not have the courage to oppose it.

The plan was simple. Many of the French Protestants, the Huguenots, had been invited to Paris under the pretense of being present at the marriage of King Henry of Navarre and Margaret, the sister of Charles IX. King Henry was a Protestant, and the Huguenots hoped that by his marriage to the princess of France, their country might come under Protestant rule. The king was afraid that with so many Protestants gathered in the city, they might decide it would be a good time to rebel. To prevent such an uprising, Charles ordered that the Huguenots be killed.

Massacre

The time of the massacre was set for Sunday, August 24, 1572, St. Bartholomew's Day, at three o'clock in the morning, when the victims would be sleeping. The signal was to be the tolling of the bells of one of the churches in the city. The gates were closed, and guards were posted everywhere. Lights were placed in the highest points in the city, so that the assassins could clearly see the marks placed on the houses of those about to be killed. The murderers wore a piece of white linen on their arms, a white cross on their caps, and the image of the Virgin Mary around their necks. Their reward was to be the property of those whom they murdered.

In the palace of the Louvre that Saturday evening, the king was restless and troubled. He couldn't get rid of the feelings of guilt for what he had consented to allow. Perhaps he would have changed his mind, but his mother, Queen Catherine, entered his bedroom shortly after midnight to convince him he was doing the right thing. She then led him to the window and stood by him while he watched and even took part in the murder of thousands of innocent people.

The silence of the night was broken by the tower clock solemnly striking three. Suddenly, the sharp sound of gunfire reverberated throughout the city. Armed men sprang from their hiding places, shouting, "Kill! Kill! Death to the Huguenots!"

The man in charge of the armed guards, the Duke of Guise, led his men to the house where Admiral Coligny lived. They found him lying on a couch, suffering from a shot in the arm. A few days earlier, some men had tried to murder him. The admiral awoke when he heard the men enter his house. He tried to get up from the couch. One of the soldiers asked him, "Are you the admiral?"

"Yes, I am," fearlessly replied Admiral Coligny, "but, young man, respect my gray hairs and do not stain them with my blood."

The young soldier did not listen, but killed the admiral with his sword. Then they threw his body out of the window. When one of the French princes saw whose body it was, he shouted, "Courage, my friends! We have had a lucky beginning; let us finish in the same way!" Heartlessly, the soldiers cut off Coligny's head and hands and then dragged the faithful admiral's body through the streets. The head was embalmed and sent to Rome as a present for Pope Gregory XIII.

The dreadful massacre was carried out throughout the city. Everywhere was heard the dreadful cry, "Kill! Kill! Kill every one of them! It is the order of the king!" In every street lay the bodies of murdered Huguenots. For three days and nights the massacre continued in Paris.

The death of Coligny

In their thirst for blood, messengers were sent to the surrounding town and villages, urging them to do the same in their towns. Thousands of Huguenots were killed in the most cruel ways. Children were killed too, while others were left orphans.

When letters from the court containing the command to kill the Huguenots were brought to the governor of the city of Lyons, he ordered all the Protestants to appear before him. Not suspecting any danger, the Protestants obeyed and were thrown into prison. The soldiers were ordered to kill all of them, but they refused. Furious, the governor hired cruel, wicked men to torture and kill the prisoners.

one executioner." He refused to murder innocent people. He protected the Huguenots as much as he could, but it later cost him his life.

King Charles did his part, too. He closed his conscience and willingly joined in the murder of innocent people. From his bedroom window, he shot at the fleeing Huguenots. Later, he invited the Protestants who had escaped to the woods and forests to return to their homes. The poor, hunted Huguenots were tricked into believing that the king felt pity for them and that the massacre was over, but they were seized and killed.

The year after the massacre, one historian wrote, "For thirty days together there was no end of killing, slaying, and robbing; so that at this day there are thousands of little children now fatherless and motherless, having to beg for their food."

The Roman Catholic Church rejoices

The messenger who carried the news to Rome was rewarded with a lot of money, and the pope joyfully cried, "Good news! Good news!" People celebrated in the streets. A procession was formed of the pope, cardinals, and officers of state. They went into a cathedral and offered up thanks to God for "the uprooting of the heretics."

To keep a memory of the event, Pope Gregory ordered a medal to be made. On one side was the portrait of the pope; on the other, a destroying angel holding a cross in one hand and a sword in the other with which he was killing the Protestants. On this medal were the words, *Ugonottorum strages*, which means, "The slaughter of the Huguenots."

Charles IX assisting at the massacre of St. Bartholomew

In some towns, the governors refused to obey the orders of the king. One, named Ortezto, responded, "Sir, I have received your letter requesting the inhabitants of Bayonne to a massacre of the French Huguenots. Your majesty has many faithful servants and brave soldiers in this city, but not

Slaying the Huguenots

King Charles IX

As for King Charles IX, he was miserable for the rest of his life. The Scripture was fulfilled, "Whoso rewardeth evil for good, evil shall not depart from his house" (Proverbs 17:13). His kingdom was in turmoil, and he lost the confidence of his subjects. His own family was in a continual state of strife. After the massacre of St. Bartholomew's Day, King Charles became sad and depressed. His guilty conscience haunted him. He had walked so proudly and triumphantly through the streets of Paris, viewing the bodies of the murdered Huguenots, but now those scenes would not leave him. He became weaker and weaker. In his last hours, he endured terrible pain and died miserably at the age of twenty-four.

The Bible says, "The wicked plotteth against the just.... The wicked have drawn out the sword, and have bent their bow, to cast down the poor and needy, and to slay such as be of upright conversation. Their sword shall enter into their own heart, and their bows shall be broken" (Psalm 37:12a, 14–15). "LORD, how long shall the wicked, how long shall the wicked triumph? How long shall...all the workers of iniquity boast themselves? They break in pieces thy people, O LORD, and afflict thy heritage.... [The LORD] shall bring upon them their own iniquity, and shall cut them off in their own wickedness; yea, the LORD our God shall cut them off" (Psalm 94:3–5, 23).

The early church father Tertullian said that "the blood of the martyrs is the seed of the church."[1] This was certainly the case in France. Thousands of God-fearing Huguenots were killed, but others took their place. Some Huguenots remained in France, working in secret, but many fled to the Netherlands and England, and ultimately to America, escaping the dreadful persecutions. Wherever they went, God used them to instill fresh life and zeal in the church. As for France, however, though the Lord keeps a faithful remnant, the Reformed church there never fully recovered from the St. Bartholomew's Day Massacre.

---

1. Tertullian, *Apologeticum* (The Apology), Chapter L, Elucidation XII; see www.tertullian.org/works/apologeticum.htm

~ 28 ~

Charlotte
the Nun of Jouarre

(c. 1550–1582)

From Charlotte's life, we learn that God has a perfect plan for each of His children.

Her family

Charlotte de Bourbon was born in the middle of the sixteenth century in a small town named Jouarre, in Normandy, France. Her father was the Duke of Montpensier and her mother's name was Jacqueline de Longvic. The family had lost quite a bit of money, and the duke had to admit that he could not provide well enough for his daughters. He decided that the best thing to do was to place Charlotte and two of her sisters in a convent, or abbey. That was one of the reasons for his decision. The other reason was that Charlotte's mother was a Protestant and was secretly training her daughters in the truths of Scripture. The Duke of Montpensier was a devoted Roman Catholic and was angry when he discovered his daughters were being trained in the Protestant faith. If they were away from their mother, hidden in a convent, the duke believed his daughters would be out of reach of the Protestant teachings.

Of course, Charlotte and her mother and sisters were very sad when they heard the duke's decision, but there was nothing they could do to change

Charlotte's mother secretly training her

his mind. In the remaining time before her daughters entered the convent, Mrs. Bourbon often took Charlotte and her sisters into a quiet room of their home. They wept, prayed, and searched the Scriptures together. Charlotte and her sisters listened carefully as their mother told them the precious truths of the gospel.

She is sent to a convent

Charlotte was only thirteen when her father decided the time was right for her to enter the abbey. It was very hard for Charlotte to say goodbye to her parents and to her beautiful home. She was an active girl, and now she was being asked to live in a world where quiet and solitude were considered pious qualities. The Roman Catholic Church taught that the surest way of pleasing God and of leading a holy life was to separate from those around you and live in a convent or a monastery. They thought that saying prayers many times a day, doing good works, speaking very little, and living away from family and friends meant that you could live a holy life more easily. The piety that the Bible teaches, however, is that of an active life. It does not destroy the family. We do not read anywhere in God's Word that we can practice meekness, patience, and love only when we are alone. Rather, we must live a godly life in the midst of society. We are to be *in* the world, though we are not to be *of* it (John 17).

Before Charlotte left for the convent, Mrs. Bourbon secretly wrote a protest stating that Charlotte should not be forced to go to a convent, and that she should have the right to leave the convent if she chose to do so. Both Charlotte and her mother signed this paper. Mrs. Bourbon hoped that one day freedom would be granted to her beloved daughter.

She did not live to see her wish realized, but she prayed for her every day.

Charlotte was taken by her father to the abbey of Jouarre in Normandy. Her flowing hair was cut off, and she had to exchange her pretty dress for a scratchy, brown, unshapely garment with a rope for a belt. She was taught to walk with her eyes looking down. Her room was like a prison cell. It had bars on the window, and she had to sleep on the cold floor. Do you think this made her feel holy? Was she happy? How could she be happy when she missed her parents and was cold and uncomfortable? Did she find the peace that the revered mother, the head nun of the convent, promised her? No, for although she lived in a silent world, she had no peace in her heart.

Her sadness grew when she was told that her mother was very sick. She was not allowed to visit her. No one comforted Charlotte when she cried. And when her beloved mother died, she was not allowed to attend the funeral. Poor, lonely Charlotte! The Lord, however, uses pain and suffering in the lives of His children to their benefit. Charlotte thought about her mother often and remembered her mother's instructions from the Word of God. Of course, the lessons that Charlotte's loving mother had taught her were far superior to the unbiblical teachings of the Roman Catholic Church she received in the cold, dreary convent.

The years passed, and slowly Charlotte became used to her surroundings. She was told by the other nuns that her sufferings and self-denial were pleasing to God, and that the reward of her life would be the glory of heaven. While she was still relatively young, she was put in charge of the convent of Jouarre. She now had the distinguished title of Lady Abbess.

Her conversion

Around the same time, light entered the dismal abbey in the form of Protestant tracts. Someone managed to smuggle these tracts into the convent, and Charlotte read them. Their message made her think of her dear mother's words to her before she entered the abbey. Charlotte thought again of her mother's treasured Bible, her prayers, and her tears. She thought of the paper she and her mother had signed. These precious memories, together with the words of the tracts, were blessed by the Holy Spirit to Charlotte's heart, and she was led to Jesus Christ. Now Charlotte felt peace and joy and happiness! Only in Jesus is true joy to be found.

Could Charlotte keep quiet about her newfound peace? She felt it was her duty to tell the other nuns. She began to teach them that they must not try to win heaven by doing

Charlotte instructing the nuns of Jouarre

good works, but that salvation was by grace, through faith in Christ Jesus alone. Charlotte saw now that counting beads on a rosary, kneeling before an image of Mary, and praying to the saints could not save her. Actually, it was sin and an offense to God.

More than ever, Charlotte felt that living in the abbey was like being in prison. She wanted to leave, but where could she go? If she went to her father's house, he would certainly not welcome her. If she tried to go to someone else in her family, they would despise her. Leaving a convent or monastery was regarded as a terrible sin, since it meant breaking a solemn vow. She couldn't ask anyone for advice. So she prayed and continued to teach the other nuns about the only Savior, Jesus Christ.

Her escape

At the same time as her conversion, Charlotte heard that war had broken out in France. The Huguenots, after suffering so much, had begun to fight back against the Roman Catholics. Their leader was Gaspard de Coligny, of whom we told you in the previous chapter. It was a sad time, with much bloodshed and sorrow. In 1572, the year of the massacre on St. Bartholomew's Day, the noise of battle was heard near the convent. The shouts came closer and closer and then, suddenly, the doors of the abbey were broken down! The terrified nuns fled into the woods to escape.

Charlotte de Bourbon also fled. What a strange way to be set free, she thought. She needed a safe place to hide. She wanted to find a place where she could freely speak about the Lord Jesus Christ. Could she find such a place in France? Somehow, she found other clothes; it was far too dangerous to be seen in nun's clothing. Praying for the Lord's protection, she left France. First, she fled to her sister Frances, who was also a Protestant. Frances arranged transportation for Charlotte to Heidelberg to stay with the Elector of the Palatinate, Frederick III, a Protestant prince who treated her kindly. In the city of Heidelberg, Charlotte found many Protestants ready to welcome her.

As she expected, Charlotte's desertion caused a commotion in her native country. A nun had fled! Lady Charlotte de Bourbon, the daughter of a duke and member of the royal family of France, had abandoned the Roman Catholic Church! On March 15, 1572, Prince Frederick wrote a letter to the duke of Montpensier, Charlotte's father, begging him not to be angry with her for doing what she believed to be right. Her father wrote Charlotte an angry letter in return. He told her she had shamed the whole family, and that he would never forgive her if she did not return to France at once to beg forgiveness for what she had done. If she did not return as a Roman Catholic, wrote her father, he did not want her to come back at all.

Charlotte had known this would happen when news of her escape became known. She would have loved to make her father happy, but how could she disobey and dishonor God? The words of the Savior upheld Charlotte in her decision: "He that loveth father or mother more than me is not worthy of me: and he that loveth son or daughter more than me is not worthy of me. And he that taketh not his cross, and followeth after me, is not worthy of me. He that findeth his life shall lose it: and he that loseth his life for my sake shall find it" (Matthew 10:37–39).

In Heidelberg

Charlotte was now in a country where she could openly declare her faith, and that is just what she began to do. Standing among the Protestants of Heidelberg, upheld by their prayers and encouragements, she declared that the Roman Catholic Church was in error. She confessed that the Reformed church upheld the teachings of Scripture.

After Charlotte had lived at the palace of Prince Frederick for a few years, the prince of Orange, ruler of the Netherlands, heard of her bravery. He heard that she had left her family and her country to serve the Lord. He asked her to be his wife. Charlotte's father approved of this marriage because it meant that she would be far away from him and not be an embarrassment to him because of her religion. Also, it was an honor for Charlotte's family to be united with the royal family of the Netherlands.

Her marriage

On June 12, 1575, Charlotte became Prince William's wife. Charlotte was now the princess of Orange. She was meek, wise, loving, kind, generous, and devoted to God. She was an example of godliness to those around her. The prince and princess loved each other very much. Charlotte and Prince William served the Lord together. They were blessed with six daughters.

The prince in danger

The prince, however, had enemies. They hated him because he was a Protestant. It was the Lord's Day, March 18, 1582, and the prince and princess of Orange had returned from worshiping God in His house. As they passed along the hall of their palace, a shot was fired by someone who had managed to get into the palace. The bullet entered the neck of the prince, who fell into the arms of his servants. For some time the doctors were not sure if he would live. The princess watched over him with tender love and care. While dressing the wound, she spoke words of peace to encourage his hope in God. She prayed for his recovery. Her prayers were heard, and she had the delight of seeing him slowly restored to health.

There was great joy in the city of Antwerp when the prince and princess went to the cathedral to thank the Lord for His merciful deliverance from the hands of the assassin. Many people joined in the songs of praise and gladness that filled the land.

Charlotte's death

The shock had been too much for the princess, however. Day and night she had sat by the side of her beloved prince. As soon as she returned from the church service, she went to her bed. She became weaker and weaker. For her, death was not a dreadful thing. She had been through many trials, but she believed in her Savior. Relying on His merits, she looked forward to spending an eternity with Him in glory. On May 5, 1582, Charlotte died. Upon her death, there was great mourning in the land, and weeping crowds followed her body to its grave in the cathedral of Antwerp.

From Charlotte's life, we learn that God has a perfect plan for each of His children. When Charlotte was taken to the abbey as a young girl, she was sad. Perhaps she wondered why God would ask her to suffer at such a young age. Maybe she wondered if there was a purpose for her separation from her parents, especially her dear

Charlotte tending the wounded Prince

mother. But God had a reason for every event in Charlotte's life. She brought the gospel to the nuns in the monastery. It could be that some of them were led to the Savior through her teachings. She also set an example of godliness for the country of the Netherlands. "As for God, his way is perfect" (Psalm 18:30a).

~ 29 ~

William Perkins

(1558–1602)

William Perkins was called "the father of Puritanism" because of his great influence on later Puritans.

His youth and education

William Perkins was born in 1558 in the village of Marston Jabbett, Warwickshire, England. His parents were Thomas and Hannah Perkins. As a young man, Perkins was rebellious and disobedient. He lived recklessly, used bad language, and often drank too much. It seemed he was on his way to a wretched, useless life. The Lord, however, had other plans for him.

In 1577, he entered Christ's College, Cambridge, as a pensioner. This meant that he could earn his way through college by performing services for others. He was a bright student; he had earned his bachelor's degree by 1581, and his master's degree by 1584.

His conversion

The Lord powerfully converted Perkins when he was still a young man. It was said that the Holy Spirit began to convict him by way of the words of a young mother to her child. Perkins overheard a woman scolding her disobedient child, saying, "Hold your tongue, or I will give you to drunken Perkins, yonder." Shocked that even strangers knew of his wild behavior, he was deeply convicted. He was ashamed of himself, and by God's grace, he was converted and gave up his former ways.

He changed his course of study from mathematics to theology. He also was no longer interested in black magic and the occult; now the study of God and His Word held his full attention. This shows that no one is ever too deeply involved in sin for God to rescue.

William Perkins

At Cambridge, he came under the influence of Laurence Chaderton, who became his mentor, or guide, throughout his years of study. Chaderton became his personal tutor and lifelong friend. Other men such as Richard Greenham and Richard Rogers became close friends as well, and together they formed a spiritual brotherhood.

His ministry

From 1584 until his death in 1602, Perkins was a preacher and lecturer at St. Andrew's Church at Cambridge. His style of preaching was plain and straightforward, so that everyone could understand his messages. He was very direct in his preaching, urging people to examine their hearts in the presence of God. Erroll Hulse wrote: "His was an awakening ministry, which stirred lost souls to see the reality of eternal condemnation. Perkins was so gifted in speaking that it was said that the very way he uttered the word 'damn' made sinners tremble."[1] Many people were saved under his preaching. His simple style attracted many people, and through his preaching, they were attracted to Jesus Christ. He not only preached to the educated people, but he also made it his goal to reach the common people.

His work

Perkins was also a fellow at Christ's College, which meant that he was very involved in the lives of the students there, preaching, lecturing, tutoring students, as well as helping them in other areas of life. He urged students to read Protestant writers as well as the Bible. He himself was a man who lived a godly life, modeling it for the students and faculty of the college. He influenced many

---

1. Erroll Hulse, *Who are the Puritans?… and what do they teach?* (Darlington, England: Evangelical Press, 2000), 44.

students at the college, some of whom became influential Puritan theologians, including William Ames, Richard Sibbes, John Cotton, John Preston, and Thomas Goodwin.

In 1595, he resigned from being a fellow to marry Timothye Cradocke on July 2 of that year. During his marriage, he and his wife had seven children—one not yet born when Perkins died, and three who died from illnesses when they were very young.

After resigning his fellowship at Cambridge, William Perkins continued to work at the university in several ways. He was dean of Christ's College from 1590 to 1591. Every Thursday afternoon he would catechize students at Corpus Christi College. During his catechism teaching, he would lecture on the Ten Commandments in a convicting way. He made himself available on Sunday afternoons to advise God's people and to counsel those who were convicted. He also preached to people in prisons. His desire was to be useful in pointing people to the Lord Jesus Christ as the only Savior.

Perkins, like the other Puritans, realized that outward reformation of the church and of individual people was not enough. Inward cleansing worked by the Holy Spirit was needed. The Reformation had opened many people's eyes to the truth of the gospel and the errors of the Roman Catholic Church, but every person needs to be inwardly renewed in order to be saved. "Jesus answered and said unto [Nicodemus], Verily, verily, I say unto thee, Except a man be born again, he cannot see the kingdom of God" (John 3:3). No matter how "reformed" a person may be in his talk and behavior, he must have the cleansing blood of Jesus applied to his heart by the Holy Spirit.

Perkins's writings were very helpful to people living in his time but also in later years. He tried to explain Calvinist teachings from Scripture in a way that everyone could understand. He was not afraid to stand boldly for the truth. He openly opposed the false doctrines of the Pelagians (who taught that God chose the people whom He saw beforehand would accept His grace), the Semi-Pelagians (who taught that salvation is partly mercy and partly works), and the Lutherans (who taught that God chose some people but rejected those whom He saw beforehand would reject Him). He not only exposed these errors, but he also explained the scriptural view on these doctrines.

Several of his books are well known. *The Art of Prophesying* is a book on preaching and speaking the truth of God's Word. *The Works of William Perkins* contains 2,000 pages of his writings, including many of his theological and practical writings as well as writings on worship and preaching. *The Foundation of Christian Religion, Gathered in Six Principles* was written to correct people's lack of knowledge about the true Christian religion. Perkins was also very gifted in speaking to the consciences of the people in his preaching and pastoral work. His writings in this vein can be found in *A Discourse of Conscience* and *The Whole Treatise of Cases of Conscience.* He also wrote several commentaries.

His works were translated into many languages: Dutch, German, Spanish, French, Italian, Irish, Welsh, Hungarian, and Czech. God used this man to help spread the truth of Scripture all over the world. Even today, his books can be purchased for us to read and benefit from.

When he died in 1602 of kidney stones, he was greatly mourned by his family, students, congregation, and fellow theologians. Many people thought there could be no better preacher. He was called "the father of Puritanism" because of his great influence on later Puritans.

~ 30 ~

William Ames

(1576–1633)

William Ames's Marrow of Theology *greatly influenced Reformed Doctrine and Puritan piety in the Netherlands, North America, and England.*

His youth and education

William Ames was born in 1576 at Ipswich, a city in Suffolk County, England, an area in which many Puritans lived. His parents died young, leaving his mother's brother, Robert Snelling, to raise the orphan. Robert Snelling was also a Puritan and raised his nephew in the Puritan tradition.

In 1593, when Ames was seventeen, he was sent to Christ's College at Cambridge University. There he received a Bachelor of Arts degree in theology in 1598. In 1601, he received a Master of Arts degree, he was elected fellow at Christ's College, and he was also ordained to the ministry.

His conversion

Although Ames was raised in a Christian home, he was not saved until 1601, under the preaching of William Perkins, a professor at the university. His conversion was a major turning point in his life. Ames began speaking to his fellow students about the need for godliness and sorrow for sin. He was like Nicodemus, who realized through the teaching of Jesus in John 3 the importance of the new birth, even for outwardly religious people.

The Puritans

In 1604, King James signed into law the Edict of Tolerance. *Tolerance* is the practice of allowing people to worship as they please. This edict stated that there had been enough reform in the Church of England. There was to be no more criticism of the state church. Any Puritan writings and preaching against the Church of England must be stopped.

There were many students and professors at Cambridge University who were Puritan. They could not, with a clear conscience, stop their scriptural teachings. They wanted people to realize the importance of inward cleansing, not only outward reform. They continued their teachings and writings, with serious consequences. Many who taught or believed Puritanism were stripped of their degrees and dismissed from the university. This situation was a great disgrace.

A few years later, a man named Valentine Cary was appointed to be head of Christ's College instead of William Ames. Cary was strongly opposed to Puritanism. After Ames preached a sermon at the university against gambling and other sins, his degrees were suspended. He was not officially dismissed, but he knew he was no longer welcome at the university.

The Netherlands

After seeking the Lord's guidance, Ames went to the Netherlands, where he remained until his death. In Rotterdam, he met some of the people who had fled from persecution in other countries. The people there were glad to have such an able Puritan theologian in their

William Ames

midst. Some of these people were the Pilgrims who sailed for Plymouth soon afterward.

From 1611 to 1619, Ames became the military chaplain of the English forces stationed at The Hague. Around this time, a new doctrine called Arminianism was gaining a foothold among the people. During his years as military chaplain, Ames wrote many helpful papers against this false doctrine.

Writes against Arminianism

Arminianism was taught by Jacobus Arminius (1560–1609), a Dutch theologian. He opposed the scriptural doctrine of predestination and taught instead that man, not God, decides who will be saved. He stated that each person has a free will to choose or reject salvation.

Ames saw that Arminianism is not scriptural. God has chosen His elect from eternity. "For whom he did foreknow, he also did predestinate to be conformed to the image of his Son, that he might be the firstborn among many brethren. Moreover whom he did predestinate, them he also called: and whom he called, them he also justified: and whom he justified, them he also glorified" (Romans 8:29–30). We have no will of our own except to do evil, because we are totally depraved. "The whole head is sick, and the whole heart faint. From the sole of the foot even unto the head there is no soundness in it; but wounds, and bruises, and putrifying sores: they have not been closed, neither bound up, neither mollified with ointment" (Isaiah 1:5b–6). No one will choose salvation by his own will because even our wills are depraved. "As it is written, There is none righteous, no, not one: There is none that understand, there is none that seeketh after God" (Romans 3:10–11). It is only God, by way

of the atoning sacrifice of Jesus Christ, who saves anyone at all. "No man can come to me, except the Father which hath sent me draw him" (John 6:44a).

Synod of Dort

This debate finally resulted in the Synod of Dort, or Dordrecht, from 1618 to 1619, which took place after the death of Arminius. The synod met for the main purpose of deciding what Scripture teaches. William Ames was asked to be one of the clerks at the synod. The synod discussed many issues. They especially focused on the teachings of Jacobus Arminius. After much discussion, the synod ruled in favor of Calvinism and rejected Arminianism. The Canons of Dort is a document that summarizes the decisions of the Synod of Dort. God used this group of men to write a clear statement declaring the scriptural view on several important doctrines. These can be summarized using the word TULIP: T—total depravity; U—unconditional election; L—limited atonement; I—irresistible grace; P—perseverance of the saints.

Marriage and teaching career

Ames's first wife died shortly after they married. He married for the second time in 1618, to a woman named Joan Fletcher. During their marriage, they were blessed with three children: Ruth, William, and John. To support his family, Ames lectured and tutored privately for three years after the Synod of Dort. He established a "house college": several students lodged in his home, and he taught them there. Some of his lectures became part of a book he later wrote, *The Marrow of Theology*, which is a summary of Calvinist doctrine. This book became very important for the training of Puritan pastors of later generations. It emphasized the practical aspects of Christian doctrine.

In 1622, Ames moved to Friesland, a province of the Netherlands. On May 7, he was inaugurated as a professor of theology at the Franeker University. Four days later, he received an honorary Doctorate of Theology. Ames's main focus during his eleven years at this university was to teach students that godly living is essential to the Christian life.

Not all the other professors and students at the university liked Ames's practical teachings. They challenged Ames and made things unpleasant for him. Even though most of the professors and students at the university agreed on doctrinal points, this matter of Christian living caused controversy.

Franeker University was marked by riotous living before Ames arrived in March of 1622. Ames was very disturbed at the lives of many who attended the university. He was distressed at finding much "coldness in religion and little piety."[1] As the rector of the university, Ames tried to promote piety among his students, speaking against their practices of breaking the Sabbath day, swearing, gambling, heavy drinking, and oaths. His attempts were met with ridicule and scorn, but he opened his house to those students who wanted to practice piety.

---

1. Keith L. Sprunger, "William Ames," in *Oxford Dictionary of National Biography* (Oxford: Oxford University Press, 2005), 1:943.

His last move

This constant debate at Franeker and the damp sea air were not good for Ames's health. Besides, his wife wanted to go back to England. They decided it was time to move. They asked the Lord to direct them to a new place to live.

In 1632, Ames was invited by Hugh Peter to be a pastor along with him in the English-speaking church at Rotterdam, the Netherlands. Peter and his congregation believed, like Ames, that a person should live a godly life if he professed to be a Christian. They told Ames that they would like to begin a Puritan college in Rotterdam.

In late summer of the following year, he headed to Rotterdam with his family to make his home there. It was a very wet fall, and the Maas River flooded its banks. The Ames family was one of many whose homes were flooded. Ames, who already suffered from poor health, caught pneumonia. On November 11, he died in the arms of his friend, Hugh Peter, at the age of fifty-seven.

Four years later, Ames's wife and children sailed across the ocean and made their home in Salem, Massachusetts. Ames's books accompanied them. Many of these books were part of the original library of Harvard College, most of which were later destroyed in a fire.

~ 31 ~

Willem Teellinck

(1579–1629)

As the "father of the Dutch Further Reformation," Willem Teellinck was concerned with the reform of the church, not only in doctrine but also in life and practice.

His youth and education

Willem Teellinck was born on January 4, 1579, in Zerikzee, a main town on the island of Duiveland, Zeeland. He came from a godly family and was the youngest of eight children. His father, Joost Teellinck, was the mayor of Zerikzee, and he died when Willem was only fifteen. His mother lived longer but was often sick.

Young Teellinck was well educated in his youth. He studied law at St. Andrews in Scotland, graduating in 1600. He also studied at the University of Poitiers, France, where he obtained his doctoral degree in 1603. After this, he had the privilege of spending almost a year with a godly family who lived in the Puritan community of Banbury, England. It was during this time that the Lord converted Teellinck and taught him many things about living a godly life.

Becomes a Puritan

The Puritans were people who tried to live God-centered lives according to the Scripture. They were often accused of being fanatical in their devotion to God. All religions have members who only observe the outward rituals in order to try to gain the favor of God, but many Puritans served the Lord with their whole heart. They lived a strict, simple life because they did not want worldly things to interfere with their relationship to God.

While in England, Teellinck learned the value of time spent alone in prayer. He participated in sermon discussions after church. Keeping the Sabbath day holy was important to the Puritans, as was observing fast days.

Self-examination was encouraged in order to weed out sin. Doing good for others was regarded as an important part of a life of thankfulness. Even children could join in by singing the Psalms with the adults. Joy in the Lord was an important part of their lives.

The Puritans were regarded by many as somber, long-faced, sour people, but this was not true for most of them. True, they took life seriously, as we should. We are created to serve God and we must spend our time on earth in light of eternity. People often shunned and avoided the Puritans because of their godly lifestyle, but we can learn much from them, as Teellinck did.

This group of godly Puritans did not feel at home in the Church of England, not only because of people's attitudes toward them, but also because of the doctrines they heard there. When the Puritans heard the teachings of the Reformation, they were delighted and wanted to learn more. Teellinck also heard about the Reformers and their work. Teellinck decided, with the Lord's blessing, to study theology at Leiden, in the Netherlands. He was there for two years and studied hard.

By this time Teellinck was married to a young Puritan woman, Martha Greendon. Together they had six children: four sons (the first died as a baby, and the other three became Reformed ministers) and two daughters. Teellinck did not live to see his two younger sons ordained to the ministry, but he did witness his eldest son become a pastor. Teellinck was always a godly example for his family. He was a generous

Willem Teellinck

man, giving to those who lacked. He was a very spiritual man. In his life as husband and father, he directed his children to worship God with their whole lives.

Ordained minister

In 1606, at age twenty-seven, Willem Teellinck was ordained a minister of the gospel. For seven years he served the church of Burgh-Haamstede on the island of Duiveland. His sermons stressed the necessity of repentance and the new birth. Jesus said, "Verily, verily, I say unto thee, Except a man be born again, he cannot see the kingdom of God" (John 3:3). He also emphasized the importance of a godly lifestyle, but he was not cold nor harsh in his preaching. Rather, he was loving but urgent in his callings on his Master's behalf. He told the people it was not enough to live an outwardly clean life, but the love of Christ and the work of the Spirit are necessary.

His work

During this time, Teellinck wrote several books and papers. His writings were very influential. He worked very hard to get the Dutch government to make laws that would govern the lives of the people. He saw the ungodliness of much of society and he wanted to reform it to a closer walk with God. What Teellinck brought to the Reformation more than nearly anyone else was the truth that head knowledge must be coupled with a godly walk. Romans 1:17b says,

"The just shall live by faith," but James adds the other side of the coin when he warns, "Even so faith, if it hath not works, is dead, being alone" (James 2:17).

Sometimes people, even Calvinists, became frustrated with Teellinck because he challenged people to *live* their faith, not only to *talk* about it. This was, in part, because some people did not practice what they professed to believe. Sometimes Teellinck laid down rules that were quite strict, and when some people complained, he explained that he was only trying to urge people to live godly lives, close to the Lord. He had only their spiritual good in mind.

From 1613 until 1629, he was pastor in Middelburg, where there were quite a few other Reformed churches: four Dutch, one English, and one French. Teellinck was a kind, sincere man who walked close to the Lord he loved. He was friendly and humble, never putting himself above another person. The burden of the salvation of the souls of his congregation prompted much prayer from this faithful pastor. Teellinck felt that the pastor must be the godliest man in the congregation, and this showed itself through self-denial. During an outbreak of a pestilence in 1624, he visited many sick people, even though it could have been deadly for him. At the same time, he called the people to repent, both publicly and privately. His work as a pastor in Middelburg was blessed by the Lord, and he rejoiced to see his people walking in the truth (2 John 4).

The goal of Willem Teellinck's ministry was to see his people grow in holiness. His preaching and his writings aimed to do this at all times. His preaching was direct and called the people to repentance, yet he also showed them Christ in all His beauty, love, and suitability as the Savior. He was often scoffed at for being legalistic in condemning immoral behavior, but he wanted to build up believers to fear God and walk humbly before Him. As the "father of the Dutch Further Reformation," Willem Teellinck was concerned with the reform of the church, not only in doctrine but also in life and practice. He believed that correct, biblical doctrine would result in a life of godliness and piety.

His writings reflect this aim in a profound way. In all, he wrote 127 manuscripts. He wrote on a variety of subjects, but his goal was always sanctification, that is, the growth of holiness in the believer. His most well-known book in English today is *The Path of True Godliness*. This book tells the believer how he must live his life before God in a biblical way, not relying on works, but on the finished work of Jesus Christ upon the cross.

His influence continues today, mostly in the Netherlands, but also now in North America, where his works are being translated into English. More than 150 editions of his works were printed in Dutch. His life continues to be studied because it was so important to the Dutch Further Reformation that followed his death.

Willem Teellinck was often a sickly man, but he continued tirelessly to reform the church and his people. He wanted to see the truth of God's Word spoken to the mind but also applied to the hearts and lives of the people to whom he ministered. He died at the age of fifty, on April 8, 1629.

~ 32 ~

The Anabaptists

Konrad Grebel

Felix Manz

Ludwig Hätzer

Georg Blaurock

Thomas Müntzer

Jan Mattijs

Jan Beukelssen

Melchior Hoffmann

Jakob Hutter

Balthasar Hubmaier

Menno Simons

Not all the followers of Zwingli and Luther remained true to all the teachings of the Reformation. Some people had become aware of the errors of the Roman Catholic Church and for a time followed the teachings of the Reformers, but then they swerved off their path in various ways. A group of people, later known as the Anabaptists, began to doubt several doctrines the Reformers taught. Though they continued to embrace most of the Reformation's doctrines, they developed some unique teachings that, in varying degrees, made them part ways with the Reformers.

Their distinctive doctrines

The word "Anabaptist" means "re-baptized." The Anabaptists believed that infant baptism was not according to Scripture; some even said it was an attempt by Satan to deceive the church. Instead, they were re-baptized when they professed their faith. In general, Anabaptists believed that what both the Roman Catholic Church and the Reformers taught about the baptism of infants was wrong. The Roman Catholic Church taught that salvation is automatically granted when a child is baptized. The Reformers, on the other hand, taught that baptism is a sign and a seal of the covenant of grace. They taught that God makes a covenant with the baptized child, just as He made a covenant with all the male children in the Old Testament by way of circumcision. Even when children are helpless and unaware of what baptism means, the Lord comes near them and tells them in baptism that He is able and willing to save them.

The Anabaptists, however, believed that baptism is a statement of repentance, a rejection of one's former life, and a pledge of obedience to God. They taught that baptism should come after one has confessed faith—not in infancy, but in adulthood. To the Anabaptists, baptism was like making a public confession of personal salvation: the person said that he had repented of all his sins, pushed sin and worldly things away, and vowed always to obey God and follow all His commandments.

Concerning the sacrament of the Lord's Supper, the Anabaptists also rejected some of the teachings of both the Roman Catholic Church and the Calvinists. Like Zwingli, they taught that it was merely a memorial of Christ's death. The Anabaptists, however, focused on the importance of suffering and being shunned by the world because of their faith. Many of them believed that the Lord's Supper was a model to them, to teach them to be like Christ by being willing to offer oneself for God or one's neighbor. Persecution and martyrdom were considered the ultimate honors, because it was thought that in these ways one could truly imitate the Lord Jesus.

Since some Anabaptists did not treasure the Old Testament as much as the New, they taught that tithing was not necessary. Believers should only give as they were willing and able, for the good of all believers. Ideally, they taught, believers should have all things in common. Since all things are gifts of God, they taught that they ought to share what they have been given by Him.

Many of the Anabaptists also taught that a believer should not participate in government or in wars. Government was something that involved worldly people. War was something they believed Jesus forbade in Matthew 26:52:

"Put up again thy sword into his place: for all they that take the sword shall perish with the sword."

Neither were some permitted to swear an oath, not even in court. They took for their pattern Jesus' statement in Matthew 5:33–34a, 37: "Again, ye have heard that it hath been said by them of old time, Thou shalt not forswear thyself, but shalt perform unto the Lord thine oaths: but I say unto you, Swear not at all…. But let your communication be, Yea, yea; Nay, nay: for whatsoever is more than these cometh of evil."

Many Anabaptists taught that since Christians are to live separate from the world, they ought not have any dealings with the world. They established their own communities in which they tried to follow the ideal of the New Testament church when it was first established. There are still Amish, Hutterite, and Mennonite communities today that keep themselves literally separated from the world. Depending on the strictness of the particular order, they have rules limiting possession of "worldly" inventions, such as cars and electricity.

Another thing the Anabaptists taught is that their churches were to be pure. Outsiders were not permitted to join them as long as they did not follow their teachings. For someone who had been baptized and then was discovered to live in any kind of sin, Anabaptists introduced the dreaded "ban," which meant that the person was cut off from the group: no one was to speak to, eat with, or do business with that person. If the person would not repent, he was excommunicated. If the person repented, and confessed and forsook his sin, he was accepted again into the community of believers.

Not all Anabaptists believed exactly the same things. There were some major differences among themselves on several of their teachings, but what we have just described was typical of many of their beliefs. The Anabaptist teachings spread quickly, especially among the poor and uneducated. At first they had no specific written statements of beliefs, which is one reason why there were various groups, not all of them agreeing completely with one another. As the Anabaptists grew and developed, some leaders emerged among them and their doctrines were written in the Schleitheim Confession of 1527.

Grebel, Manz, and Hätzer

A few early Anabaptist leaders were Konrad Grebel, Felix Manz, and Ludwig Hätzer. These men lived in Switzerland and knew Zwingli. They tried to get him to agree with their teachings, but Zwingli stood firm on the Reformed doctrine. These men insisted that their followers be re-baptized, since they rejected infant baptism. They wanted a complete separation of church and state.

Zwingli warned people against the teachings of Grebel, Manz, and Hätzer. He wrote tracts explaining their errors and taught people what God's Word says. In one particularly strongly worded tract, written in July 1527, Zwingli said that the Anabaptists were hypocrites, acting piously but deceiving the people. He warned that they did not value the Old Testament, ascribing more value to the New Testament. He also pointed out that they had a wrong view on the doctrine of man's will. They believed a person can choose to believe the gospel or reject it. He said they were superstitious, proud people who were in error.

Konrad Grebel was born in 1498 in Switzerland and came from a fairly wealthy family. He was educated at Basel and Vienna. He was schooled in 15th and 16th century humanism, learning Greek, Hebrew, and Latin, as well as studying classical literature. At first, Grebel supported Ulrich Zwingli in his reforms at Zurich, but they gradually drifted apart. Grebel wanted reform to move much faster than it was, and he wanted to force the destruction of images in the churches. He began to correspond with Thomas Müntzer, one of the most radical Anabaptists, and set up his own church, instituting believers' baptism. He died of the plague in 1526.

Felix Manz was born around 1500. He studied with Konrad Grebel and Zwingli in Zurich. He too became a leader of the Anabaptists when the city council of Zurich ordered all illegal preaching, that is, preaching against idols, to stop. Manz had these rebel preachers meet at his house, where Georg Blaurock was baptized by Grebel. This was the first adult baptism, and it was punishable under imperial law, which stated that "the refusal of infant baptism was heretical and rebellious."[1] Eventually Manz was captured and imprisoned. He was put to death by drowning in 1527.

Ludwig Hätzer was also born around 1500. He too wanted to see reform enforced in the Swiss churches. He wrote a tract called "The Judgment of God: Our Spouse as to How One Should Hold Oneself Toward All Idols and Images." This tract caused much destruction and violence in the Swiss churches because the people were stirred up to destroy the images. In 1529, Hätzer was beheaded in Constance after a long imprisonment.

---

1. Carter Lindberg, *The European Reformations* (Cambridge, Mass.: Blackwell Publishers, 1996), 215.

Georg Blaurock (c. 1492–1529)

Some historians believe that Anabaptism officially began in January 1525. A small group of people met at Manz's home to discuss their beliefs. Grebel was there, as well as a man named Georg Blaurock. The group decided that Grebel, who was not an ordained minister, should baptize Blaurock, who, in turn, baptized several others present.

The Anabaptist movement spread so quickly that the authorities became alarmed. They made a law stating that all children who had not yet been baptized must receive that sacrament within the next eight days or be sent out of Zurich. When not everyone responded, the command was repeated. The Anabaptists did not obey. Shortly afterward, Manz, Blaurock, Grebel, and others were arrested. Zwingli tried to prove to them from Scripture that they were wrong; but they would not listen to him.

In 1526, a law was made stating that Anabaptists were to be drowned if they were found out. In January of the following year, Manz was drowned. Grebel had died of the plague before this time. Blaurock, since he was not a citizen of Zurich, was beaten and sent out of the city. In 1529, he was burned at the stake.

Thomas Müntzer (c. 1489–1525)

Thomas Müntzer was raised in a devout Roman Catholic family. When he came across some of Luther's writings, however, he began to see that the Roman Catholic Church was wrong in many of its teachings. He soon became a Protestant. In 1519, he worked with Luther in Wittenberg. Before long, however, he left Luther because he thought Luther was not going far enough in his reformation.

Believing he was called to be a minister in Prague, Müntzer traveled there and was welcomed as a follower of Luther.

Soon, however, he began openly questioning Luther's teachings. He seemed to think very highly of himself, since he said that he was the last of God's prophets. In letters he wrote, he called himself "the servant of Christ" and "the son who shakes out the wicked."

He wrote and posted a statement of his beliefs in Prague. There is nothing wrong with stating one's beliefs, but some of the things Müntzer taught were not according to Scripture. For instance, he said that the Bible itself was like a dead book, and that a person needed a special voice inside them to understand it. This may seem to come close to the doctrine that we need the Holy Spirit to open our hearts for the gospel. The Bible is God's Word, however, and no special revelations or visions are necessary in order to be blessed by it.

Because of his wrong teachings, Müntzer was not allowed to preach in Prague anymore. He left the city with his friend Marcus Stübner, who was also a preacher.

The following incident will help you to understand why Luther was so determined to leave the Wartburg Castle and return to Wittenberg. Müntzer's friend Stübner joined some other men, Thomas Dreschel and Nicholas Storch, also Anabaptists, on their way to Wittenberg. These men became known as the Zwickau Prophets. They preached that the world would soon end; they organized riots, led attacks against priests, and cursed those who did not follow their teachings. These Anabaptists accused Luther and his followers of a half-hearted religion. They said Luther only led a partial reformation and that a more radical change was needed. People began to listen to them and join in their demonstrations. Luther was distressed to hear this and returned to Wittenberg. Through preaching a series of Lenten sermons every day from March 9 to 16, 1522, and by speaking to the people, Luther was able to restore peace to the city. In his forceful, honest manner, Luther pointed out the errors of these men, calling them the "messengers of Satan." Stübner, Dreschel, and Storch soon left the city and were never heard from again. They were among the most unbiblical of the Anabaptists.

Another one of Müntzer's teachings was that God had told him that he would be the one who would bring about God's kingdom on earth. He said that if people would not yield to his teachings peacefully, then he would force them. First, he tried to persuade the princes and nobles to help him establish God's kingdom on earth. When they did not listen to him, he became angry with them. He turned his attention to the peasants, the poor and uneducated. To the peasants, this sounded like wonderful news: a kingdom of God on earth, where no princes could rule over them! Müntzer was willing to fight for his kingdom. This was obviously not in accordance with the teachings of other Anabaptists, who advocated not using force at all. This caused unrest and rebellion among the peasants, who were tired of being poor, uneducated, and oppressed. Ultimately, it resulted in the Peasants' Revolt in 1525. During the battle, Müntzer tried to escape his enemies but was found hiding in an attic. He was beheaded on May 27, 1525.

Jan Mathijs and Jan Beukelssen

Similarly, Jan Mathijs (d. 1534) and Jan Beukelssen (d. 1535) of the Netherlands said that Christ would return soon—to the city of Münster. They actually took over the city government by force, intending to set up what they termed the New Jerusalem. Other towns tried to defend Münster to prevent this from happening.

Jan Mathijs was a baker from Haarlem, the Netherlands, who was converted under the ministry of Melchior Hoffman. He believed that the godless should not be allowed to live. He set out to kill all those whom he considered godless. He was convinced by one of his friends that this killing would upset the local prince. His policies as the mayor of Münster were based on revelations he said he received from God. He wanted the people of the city to share all their possessions. Mathijs was killed when an army besieged the city; he thought the weapons of the enemy would not be able to kill him. His revelation about this did not hold true, however, and he was killed.

Jan Beukelssen, also known as John of Leiden, was even stranger. He ran through the city naked and then fell into a trance, which lasted three days. He believed this to be a spiritual experience in which he was instructed by God. He then took over the position of leader, convinced that Münster was the New Jerusalem that is described in Revelation 21:10: "And he carried me away in the spirit to a great and high mountain, and shewed me that great city, the holy Jerusalem, descending out of heaven from God." Establishing himself as king, he chose twelve elders to rule under him. He boldly stated that all former marriages were no longer valid and the practice of polygamy (having more than one wife) was introduced.

Lutheran and Roman Catholic troops surrounded the city to stop Beukelssen's reign of terror. The siege lasted approximately six months. Beukelssen was tortured and killed with red-hot irons when they recaptured Münster in 1536.

The errors of Mathijs and Beukelssen began with the sin of pride. They believed that they were special children of God, on whom God bestowed extra favors. They believed that God spoke to them not through His Word, but through special visions. This led to the disastrous establishment of their so-called New Jerusalem. How dangerous it is to stray from the teachings of God's Word!

Melchior Hoffmann (1498–1543)

Another Anabaptist leader was Melchior Hoffmann. He was born in 1498 and was a leather tanner by trade. He joined Luther as a lay preacher in 1523, but he eventually rejected Luther's view of the Lord's Supper. He was found preaching throughout northern Germany and in the Netherlands, where he had much influence.

Hoffman believed that God had appointed him to lead the believers into another New Jerusalem, which he held was in Strasbourg. There they would wait for the end of the world, which Hoffmann said would transpire in 1533. He believed that he had direct inspiration from God; that is, he believed God talked directly to him aside from the Bible, telling him what he must do as the leader of God's chosen people.

Hoffman was arrested and imprisoned in a dungeon in Strasbourg, where he died in 1543. He refused to change his beliefs about the Judgment Day until he died. After his death, the Melchiorites remained as a group within the Anabaptists, adopting his beliefs.

Jakob Hutter (d. 1536)

Jakob Hutter was an Austrian Anabaptist who led many of the Anabaptists out of Austria into Moravia, where he established more than eighty communities. Although he did not begin these Anabaptist groups himself, his name became attached to them because of his leadership. This was the beginning of the Hutterian Brethren, commonly called the Hutterites.

Because of the strange events in Münster in 1534 and 1535 and the reputation the Anabaptists had gained, the Hutterian Brethren were not left in peace for long. The Moravian government also began to persecute them, so that they were forced to live in caves and hide in the forests.

Besides believing most of the basic teachings of the Anabaptists, the Hutterites believed in living a strict moral life. They believed that work was a great blessing. Many of them became farmers, growing crops or raising cattle. Hymn-singing was an important part of their worship and everyday life. Jakob Hutter was a person who believed in the brotherhood of believers. Hutter felt strongly not only about sharing all things in common to help one another, but also about the notion of a close community. He took the idea of Christian fellowship described in Acts 2:44 and put it into practice literally: "And all that believed were together, and had all things common."

Hutter was arrested and, sadly, burned at the stake for his faith in February 1536.

Balthasar Hubmaier (c. 1485–1528)

At one time, Balthasar Hubmaier was a student and a friend of Johann Eck, Luther's opponent. Hubmaier was ordained a parish priest at Waldshut in 1521. He came into contact with the Swiss Reformation there and openly joined himself to Zwingli. Of course, in so doing, his friendship with Eck was broken. Eventually, he left Zwinglian doctrine and the Swiss Reformation, condemning infant baptism as idolatry.

Subsequently, he became increasingly interested in Anabaptist teachings. Finally, on Easter Sunday, 1525, Hubmaier was baptized in Waldshut, Switzerland. "Hubmaier and his community at Waldshut insisted on living with the Bible alone as their law, and joined the peasant revolt. When the revolt was quashed, Hubmaier was arrested, tortured, and imprisoned at Zurich, but escaped to Moravia."[2]

In Moravia, Hubmaier began to write tracts about Anabaptist doctrine, especially on the Anabaptist views of the Lord's Supper and in defense of free will. Although Hubmaier gained much support, especially among the peasants, he was burned at the stake in Vienna in 1528.

Menno Simons (1496–1561)

Anabaptism achieved a bad reputation because of some various strange, radical men and their activities. They were despised and ridiculed by Lutherans and Roman Catholics alike, but many Anabaptists were not fanatical. Under the leadership of men like Menno Simons, the founder of the Mennonites, Anabaptism grew and changed. Simons, a former priest, had a mild, peace-loving character.

Simons was born in Witmarsum, a village in Frisia, now a part of the Netherlands. He was ordained into the priesthood

Menno Simons

in 1534, but soon he began to doubt and to question the Roman Catholic doctrine of the Lord's Supper. He took up the Scriptures and began to search them, becoming convinced that baptism should not be administered to infants since it should only follow conversion, a basic doctrine of the Anabaptists.

Although Simons taught that man is sinful, justified only through Jesus Christ, and that faith is a gift of God,

---

2. William P. Barker, *Who's Who in Church History* (Old Tappan, New Jersey: Fleming Revell Company, 1969), 144.

he still agreed with most of the basic teachings of the Anabaptists. He stated that the Lord's Supper was only a memorial of Christ's death, the church was a gathering of believers only, and faith must come before baptism. He spent many years teaching and preaching as he traveled, visiting various groups of Anabaptists. He wrote papers for their instruction, as well as a book entitled *The Book of Fundamentals* (1539). He urged his followers to be simple in dress, food, and material belongings, which is what is still practiced in varying degrees in the Amish, Hutterite, and Mennonite communities today.

Summing up

Although some of these Anabaptists were fanatics and clearly unbiblical in their teaching, others, like Hutter and Simons, were sincere men who tried to pattern their lives and those of their followers according to Scripture. The problem for these latter Anabaptists lay in their taking Scripture texts literally that were not meant to be taken literally and their essentially having a Roman Catholic view of perfection—to be perfect one had to live in a community distinct from the world and society. In essence, their inspiration was the monasteries of the late Middle Ages, and not the pattern of Christian living reflected in, say, the letters of Paul. The latter Anabaptists also failed to understand the depth of total depravity.

Though the Anabaptists were wrong in some of their beliefs, the Reformers also erred in the way they treated them by having some of them executed. Yes, some of the more extreme Anabaptists were upsetting society and creating political unrest, and these had to be imprisoned. But to execute peaceful men like Hutter goes beyond what the New Testament permits and, sadly, has caused reproach to be cast upon some of the Reformers to this day.

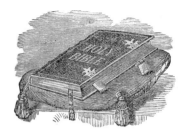

~ 33 ~

The Counter Reformation

The Counter Reformation, being spurred on by the Jesuits, helped reform the Roman Catholic Church outwardly but did not correct the wrong teachings of the church.

Just as the Pharisees hoped that the disciples and their message of a risen Christ would fade away, so the Roman Catholic Church hoped the teachings of the Reformers would eventually disappear. Since the Reformation grew stronger and spread further, however, the Roman Catholic Church grew more and more determined to stop it. Several indecisive and ineffective popes tried in vain to come up with a plan to stifle the Reformation. This was all in God's wise providence. The gospel needed time to take root and grow. Believers needed time to study the Scriptures and come to an understanding of both its simple message of salvation and its deep truths and doctrines. Just as a child is not ready to fight a war, so the Reformation needed time to grow in learning and gain strength in knowing the truth.

Through the efforts of the Reformers, people became more and more aware of the many faults and corruptions in the Roman Catholic Church. Not only were its doctrines not in accord with Scripture, but the lifestyles of the clergy were often sinful and offensive. It was time for the Roman Catholic Church to "clean up."

Since the Roman Catholic Church believed its doctrines were correct, they began to reform obvious immoral blemishes. People wanted more from the Roman Catholic Church than laws and rules. They wanted spiritual satisfaction, never realizing that as long as they rejected the Lord Jesus Christ as the only way of salvation, they could not earn atonement for sin. The Counter Reformation arose as an attempt by the Roman Catholic Church to address these needs.

The monasteries, supposed to be places of prayer and study away from the influences of the world, had become just the opposite. They were often wealthy places of parties and sin. Some monasteries changed their ways; new monasteries appeared. They went back to the original intention of their existence: places where monks who took vows of poverty would pray, meditate, and serve their fellow man. Monks studied agriculture in order to help their countries develop better farming techniques. They copied manuscripts written by learned scholars. They established schools to promote education in their communities. They studied medicine and science to benefit the sick and dying. These are mostly good things, but the emphasis was on doing good works, which should be a *fruit* of salvation, not the *means* to achieve it.

The Inquisition

The word "inquisition" has a Latin root meaning "to inquire," which means "to ask." The period in history known as the Inquisition, however, was much more sinister than simply asking people questions. When the Roman Catholic Church realized that the Reformation was there to stay and that they were losing many members of their church to the new Protestant churches, they took action. Protestants had been persecuted over the years, and many died painful deaths, but under the leadership of an Italian cardinal, Giampietro Caraffa, this persecution intensified. On July 21, 1542, Pope Paul III officially approved the Inquisition, extending its reach throughout all countries. Protestants everywhere were in danger.

Soldiers hunted down Protestants and brought them before judges called "inquisitors" who questioned them about their faith. All who did not conform to the doctrines of the Roman Catholic Church were imprisoned, tortured, or killed, whether they were Protestants, Jews, or even Roman Catholics with some "heretical" ideas. Cardinal Caraffa was pleased. He said, "If our own father were a heretic, we would carry the wood to burn him!"[1]

In 1555, Cardinal Caraffa became pope. His new name was Pope Paul IV. He wanted to purge the church of impurities, rid the world of the Reformation, and strengthen and advance the Roman Catholic Church. He was ruthless and would not tolerate any heresy. He had many willing helpers.

Many innocent people died terrible deaths because they loved the Lord Jesus Christ. Children lost their parents and relatives. Friends became traitors. It was a time of great trial for the Protestants. But they were willing to suffer. They knew that if they remained faithful, they would live forever with King Jesus, and that was worth all their suffering and pain. Jesus said, "Fear none of those things which thou shalt suffer: behold, the devil shall cast some of you into prison, that ye may be tried; and ye shall have tribulation ten days: be thou faithful unto death, and I will give thee a crown of life" (Revelation 2:10).

The Spanish Inquisition

Often the word "Inquisition" is linked to Spain. That is because Spain was a powerful Roman Catholic nation in the time of the Reformation. It became even stronger when Mary, Queen of England, married Philip II, King of Spain in 1554. This extended Spain's domain to England, and since

---

1. Lewis W. Spitz, *The Renaissance and Reformation Movements, Volume 2: The Reformation* (St Louis: Concordia Publishing House), 477.

The Inquisition

Queen Mary Tudor – "The Bloody Mary"

both Philip and Mary hated the Protestants, the Inquisition thrived. Queen Mary was King Edward VI's sister. So after his death, the remarkable progress of the Reformation in England was reversed.

> Within three months of the death of the first Protestant king of England, the whole conduct of public worship was again under the control of the Roman Catholics. The Prayer Book was abolished, the altars replaced, crosses and images which had been pulled down were set up again, and the legends of the Roman Catholic Church substituted once more for the Bible.[2]

Many Protestants were innocently imprisoned and killed during Mary's reign. It has been said of the Inquisition's work in England:

> Of the cost in human life and suffering of the last three and a half years of Mary's reign no estimate can be made.... Men and women untried, uncondemned, were crowded into the prisons. "They were beaten, they were starved, they were flung into the dark, stinking dens, where rotting straw was their bed; their feet were fettered in the stocks, and their clothes were their only covering, while the wretches who died in their misery were flung out into the fields, where none might bury them."[3]

Philip's right-hand man was the Duke of Alva (chapter 23) who terrorized the Netherlands. Alva brought the Inquisition to the Netherlands, persecuting and killing many people because of their faith. The Inquisition was also doing the same in Spain. Many people were either killed or exiled from Spain. Roman Catholicism remains the strongest religion in Spain today.

---

2. W. H. Beckett, *The English Reformation of the Sixteenth Century* (London: The Religious Tract Society, 1890), 221.

3. Ibid., quoting Froude.

The Council of Trent (1545–1563)

Several times over the years, the Roman Catholic Church held meetings to discuss the problem of "heretics." There was the Council of Constance (1414–1418), the Council at Basel (1431–1439), the Council at Florence (1438–1445), and the Fifth Lateran Council at Rome (1503–1521). The meetings were held to try to begin a reform within the Roman Catholic Church. None of these councils was very effective, however. The clergy had become too comfortable with the way things were, and they were unwilling to give up their sinful, lavish lifestyles.

As the Reformation became stronger and more widespread, the Roman Catholic Church could no longer push aside this glaring issue. They had to do something. At last the Council of Trent assembled to discuss the matter. Would they admit their faults? Would they repent? Would they make changes? Would the pope and the powerful cardinals be willing to surrender to the Word of God and its supreme authority?

Trent is located in Northern Italy, not too far from Rome. The Council lasted from 1545 until 1563. This did not mean that they had constant meetings. It was an ongoing council, and it did not reach its conclusion until 1563, when certain statements were formally written down. Some of the decisions made at the Council of Trent are outlined below.

1. Seven sacraments were affirmed: baptism, confirmation (becoming a member of the church), the Eucharist, matrimony, holy orders (becoming a priest or nun), penance, and the sacrament of the sick (extreme unction or the last rites, given to a dying person).

2. Scripture and tradition were determined to be equally authoritative. Actually, in case of doubt, the pope and the Roman Catholic Church were given the ultimate authority. The pope was said to be infallible—that is, incapable of making mistakes—when he made formal statements.

3. The best version of the Bible was Jerome's Latin Vulgate.

4. Salvation, or justification, occurs when a person has sanctified himself sufficiently for God to justify him. Good works help a person achieve salvation.

5. The doctrine of transubstantiation was declared to be true; that is, when the priest blesses the bread and the wine at the Lord's Supper, they actually become the body and blood of the Lord Jesus Christ.

6. The mass was recognized as the correct way to worship God.

7. Some reform was necessary. They decided to build seminaries to educate the clergy. The clergy needed supervision. They wrote a catechism for children, agreeing that the education of children was important. Also, a bishop needed to live in his diocese; that is, he couldn't be a bishop of a town or city in which he did not live.

8. In their vehemence against the Reformation, they compiled a list of forbidden books: the *Index Librorum Prohibitorum*. Anyone caught reading any of the books on this list would be severely punished

and the books destroyed. This list proved beneficial to the inquisitors in their work of searching for the Protestants.

The Jesuits

Iñigo López de Loyola, or Ignatius Loyola, was born in Spain in 1491. He was born into a noble family and was thus carefully educated. It was important that he learn how to be a knight and a gentleman. When he was twenty-six, however, Ignatius grew tired of court life. He became a soldier. Fighting in a battle against France, Loyola was wounded in 1521. Both his legs were badly injured, and his military career ended. What would he do now, since he was disabled?

He had been taught to read and write, but his education had focused more on court manners and knightly behavior. He was a Roman Catholic, but it was more out of tradition than conviction. Recovering slowly in the family castle gave Loyola time to think. He read some religious books and was impressed with the lives of the saints about whom he read. He decided to give his life to God and formally consecrated himself at the Shrine of the Virgin Mary at Montserrat, on March 24, 1522. During the night he alternately stood or knelt at the altar, trying to fill his mind with holy thoughts. "In the morning he received Holy Communion, put on a pilgrim's garb of rough material, and wore only one shoe, favoring his deformed leg; later he let his hair grow unkempt and in general neglected his personal appearance.... For Ignatius it was the beginning of his quest to find the will of God."[4]

For about a year after this, Ignatius lived alone, torturing himself in order to gain insight into God's will. Then he went on a pilgrimage to Jerusalem. When he returned, he decided that studying would be beneficial, so he went to Paris, where he obtained Bachelor of Arts and Master of Arts degrees.

It is ironic that he was questioned by the Inquisition because of his strange dress and intense religion, and he was even accused of heresy. How sad that all his religious devotion did not lead to a saving knowledge of the Lord Jesus Christ! His religion was mystical, vague, and rooted in Roman Catholic notions of penance, poverty, and pilgrimages.

Ignatius wrote a book called *Spiritual Exercises*. It tells the reader how to conquer oneself and respond to God. It is not in accord with Scripture. He taught that a person needed to cleanse himself in order to achieve union with God. He described a series of things that would help a person achieve this union: fasting, penance, solitude, and meditation.

How blessed are those who trust in Christ's atoning blood! Salvation is simple and free. Good deeds cannot earn salvation; confessing sins to a human being is not enough; reforming outwardly cannot save. Only Jesus' blood can cleanse from sin; only God's grace can save.

Eventually, Ignatius attracted some followers. They vowed to live in poverty and holiness, to make a pilgrimage to Jerusalem, and after that to try to save others. They wanted to give themselves to the service of the Roman Catholic Church and put themselves under the authority of the pope. On September 27, 1540, Pope Paul III approved Ignatius's new Society of Jesus. The Jesuits had come into being.

---

4. Gerrish, B.A., ed., *Reformers in Profile* (Philadelphia: Fortress Press, 1967), 237.

Many Jesuits became Roman Catholic missionaries. Ignatius's friend, Francis Xavier[5] was one of the great Jesuit missionaries. He labored especially in eastern countries such as India, Japan, and China with much success. Years later, the Jesuits traveled overseas to the New World and converted many Native Americans to Roman Catholicism.

The Roman Catholic Church saw the Jesuits, or the Society of Jesus, as a good way to help reform the Church. The Jesuits preached, taught the Roman Catholic doctrines, heard confessions, and gave penance, but they also did good works, such as caring for the sick and the poor. The Jesuits did much to help people in need. How sad, though, that the true gospel of salvation in Christ alone was not preached and taught.

The Jesuits were very influential in the courts of Europe. They gave kings and princes advice on how to run their countries and put reforms in place. They also helped to make and write the new doctrines of the Roman Catholic Church at the Council of Trent. They were a very effective order that helped the Roman Catholic Church a great deal in the Counter Reformation.

---

5. Francis Xavier (1506–1552) became a priest in 1537 and then became a Jesuit after meeting Ignatius Loyola.

~ 34 ~

The Influence of the Reformation

The Reformation had a significant impact on education, politics, the economy, and especially, religion.

The Reformation certainly had an impact on the church and religion in its day, but did the Reformation influence other areas of life at that time? Was the Reformation a passing era, or are the effects still visible today? Are Reformation doctrines, ideals, and piety still treasured today? How did God graciously use the Reformation to further His cause and kingdom? These are some of the questions that this final chapter addresses. Throughout this book, we have seen how the Reformers were used by God in various countries throughout Europe and the rest of the world. God carefully prepared the soil for the seeds of the gospel to sprout and to take root. The effects of the Reformation cannot be traced by giving one simple answer. A variety of factors combined with the Reformation have led to certain influences then and now. There is no doubt, though, that the Reformation has had a significant impact on the modern world. We would like to show four basic areas in which the Reformation had a large impact: education, politics, economy, and religion.

Influence on education

The first area to examine is the impact of the Reformation on education. At first it was thought that the Reformation as a movement was to be credited for the education of the people. Recent historical investigation has shown that this is not entirely true. Many schools already existed throughout Europe in which young men were trained, especially to become lawyers and priests. These schools were established near the end of the Middle Ages, the late

1400s.[1] The Reformation used the medieval system of schools as a basis for the education of the laity or common person.

The Reformation also used the Renaissance as a basis for its educational model. The Renaissance was a movement started in the late 1300s that emphasized a return to the languages of the Bible and antiquity: Hebrew, Greek, and Latin. It also stressed the value of philosophy, of literature, and of a careful attainment of the knowledge of history. Moreover, the Renaissance saw the importance of educating and carefully training leaders in society and the church.

The Renaissance was not a Christian movement, though it certainly influenced the church and religion. It was a movement rooted in extolling the capabilities of the human mind. Education was the key to discovery. Art, music, science, and literature proved that man could accomplish amazing things. These accomplishments, in turn, could improve the quality of one's life. For example, if a farmer's son learned to read, he could learn more about the crops and soil, the animals and their care, and he could make improvements. Education was valued because it proved that man was intelligent. For many people, it became less important to trust God because they relied on their own intelligence and ingenuity.

The Reformation approached this movement of renewed interest in education from another angle. To the Reformers, it was not the human being they revered; rather, it was God the Creator they worshiped. Education was a means of learning more about God; the human mind was a gift to be used in the service of God. By studying science, for instance, one could learn about the world God created; by studying the Bible, one could learn more about God and salvation. They embraced the ideals of the Renaissance and incorporated them into the wider context of the Reformation. To the Reformers, it was important that education include the study of such subjects as language, science, literature, history, economics, and religion. This model of education became known as a classical education and remained the model of education into the twentieth century.

The Reformers saw the need for educated men to study the Scriptures in their original languages in order to break away from the interpretations that the Roman Catholic Church had monopolized for so long. What happened when more and more people learned to read, and more and more people owned copies of the Bible? They began to ask questions. They began to realize that what the church taught was not always what Scripture taught. Teaching people to read was a powerful tool that helped spread the Reformation. The Reformers built on the medieval and Renaissance foundation, making education a priority and employing it to promote the truths of God's Word.

The five *solas* of the Reformation, *sola fide, solus Christus, sola Scriptura, sola gratia,* and *soli Deo gloria*—faith alone, Christ alone, Scripture alone, grace alone, and glory to God alone—guided the Reformers in their emphasis on education. They desired to see the people reading the Word of God for their salvation and walk of life. This desire motivated them to use education as a vehicle for helping the people to read. While only a small percentage of the population probably could read by the time of the Reformation, this percentage increased during the Reformation, so that many could read the Bible in their native language.

---

1. Hans J. Hillerbrand, *The Oxford Encyclopedia of the Reformation,* (Oxford: Oxford University Press, 1996), 2:19.

The educational system that we enjoy today is due in large part to the influence of the Reformation. The leaders of the Reformation recognized that the only way to spread the gospel was through education, through reading and teaching. The emphasis on education was not limited to the Protestants, however, because the Jesuits also recognized the effects that education was having on the people. They made it a priority to educate not only the lay people but also the clergy, who often were uneducated themselves. The Jesuits realized the edge that the Protestants had gained by using education as a tool to further the message of the gospel. The Counter Reformation sought to remedy this and educate Catholics.

The emphasis on education also led to more discoveries in science. As people studied more, they began to explore the world outside of their towns and villages. They became interested in the worlds beyond the oceans, and they wanted to learn more about astronomy and biology. As the Reformers broke away from the Roman Catholic Church, there was more freedom for this exploration to continue. Technological advances and new scientific discoveries were made, showing that the Reformation in some way helped the rise of science as it is known today.

Influence on politics

Few things changed more during the time of the Reformation than the politics of sixteenth-century Europe. Europe was roughly divided between four major powers during the sixteenth century: England, France, the Holy Roman Empire (which consisted of Spain, the Netherlands, Germany, Austria, and Hungary), and the papacy (that is, the power that belonged to the popes who ruled in Italy).

As the Reformation progressed, various monarchs and princes began to align themselves with either the Protestant or the Roman Catholic cause. Some, of course, made their choice because of political reasons rather than strictly religious convictions.

Nevertheless, as the political landscape began to change, so did the views on the king's source of authority. People used to believe that a king ruled by divine right, deriving his power from God alone. This view, as well as the papacy's claims to absolute authority over the Church, began to be questioned. Luther especially played a large role in this shift when he wrote pamphlets such as *The Freedom of a Christian Man* and *The Priesthood of All Believers*. These pamphlets, however, were often misapplied by those who sought to take advantage and rebel against the ruling authorities. Eventually this led to the Peasants War of 1524–26.

John Calvin, too, played an important role in the rise of a form of democracy in the time of the Reformation. This can be seen in the city of Geneva. Groups known as the Council of Twelve, the Council of Sixty, the Council of Two Hundred, and the consistory (ministers and elders in the church), all played a large role in the government of the city. The city was no longer controlled by just one noble or bishop, but by several groups of men. Although this is not democracy as we know it today, the beginnings of it are visible.

The change in the political scenery of Europe took place within the church as well. The Reformers rejected the sole authority of the pope over the church and argued for freedom of conscience bound to the Word of God. This was an echo of Martin Luther's statement at the Diet of Worms: "My conscience is captive to the Word of God. I cannot and will not retract anything, for it is neither safe nor right to go against conscience. I cannot do otherwise, here I stand, may God help me, Amen."[2] Monarchs as well as common people began to question the authority of the pope over spiritual matters, especially over their own hearts and their salvation. The Reformation sowed in the mind of the European man thoughts that began to change his thinking about his government, his society, and his church.

Part of the Reformation's impact on politics pertains to the rise of democracy in the West. Certainly the Reformation is not the only factor, but it is one of the factors. Democracy generally arose in the countries that became Protestant after the Reformation, manifesting itself first in Switzerland, the Netherlands, and England. From there, it spread to the United States. Did Protestantism have anything to do with this democratic form of government? More specifically, did Calvinism or Reformed Christianity have an effect on government? After all, England, the Netherlands, and Switzerland are all areas in which Reformed Christianity dominated.

A simple answer to these questions cannot be given easily, but it is important to recognize the major issues facing these countries in the sixteenth century, particularly the struggle for power and stability in Europe, both in the relation of the vassal (servant) to his lord, and the lord to his monarch. The whole medieval structure of authority was being challenged. This issue of acceptance of authority, or at least absolute authority, was found in the countries in which the Reformation had taken hold, and the people of these countries struggled with whether they should be ruled by an absolute monarch or by a body of people chosen from among the people. There are no quick answers to tell whether democracy is a direct fruit of the Reformation, but at the very least, most scholars agree that the Reformation contributed to the rise of democracy.

Influence on economics

Another area in which the Reformation is thought to have had an impact is in the rise of capitalism in the West. Capitalism is an economic system that exists through labor, capital, trade, investments, private ownership, and a free market. Our present economy runs on this economic model. The rise of capitalism is connected to the previous section on the change in politics; these two areas basically changed together and complemented each other. The medieval system of trade was changing. Cities began to play an important part in the economy, especially those cities along rivers and routes of transportation. European cities became economic centers and prospered as a result. Together with this trade and commerce came the spread of the ideas of the Reformation, and the Reformation ideas strengthened the economic ideas of the time.

A crisis had also taken place in the economy in which the lord could no longer rely on his vassal for economic prosperity. Many nobles and the upper level of the peasants began to produce raw materials for manufacturing. Luther's father was a prosperous miner near Wittenberg, and by the time Luther arrived on the scene, there seems to have been a shift in prosperity, especially among the peasants. The peasants were no longer as poor as they once were; wealth was no longer only controlled by the nobility. There were no longer just two classes of people, rich and poor: a middle

---

2. Carter Lindberg, *The European Reformations* (Oxford: Blackwell Publishers, 1996), 361.

class began to emerge. This middle class tended to be quite educated and prosperous, and the Reformation took hold mostly among this class.

The Puritans in England, as well as the Reformers, valued hard work, and reclaimed the work week of six days and the Sabbath as a day of rest. They rejected the days dedicated to saints and saw these as a disruption of the work week. Performing the duties of the clergy was no longer the only "sanctified" work that a person could do. Dignity and worth were given to ordinary jobs, and people were urged to see that even in the most menial job they could serve the Lord, even though they were not pastors. The Puritans stressed the value of self-denial in regard to spending large amounts of money on oneself, and they encouraged saving money for the future. The medieval opposition against charging interest on money loaned was rejected, and it soon became part of usual business practice.

In some part, this analysis helps answer the questions: Where does capital come from? Where does the will to save and to invest, to deny oneself in the present for the sake of future gain, come from? Again, there are no simple answers to these questions, but it cannot be denied that the Reformation had some influence on the rise of capitalism.

Influence on religion

The most obvious and greatest impact that the Reformation has had is in the area of religion. The Reformation sought to restore true religion of mind, heart, and hands. It broke away from a Roman Catholicism that was mired in superstition, corruption, and legalism. The five watchwords of the Reformation help to understand the impact of the Reformation in this area.

First there is *sola Scriptura*—"Scripture alone." The Reformers sought to live by Scripture and to see the lives of the people transformed by Scripture. They wanted to see the Word of God in the hands of the people, and they worked very hard to translate the Bible from Latin, Greek, and Hebrew so that the people could understand what they read. This desire to have the Bible in the language of the people also resulted in the preaching of sermons in a language that the people understood. The Reformers made every effort to ground their theology and their piety in the Word of God. They recognized the power of the Word of God to change people's hearts and lives through the work of the Holy Spirit. They have handed the present generation a wealth of resources that can encourage spiritual growth. In a time when many are turning their backs on the Reformation, a return to Scripture is required, as it was in the days of the Reformation. Scripture alone is the foundation of the Christian faith.

The second watchword is *sola fide*—"faith alone." This doctrine is in direct contrast to the teaching of the Roman Catholics that salvation could be gained through faith and works. The Reformers said that it is through faith alone that a sinner is justified before God. Though there are still those who live by this scriptural principle, errors are creeping in against this precious doctrine in many churches, including evangelical churches that formerly clung to the truth of salvation by faith alone. A return to Scripture is necessary to see that it is *only* by faith that a sinner can be justified before God.

The third concept is *sola gratia* or "grace alone." This cannot be separated from faith because it is only by grace that a sinner receives faith. This grace not only justifies but it sanctifies as well. As the Reformers prayed for revival and the work of grace in the hearts of the people, so too, must we pray this way in the present day. Nothing but the free and sovereign grace of God in Christ Jesus can free people from sin, Satan, and self.

That truth introduces the fourth watchword, which is *solus Christus*—"Christ alone." This watchword governs faith and grace, because without Christ's finished work, there would be neither. The Reformers recognized the importance of keeping their focus on Christ. Throughout their sermons and writings, they extolled Christ as the only name under heaven given among men whereby we must be saved (Acts 4:12). Their religion was anchored in Christ, His atonement, His finished work on the cross, His blood, and His righteousness. These were important themes throughout their theology, and they sought to live fully unto Christ. In passing this legacy on to succeeding generations, the Reformers offer examples of how to live the Christian life—not legalistically or without the law, but in walking by faith in Christ.

The final watchword is *soli Deo gloria*—"glory to God alone." Despite all the setbacks, the persecutions, and their own shortcomings, the Reformers sought to do all to the glory of God. Their lives smell of a sweet, godward fragrance. Today's society is largely focused on how one can gratify oneself, but the Reformers give us a view of how one must and can gratify God. Their theology was not just written in a book or preached from the pulpit, but it was also practiced in their lives. They sought to instill principles of holiness and piety in the lives of the people so that they might glorify God. There is much we can learn from the Reformers in this area, as well.

So much more could be said about the impact of the Reformation, but we hope this book has increased your appetite for these things and that the Lord will bless you as you continue to study them further.

Conclusion

This book should teach us to be thankful for the freedom we enjoy today. Think what it would have been like to live in the early sixteenth century. Very little was known about the Bible and the truths it contains. Our lives would have been in danger if we read the Bible or attended a worship service.

In many countries today, Christians suffer persecution and death, just as they did in the time of the Reformation. In fact, many more Christians suffered and died for their faith in the twentieth century than in the sixteenth century! How blessed we are to be able freely to enjoy the Bible, church services, catechism and Sunday school classes, our parents, ministers, sound books, and Christian schools! God has given us many means to teach us the way of salvation. Do you appreciate the many blessings God has given you? Are you, by God's grace, a true son or daughter of the Reformation?

Appendices

Appendix A

Countries Influenced by the Reformation

REFORMER	Bohemia	England	France	Germany	Italy	Lowlands	Navarre	Poland	Scotland	Switzer-land
Waldo			░							
Wycliffe		░								
Anne of Bohemia	░	░								
Huss	░									
Luther				░						
Melanchthon				░						
Bucer		░		░						
Bullinger										░
Tyndale		░								
Olevianus				░						
Ursinus				░						
Frederick III				░						
Edward VI		░								
Foxe		░								

REFORMER	Bohemia	England	France	Germany	Italy	Lowlands	Navarre	Poland	Scotland	Switzer-land
Cranmer		X								
Latimer		X								
Ridley		X								
Knox		X							X	
de Brès			X			X				X
Zwingli										X
Calvin			X							X
Beza			X							X
Łaski		X				X		X		
Prince of Orange						X				
Marguerite of Navarre			X				X			
Jeanne d'Albret			X				X			
Admiral Coligny			X							
Charlotte			X	X		X				
Vermigli		X		X	X					
Dathenus		X		X		X				
Perkins		X								
Teellinck		X				X				
Ames		X				X				

Atlantic Ocean

IRELAND

ENGLAND

London

North Sea

DENMARK

POLAND

Warsaw

Breslau

HOLY ROMAN EMPIRE

Amsterdam

LOWLANDS

BOHEMIA

Prague

Husinec

Paris

Munich

Vienna

HUNGARY

Bay of Biscay

SWITZERLAND

AUSTRIA

FRANCE

Geneva

Brescia

Trent

Padua

Milan

Venice

PAPAL STATES

Genoa

Lucca

Florence

OTTOMAN EMPIRE

NAVARRE

Pisa

Spoleto

Adriatic Sea

KINGDOM OF ARAGON

Corsica

Rome

PORTUGAL

Piedrahita

Naples

KINGDOM OF NAPLES

Lisbon

SPAIN

Sardinia

Sicily

Mediterranean Sea

Mediterranean Sea

EUROPE IN 1550

Appendix B

Kings and Queens of England and Scotland

b = born   r = ruled

ENGLAND

The House of Plantagenet:
  Edward II: b 1284, r 1307–1327 (murdered)
  Edward III: b 1312, r 1327–1377
  Richard II: b 1367, r 1377–c. 1399, Son of the Black Prince
      by Joan, Countess of Kent; married Anne of Bohemia

The House of Lancaster:
  Henry IV: b 1366, r 1399–1413
  Henry V: b 1387, r 1413–1422
  Henry VI: b 1421, r 1422–1461 (murdered)

The House of York:
  Edward IV: b 1442, r 1461–1483
  Edward V: b 1470, r 1483 (deposed, then most likely murdered)
  Richard III: b 1452, r 1483–1485

The House of Tudor:
  Henry VII: b 1457, r 1485–1509
  Henry VIII: b 1491, r 1509–1547
  Edward VI: b 1537, r 1547–1553, Henry VIII's son by
      Jane Seymour
  Lady Jane Grey: b 1537, r 1553 (beheaded)
  Mary I: b 1515, r 1553–1558, Henry VIII's daughter by
      Catherine of Aragon

Elizabeth I: b 1533, r 1558–1603, Henry VIII's daughter
      by Anne Boleyn

The House of Stuart:
  *James I: b 1566, r 1603–1625
  Charles I: b 1600, r 1625–1649

SCOTLAND

The House of Bruce:
  Robert I (the Bruce): b 1274, r 1306–1329
  David II: b 1324, r 1329–1371

The House of Stewart:
  Robert II: b 1316, r 1371–1390
  Robert III: b c. 1340, r 1390–1406
  James I: b 1394, r 1406–1437 (murdered)
  James II: b 1430, r 1437–1460 (killed by an exploding cannon)
  James III: b c. 1451, r 1460–1488 (killed in battle)
  James IV: b 1473, r 1488–1513 (killed in battle)
  James V: b 1512, r 1513–1542 (killed in battle)
  Mary Queen of Scots: b 1542, r 1542–1567 (executed)
  *James VI: b 1566, r 1567–1603

* James I of England is the same person as James VI of Scotland

HENRY VIII'S WIVES AND CHILDREN

b = born   m = married   div = divorced   C = Catholic   P = Protestant   ex = executed   d = died

His wives

Katherine of Aragon (C)
    b 1486; m 1509; div 1533; d 1536

Anne Boleyn (P)
    b ~1509; m 1533; ex 1536

Jane Seymour (P)
    b 1506; m 1536; d 1537

Anne of Cleves (P)
    b 1515; m 1540; div 1540; d 1557

Catherine Howard (C)
    b ~ 1522; m 1540; ex 1542

Katherine Parr (P)
    b ~ 1512; m 1543; d 1548

His children

- >   Mary Tudor (Mary I; "Bloody Mary": C)
    b 1516; d 1558

- >   Elizabeth Tudor (Elizabeth I: P)
    b 1533; d 1603

- >   Edward VI (P)
    b 1537; d 1553

Appendix C

Cambridge University

Cambridge University is in Cambridge, England, and consists of thirty-one colleges. Here is a list of the colleges in order from oldest to newest, including the date when they were established. The map shows only the colleges built between 1284 and 1596.

Peterhouse, 1284
Clare College, 1326
Pembroke College, 1347
Gonville & Caius College, 1348
Trinity Hall, 1350
Corpus Christi College, 1352
Magdalene College, 1428
King's College, 1441
Queen's College, 1448
St. Catharine's College, 1473
Jesus College, 1497

Christ's College, 1505
St. John's College, 1511
Trinity College, 1546
Emmanuel College, 1584
Sidney Sussex College, 1596
Downing College, 1800
Girton College, 1869
Newnham College, 1871
Selwyn College, 1882
Hughes Hall, 1885
St. Edmund's College, 1896

New Hall, 1954
Churchill College, 1960
Darwin College, 1964
Clare Hall, 1965
Lucy Cavendish College, 1965
Wolfson College, 1965
Fitzwilliam College, 1966
Homerton College, 1976
Robinson College, 1979

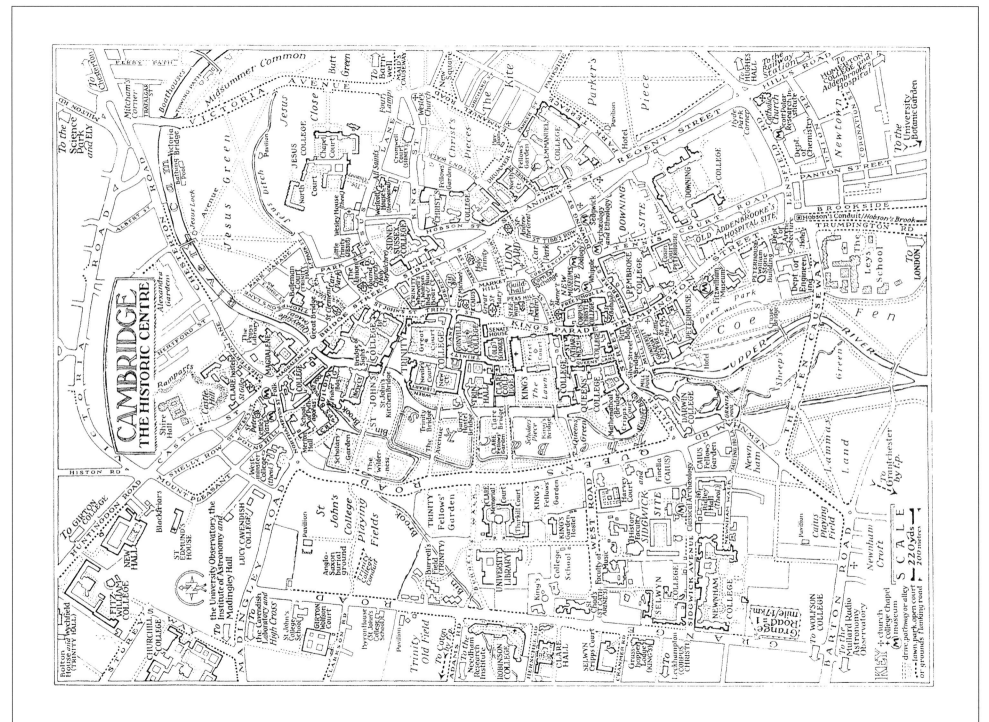

Oxford University

Oxford University is in Oxford, England. It has on its campus forty-five colleges and halls (smaller colleges). Here is a list of the colleges, beginning with the oldest, including the date when each college was established. The map shows only the colleges built between 1249 and 1624.

1. University College, c. 1249
2. Balliol College, c. 1263
3. Merton College, 1264
4. Hertford College, 1282
5. Worcester College, 1283
6. Blackfriars Hall, 13th century
7. Greyfriars Hall, 13th century
8. St. Edmund Hall, 13th century
9. Exeter College, 1314
10. Oriel College, 1326
11. The Queen's College, 1341
12. New College, 1379
13. Lincoln College, 1427
14. All Souls College, 1438
15. Magdalen College, 1458
16. Brasenose College, 1509
17. Corpus Christi College, 1517

18. Christ Church, 1525
19. St. John's College, 1555
20. Trinity College, 1555
21. Jesus College, 1571
22. Wadham College, 1612
23. Pembroke College, 1624
24. Harris Manchester College, 1786
25. Regent's Park College, 1810
26. Mansfield College, 1836
27. Keble College, 1868
28. St. Catherine's College, 1868
29. Wycliffe Hall, 1877
30. Kellogg College, 1878
31. Lady Margaret Hall, 1878
32. Somerville College, 1879
33. St. Anne's College, 1879
34. St. Hugh's College, 1886

35. St. Hilda's College, 1893
36. St. Benet's Hall, 1897
37. St. Peter's College, 1928
38. Nuffield College, 1937
39. Campion Hall, 1940
40. St. Antony's College, 1948
41. Linacre College, 1962
42. St. Cross College, 1965
43. Templeton College, 1965
44. Wolfson College, 1966
45. Green College, 1979

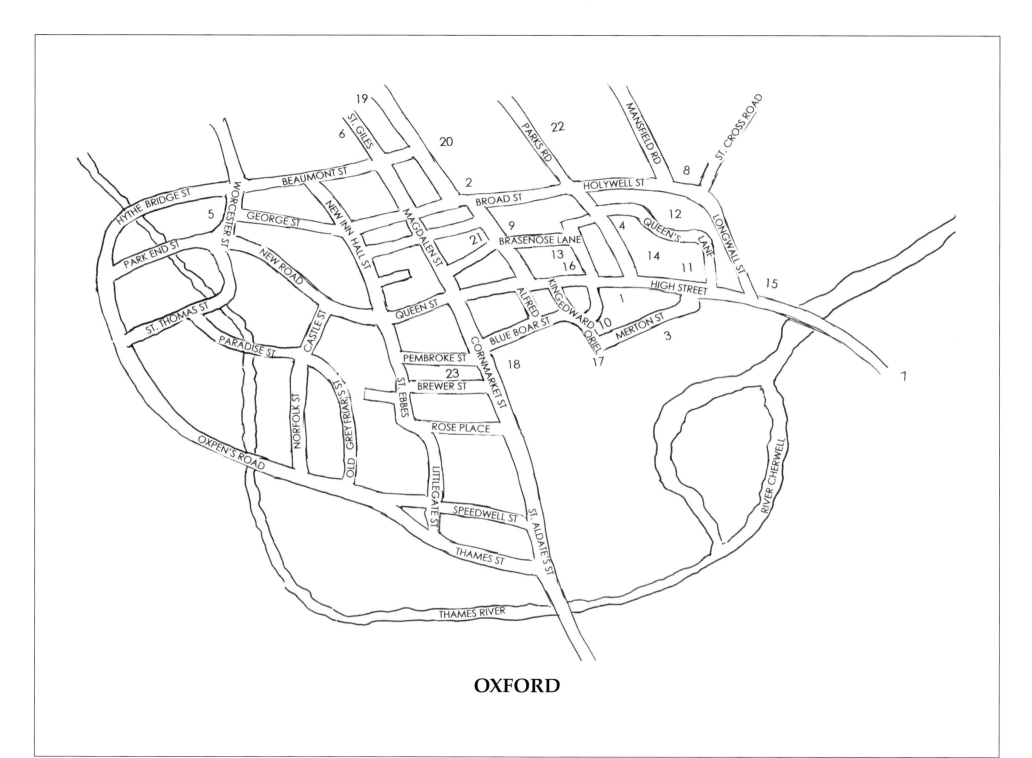

OXFORD

Appendix E

Glossary

Abbey. This word comes from the word *abba* which means "father." An abbey is a home for monks or nuns, who are under the care of an *abbot* (a priest or monk in authority over a group of monks) or an *abbess* (a nun in authority over a group of nuns).

Absolution. Forgiveness. The Roman Catholic priest, as part of the sacrament of penance, gives the confessing person absolution. This means the person is believed to be forgiven by God.

Accursed, Anathema, Anathematized. To be under or be placed under the wrath of God in the form of His curse; opposite of "blessed." Anathema means, "a person or thing under a curse," and when, in the Roman Catholic Church, something (either a person, teaching, or practice) is "anathematized," it is both cursed and condemned. If a person, he or she is consigned to hell; if a teaching or practice, those who adhere to it are likewise cursed and condemned.

Admiral. The top commander of a navy.

Anabaptists. Literally, Anabaptism means "re-baptism." The Anabaptists disagreed with both the Lutheran and the Roman Catholic Churches. They think that infant baptism is unbiblical.

Annul. To undo. For example, if two people have their marriage annulled, it is as though they were never married. Since the Roman Catholic Church believes that marriage is a sacrament, it does not allow divorce in any situation—not even adultery. A marriage may be annulled, if proper reasons are presented to church leaders.

Antichrist. Literally, "against Christ." Some of the Reformers claimed that the pope was antichrist because he claimed to have authority equal to or beyond Scripture.

Archbishop. The highest level of bishop, though he is under the bishop of Rome, that is, the Pope. An archbishop oversees a number of bishops and churches in his area of rule.

Archduke. A rank equal to that of a prince.

Arminianism. The doctrine of Jacob Arminius, which taught that man has a free will to choose good or evil, and so can choose or reject salvation. He rejected the doctrine of election, which teaches that God has graciously chosen from eternity those whom He will save. He also rejected the doctrine of reprobation, which states that God, in choosing the elect, justly rejects others who will go to hell.

Assassination. Murder committed by treachery or undercover means, by secret agents known as assassins.

Assumed name. A name other than your own, used to hide your identity.

Augustinian Order. A type of monastery that aimed to follow the Rule—a set of commands—of Augustine, Bishop of Hippo, who lived from 354–430. After being converted, he left behind his wicked lifestyle, and wrote much on God's saving grace and against sin and its evil effects. At Hippo, he opened the first monastery in North Africa. By the time of the Reformation, the Augustinian Order had become a very strict type of monastery, where the monks tried to live separate from the world in order to please God.

B.A. Bachelor of Arts degree, which indicates a certain level of mastery in a particular course of study, much like a college or university degree today. For instance, a B.A. in Science means that you have studied science and achieved a certain level of knowledge in science at the college or university.

Bailiff. A person who is appointed by a court to help the sheriff in various duties, such as taking care of prisoners, protecting the jury, and maintaining order in the courtroom.

Ban. A term meaning that a person caught in sin is excluded from church and social contact with other believers as a form of discipline.

Banished. Forced to leave; sent away.

Belgic Confession of Faith. Thirty-seven articles of faith, authored by Guido de Brès in 1561. This confession represented a statement of beliefs held in common by the Reformed churches. De Brès wanted to explain to those who persecuted the Protestants that the Reformed faith was according to Scripture and was held dear by law-abiding citizens. This confession was revised and then adopted by the Synod of Dort in 1618–1619 as one of the doctrinal standards of the Reformed churches.

Bishop. The word "bishop" comes from a Greek word meaning "guardian" or "overseer." A bishop is in charge of an area that usually includes a number of churches.

Book of Common Prayer. The book of services and prayers used in the Church of England, it replaced the Roman Catholic service book. Thomas Cranmer helped write this book, and he urged King Edward VI to have it placed in all the churches of England. It was intended to help people learn to pray and to help ministers of the Protestant faith with prayers and services. For instance, there was a certain prayer to pray for the sick, for a wedding, etc.

Burned at the stake. See *stake*.

Canon, Canons. Canon means "a rule." Statements of belief, laws of the church, and rulings on particular points of controversy, when issued by church councils or assemblies, are known as "canons." The Canons of Dort were rulings issued by the Synod that met in the Dutch city of Dordrecht (1618–19) in response to the controversial teachings of Arminianism.

Capital. Wealth in the form of money or property.

Cardinal. A word that means "most important." Cardinals in the Roman Catholic Church are chosen by the pope and fill a very important role in the church. One of their tasks is to choose a new pope when the previous pope dies.

Carmelite Order. A monk or friar belonging to the order of Our Lady of Mount Carmel, founded at Mount Carmel in about 1155.

Catechism. A short book, written in question and answer form, which gives a brief summary of the basic doctrines of Scripture. Many of the Reformers wrote catechisms as a way to instruct people, especially children. See *Heidelberg Catechism.*

Chancellor. Secretary to the king or a nobleman.

Chaplain. A minister or priest who serves in a chapel, or place of worship other than a church. Kings, bishops, and noblemen have such private chapels; private schools, religious colleges, orphanages, and units of the armed forces have both chapels and chaplains.

Clergy. Men who have been ordained to the ministry.

Commerce. The buying and selling of goods.

Communion. The act of partaking of the Lord's Supper, by eating the bread and drinking the wine. "Holy Communion" is another name for the sacrament of the Lord's Supper. The Roman Catholic Church did not allow ordinary Christians to drink the wine. Protestants insisted that Christ commanded all Christians to receive both elements. Roman Catholics hold that the bread and wine are changed into the actual flesh and blood of Christ, whereas Lutherans believe that the bread and wine are joined with the actual flesh and blood of Christ. Calvinists hold that the bread and wine are not changed, but that believers feed upon the heavenly Christ in their hearts, by faith, while eating and drinking the earthly elements.

Confession of Sins, Confessionals. In the Roman Catholic Church, believers are to disclose their personal sins to a priest, who guides them in confessing their sins, offers counsel, and prescribes some kind of penance, or good work to be done to atone for those sins. Roman Catholics must "go to confession" and "do penance" before they are permitted to have communion; booths for this purpose or "confessionals" are placed in Roman Catholic churches.

Confession of Faith. The word "confess" means to "admit" or "to say together." We admit that we have sinned when we confess our sins. When we confess our faith, we declare that we believe what all Christians should believe, in accord with the Bible; and so we "say together" with our fellow believers just what it is that we all believe.

Consecrate. To declare or set apart as sacred; to dedicate to a special service or goal.

Controversy. A dispute, or disagreement.

Convent. A building in which nuns live.

Coronation. The act or ceremony of crowning a king or queen.

Corrupt. Rotten, decayed, polluted, sinful.

Council. A group that meets together, usually to make decisions that impact those whom they represent.

Counselor. An advisor.

Count. In some European countries, a noble whose rank corresponds to that of an earl in Britain.

Court preacher. A preacher hired by the king to preach at the palace chapel.

Dean. A clergyman in the Roman Catholic Church who is in charge of one or more churches.

Debate. To discuss different points of view.

Degree. An academic title given by a college or university to a student who has completed a course of study.

Democracy. Government by the people, usually through elected representatives.

Depose. To remove from office. The pope can appoint a man to an office, and he can depose a man if he feels the man is no longer worthy of his position.

Diet. A meeting attended by royalty and high-ranking clergy, for example, the Diet of Worms, the Diet of Augsburg, and the Diet of Speyer.

Divinity. God. A degree in divinity means that the person studied about God and His doctrines.

Doctor, doctorate. "Teacher." A doctor of theology is a scholar, or minister of the Word, whose ability, learning, and experience are proven to be of the highest order, and so he can teach theology to others; a doctorate is the highest degree granted by a university.

Doctrine. Something that is taught; a principle or system of principles presented for acceptance or belief. The word "doctrine" comes from the Latin word "doctrina" meaning "teaching, learning."

Document. A paper that gives evidence or information.

Dominican Order. Originated from the order of preaching friars established in 1216 by St. Dominic.

Duke. A man who is one of the most important in the nobility. A duke owns land, called a "dukedom" or a "duchy." This title is passed down from father to son. A duke's wife is called a "duchess."

Earl. A British peer next in rank above a viscount and below a marquis.

Economy. The management of the resources of a country.

Edict. An official decree or proclamation; for example, the Edict of Worms.

Edition. A publication printed from a single typesetting. The first time a book is printed is the first edition. Sometimes changes are made, errors removed, or additional copies are needed, and the book is reprinted. This is the second edition. A book can have many editions.

Effigy. A crude image or dummy fashioned in the likeness of a person, often as an expression of mockery or hatred.

Elector. A German prince in the Holy Roman Empire who was entitled to elect the emperor.

Emperor. The ruler of an empire.

Eucharist. "Blessing, Thanksgiving." Another name for the Lord's Supper; see *Communion*. The term refers to the prayers of thanksgiving connected with the Lord's Supper, in which God is praised or "blessed." Sometimes used to refer to the bread and wine, or elements, of the Lord's Supper, because these elements are "blessed" or consecrated for this use. To receive these elements is to receive the "eucharist."

Excommunicated. To be put out of the church. A person who is excommunicated has no rights or privileges in the church anymore. For a Roman Catholic person to be excommunicated means that he is doomed to hell, since he can no longer make atonement in any way for his sins.

Execution. Death at the command of the government (to execute means "to kill"). At the time of the Reformation, death was by means of burning at the stake; the guillotine, which was a large knife; hanging; or by the sword.

Executioner. A person whose job it is to kill those condemned to death by the government.

Exhorter. Someone who *exhorts*. The word "exhort" literally means "to encourage out of." So an exhorter is someone who strongly urges people. Often, an exhorter is someone who is not an ordained minister, but who speaks to people from the Bible about their need for salvation; thus, he exhorts them to be saved.

Expel. To send away.

Fanatic. A person overly enthusiastic and devoted to a religious or political cause.

Fast. To go without food or drink, or to limit eating or drinking, for a period of time, as a form of self-control, or to be more completely devoted to prayer. Roman Catholics are required to fast during the season of Lent, and before they partake of the eucharist.

Fellow. A graduate student appointed to a position of assisting fellow students and of being granted financial aid for a period of research.

Franciscan Order. St. Francis of Assisi (1182–1226) was the founder of the Franciscan order. He served for a time as a soldier, but in 1206, he devoted himself to a life of poverty. He was also known for his love of nature.

Friar. A type of monk who depends on begging to earn his food.

Galley. A large medieval ship that had a single deck, was propelled by sails and oars, and was used as a merchant vessel or warship. Often the men who worked the oars were captured slaves and thus became known as galley slaves.

Heidelberg Catechism. Written by Caspar Olevianus and Zacharias Ursinus, and first published in 1563, the Heidelberg Catechism is one of the three doctrinal standards of the Reformed churches. To encourage its use in preaching, it was divided into fifty-two Lord's Days. It is called the Heidelberg Catechism because it was drafted and first printed in Heidelberg, capital city of the Palatinate. Elector Frederick III was ruler of the Palatinate, and he requested Olevianus and Ursinus to write the catechism in order to further the Reformation.

Helvetic Confession of Faith. Under the teaching of Henry Bullinger, this confession was accepted by the Reformed churches in Switzerland, Germany, Poland, and Hungary. (*Helvetia* is the Latin name for Switzerland.)

Heresy, Heretic. A doctrine that is declared to be false by a church because it does not agree with the official teaching or confession of that church. Anyone who teaches such false doctrines, or who believes them, is a heretic.

Hermit. Someone who has separated himself from other people, often in order to try to please God.

Homily. A sermon.

Huguenot. A French Protestant.

Iconoclasm. The destruction of things held sacred. Someone who participates in this type of destruction is called an iconoclast, which literally means "image-breaker."

Inauguration. A formal beginning or introduction to an office or position of authority. For example, when a minister begins his ministry at a certain location, there is an inauguration service.

Incense. A substance that burns with a pleasant odor.

Indulgence. "The act of giving or granting something." In the Roman Catholic Church, the "gift" or "grant" of the forgiveness of sins, promised to those who perform certain acts of religious worship, or make specified gifts of money to the church.

Infallible. Incapable of error. The Bible is infallible.

Inquisition. This word comes from the word "to inquire," which means "to seek or ask." The Inquisition was a ruling body in the Roman Catholic Church, established for the purpose of rooting out Protestants.

Investment. Money spent in order to gain profit or interest.

Jesuit. A member of the Society of Jesus, a Roman Catholic Order founded by Ignatius Loyola in 1534.

Lady Abbess. An abbess is a nun in charge of an abbey. Charlotte was the daughter of a duke and therefore had the title of "lady." When she became an abbess, this title was added to the title of "abbess."

Lay people or **laity.** (1) A member of a congregation who is not of the clergy; (2) one who does not have special or advanced training or skill; nonprofessional.

Legalism. The doctrine of salvation by works or by works and grace rather than by grace alone.

Lent. The forty days before Easter (beginning on Ash Wednesday), observed as a season of penitence.

M.A. Master of Arts degree. This is an advanced degree that a student pursues after he completes a Bachelor of Arts degree.

Martyr. This word comes from a Greek word meaning "witness." In the history of the church it came to mean a person who is killed for his faith.

Marshal. In some countries, a military officer of the highest rank; a federal officer who carries out court orders.

Mass. The most important worship service of the Roman Catholic Church, conducted on every day of the year except Good Friday. The Roman Catholic Church teaches that in every mass, the communion bread is changed into the actual flesh of Christ, and sacrificed again, to atone for sin. Protestants reject the mass as "an accursed idolatry," because earthly bread is worshipped as a heavenly being; moreover, the mass is not the true sacrament of the Lord's Supper because Christ "offered one sacrifice for sins forever" (Heb. 10:12) when He died on the cross, and so no more sacrifices are needed.

Massacre. The cruel killing of many people at once.

Medieval. Pertaining to the Middle Ages, which was the period in history from approximately 590 to 1517.

Merchant. Someone whose business it is to buy and sell goods.

Monastery. A building in which monks live. The word "monastery" comes from Greek and Latin words which mean "to live alone." Monks spend much time alone to pray, meditate, and fast.

Monk. A man who lives in a monastery. A monk promises (makes a vow) to live a life of poverty, purity, and obedience to God. Monks believe that they can be holier if they live in a monastery, away from the temptations of the world. They are not permitted to marry.

Ninety-five theses. Martin Luther wrote a list of ninety-five statements explaining various errors in the Roman Catholic Church as well as what Scripture stated about these doctrines. He nailed them to the church door in Wittenberg on October 31, 1517.

Nobleman. A man who is of the nobility. The nobility includes such titles as duke, marquis, earl, viscount, and baron.

Nun. A woman who lives in a convent. Just as monks do, nuns promise (make a vow) to live a life of poverty, purity, and obedience to God.

Nunnery. A convent, the building in which nuns live.

Ordain. To bestow with ministerial or priestly authority by virtue of God's authority. For example, a minister may ordain a man into the ministry by the authority of God. This event is called ordination.

Order. A group to which a person belongs. For example, there are different types of monks and nuns. Some are stricter than others. Each convent or monastery belongs to a certain order. Sometimes "order" can mean the office and rank of an ordained minister or priest: the order of priesthood.

Palatinate. Either of two former regions of southwestern Germany.

Papal bull. An official document that comes from the pope, sealed with a special seal.

Papist, papacy. From *papa*, the Latin word for "pope." A papist is someone who follows the pope. Papacy is the term used for the office and rule of the pope in the Roman Catholic Church. Roman Catholics are papists.

Pardon. Forgiveness.

Parish. An area that has its own church.

Parliament. A public assembly in which laws are proposed, debated, and enacted for the nation.

Peasant. A farmer working on land belonging to nobility. Usually peasants were poor people.

Peddler. A person who traveled throughout the country selling things. People living in the country were glad to have the peddler stop by their homes since they lived too far away from the shops in the city.

Penance. A means of making payment for one's sins. If a Roman Catholic person sins, he must be sorry for that sin, confess it to the priest, receive a punishment from the priest, and then be pronounced forgiven. The punishment might be to say the Lord's Prayer a hundred times, to crawl up and down the stairs on one's knees, to fast for three days, or anything the priest might think is appropriate punishment.

Persecute. To oppress or harass with ill-treatment; to subject to severe penalties because of political or religious disagreement.

Philosophy. This word stems from a Greek word meaning "love of wisdom." Philosophy, basically, is the study of why things are the way they are. It is an inquiry or study of things using logic and reasoning rather than using scientific experiments.

Pilgrimage. A journey to a sacred place.

Ploughboy. A farm boy. Boys were often left in charge of guiding the oxen that were used to plow the fields. People who lived on farms were seldom educated in the times of the Reformation.

Politics. Matters related to government and how it functions.

Poor men of Lyons. Men who agreed with Peter Waldo's teachings of poverty. They traveled around the countryside in groups of two, teaching people about the Bible.

Pope. The special title given to the Bishop of Rome as the supreme head of the Roman Catholic Church. At the time of the Reformation, the pope claimed to have authority greater than any other Christian leader in the world, in both church and state. Many of the corrupt teachings and practices of the Roman Catholic Church were connected with the pope and the way he used his authority. The pope also used that authority to oppose the Reformation, and to persecute and condemn Reformed Christians, and to have them put to death by the state.

Presbyterian. A presbyter is an elder. When a church is governed by assemblies of elders, rather than by priests and bishops, it is said to be a Presbyterian church. The Reformer, John Calvin, insisted that the biblical form of church government was Presbyterian, and so the Reformed churches adopted Presbyterian "polity" or government. Calvin's friend and student, John Knox, brought Presbyterianism to the Reformed churches in Great Britain; it was accepted in Scotland, but not in England. In America, churches with a Scottish background are called Presbyterian; churches with a Dutch or German background are called Reformed.

Priest. An ordained clergyman in the Roman Catholic Church. He ranks below a bishop and has authority to pronounce sins forgiven and to administer the sacraments.

Primer (prim-ər). An introductory book.

Procession. A religious parade.

Proclamation. An official declaration.

Professor. A teacher at a university or college.

Protest. To disagree or object. The word "protest" comes from two words meaning "to publicly testify." From this word "protest" comes the word "Protestant," a person who protests against or disagrees with the Roman Catholic Church.

Purgatory. From "purge," meaning "to cleanse." The Roman Catholic Church teaches that when they die, nearly all persons, no matter how truly they believe, or how holy their earthly lives have been, must undergo further cleansing or "purging" before they may enter heaven. The place where they undergo such purging is known as "Purgatory." The Roman Catholic Church also teaches that we who are still alive can help the dead with our prayers and gifts, and shorten the time they must spend in the fires of Purgatory. Along with such prayers and gifts, small candles are lighted before images of deceased saints, seeking their help on behalf of the dead. Priests are paid to say special masses for the dead, and prayers for the dead are said at every mass.

Puritan. From Latin, purus, "pure." The Puritans were English Christians who regarded the Church of England as impure, because its worship and government did not strictly agree with the pattern found in Scripture. They called for the pure preaching of God's Word; for purity of worship, or worshipping God as He commands in His Word, and in no other way; and for purity of church government, replacing the rule of bishops with the Presbyterian government taught in God's Word. They also called for greater purity, or holiness of life, among Christians, in obeying God's Word. The Puritan movement lasted from the late 1500s to the early 1700s. Though despised and often persecuted, the Puritans had a great impact on Britain, the Netherlands, and other parts of the world. Large numbers of Puritans left the mother country to settle in New England and other places in North America. Many of their books are still read and treasured today, because of the depth of knowledge and the spiritual power found in them.

Queen-mother. The widowed mother of the king or queen who is ruling the country.

Recant. To take back something you said you believed was true. Sometimes Protestants "recanted" when they were threatened with torture or death because they were frightened.

Rector. The person in charge of a church, university, or seminary, usually a priest. The rectory is the house in which the rector lives.

Reform. To change; to improve.

Refugees. A person who flees to find **refuge** or safety from oppression or persecution, often to another country.

Relic. Based on an ancient Roman idea that holiness can be contained in physical objects, relics are things the Roman Catholic Church says are holy. A piece of cloth said to be from Peter's coat, some hair said to belong to Mary, a piece of wood said to be from the cross of Christ, or human bones said to belong to one of the apostles are regarded as filled with holiness by Roman Catholic people. Often people make pilgrimages to see the relic because they think that seeing the relic gives them holiness and will lessen their time in purgatory.

Renounce. To give up or reject. A few Protestants "renounced" the Roman Catholic faith.

Repeal. To undo or take back; recant.

Retract. To take back. When Protestants were put on trial, they were often asked to "retract" their words or writings.

Rosary. A rosary is a set of prayer beads joined by a religious medal, with a crucifix attached. Roman Catholics "say the rosary" as an act of devotion, by reciting certain prayers connected with the crucifix, the medal, and each of the beads on the string.

Sacrament. A sign and seal of God's promises of salvation in Jesus Christ to believers. The Roman Catholic Church has seven sacraments: baptism, confirmation, the Eucharist (communion), marriage, holy orders, penance, and the sacrament of the sick (also called "extreme unction" or "the last rites"). The Protestants believe that Jesus Christ instituted only two sacraments: baptism and the Lord's Supper.

Safe conduct. Official promise of protection.

Sancta Scala. Latin words for "holy stairs." These stairs in Rome are said to have been the very stairs that Jesus climbed when He was going from Pilate's judgment hall to Calvary, and that an angel had brought them from Jerusalem to Rome.

Scholar. A student.

Stake. A post. In the time of the Reformation, many people were tied to a post and burned to death.

Summons. A call or order to appear in court.

Superintendent. A person who supervises something.

Superstition. Any religious belief or practice that is false, that is, not taught or commanded in Scripture. The Reformers showed that many Roman Catholic beliefs and practices of worship were only superstition, such as the idea of Purgatory, or that the communion bread and wine can be changed in Christ's body and blood, or that one should pray to the saints for help. Likewise, doing things that are commanded in Scripture, but without true faith in God and His promises, is to do them out of mere superstition. That which is not of faith is sin (Rom. 14:23).

Synod. A council or assembly of churches or church officials.

Theology. The study of God and the doctrines of the Bible. A theologian is someone who studies theology.

Theses. The statements of beliefs or opinions.

Thirty-Nine Articles of Faith. The confession of faith of the Church of England, finalized in 1563.

Tract. A little booklet containing a scriptural message.

Translate. To express in another language.

Transubstantiation. The doctrine that teaches that the bread and wine at the Lord's Supper actually become the body and blood of the Lord Jesus.

Treason. A betrayal of one's country or government.

Tutor. A teacher.

Vatican. The official residence or palace of the pope at Rome. The area around it is known as Vatican City, including St. Peter's Basilica, where the pope officiates as the Bishop of Rome; and the Sistine Chapel, his private place of worship, and the place where new popes are elected.

Vicar. A clergyman.

Wharves. Platforms where ships dock to unload their cargo.

Worship of images and saints. Roman Catholics are taught to pray to idols of the apostles, of Mary, and of other saints, who are believed to speak to God on their behalf.

Appendix F

Study Questions

Chapter 1: Peter Waldo

1. What unexpected event began Waldo's search for God?
2. Why did he sell all his possessions? (See Matthew 6:19–20; 19:21; Luke 12:33–34.) How did that benefit him?
3. What great work did Waldo do?
4. Who were the "poor men of Lyons"?
5. What happened to the Waldensians?
6. Does God expect everyone to sell all that they have? Why or why not? Can rich people be of service to God? How? (See Exodus 35:21–29; 1 Chronicles 29:1–22; Proverbs 11:25; 22:9; Matthew 10:8; Luke 6:38; 2 Corinthians 9:6–7.)
7. How would you react if God asked you to give up your possessions and work for Him?

Chapter 2: John Wycliffe

1. Why did large crowds come to hear Wycliffe preach?
2. Why did Wycliffe criticize the monks and friars?
3. What was the Roman Catholic Church's view on the Lord's Supper?
4. What was Wycliffe's view on the Lord's Supper?
5. What was Wycliffe's great contribution to the Reformation?
6. Who were the Lollards and how did they benefit the Reformation?
7. Wycliffe became less and less popular. Why? (See John 15:18–21; 1 John 3:13.) Are you true to God's Word or do you shy away from its truths? Have you ever had to choose between popularity and God? Was your decision a good one? (See Matthew 10:32–33.)

Chapter 3: Anne of Bohemia, Queen of Richard II

1. How did Anne's early training prepare her to be queen of England?
2. Why was she called "good Queen Anne"? (See 2 Corinthians 9:8; Colossians 1:10.)
3. How did she help Wycliffe?
4. How was she helpful to the Reformation?
5. Why was Richard unhappy even though he was a king? What lesson can we learn from this? (See Proverbs 11:4; 13:7; Zephaniah 1:18; 1 Timothy 6:9–10.)
6. What makes you happy? What makes you unhappy?

Chapter 4: John Huss

1. How did the church react to Huss' preaching?
2. What is a "safe conduct"? Did the pope honor the safe conduct he promised to Huss? Why not?
3. How could Huss be happy when he was treated so badly? (See Psalm 146:5; Proverbs 16:20; Isaiah 61:10; Jeremiah 15:16; Matthew 5:10–12; John 15:11; Acts 5:41; 1 Peter 1:6–9; 4:12–16.)
4. How did Huss benefit the Reformation?
5. What would you do if you were imprisoned and sentenced to death because of your faith?

6. Huss still adhered to some Roman Catholic doctrines. How should we treat Christians who don't always agree with us? How should we treat non-Christians? (See Leviticus 19:17–18; John 15:12, 17; Romans 13:8, 10; Galatians 5:22–26; 1 Thessalonians 3:12; Hebrews 13:1–2; James 3:8–14; 1 John 2:9–11; 4:7–11, 16, 20–21.)

Chapter 5: Martin Luther

1. What two things made Luther change his course of study?
2. How did Luther try to earn God's forgiveness? Why could he find no peace? Have you found peace? (See Isaiah 9:6; 26:3; 48:17–18; Jeremiah 8:11, 15, 21–22; John 14:27; Romans 5:1–2; Ephesians 2.)
3. Why did Luther write ninety-five theses and nail them to the church door?
4. Why was the Roman Catholic Church so determined to stop Luther?
5. How was Luther's "capture" a blessing?
6. How was Katie a blessing to Luther and to others?
7. What negative and positive things can we learn from Luther's strong character?
8. Why is it important to pray for our church leaders? Do you pray for them? (See Romans 15:30–32; Ephesians 6:18–20; Colossians 4:2–4; 1 Thessalonians 5:25; 2 Thessalonians 3:1.)

Chapter 6: Philip Melanchthon

1. How was Melanchthon's character different from Luther's?
2. How was Melanchthon's character a benefit to the Reformation? How was it a hindrance?
3. Why did Luther beseech God to let Melanchthon live?

4. Why was Melanchthon eager to die?
5. What is necessary to die in peace? Would you be glad if you knew you were dying?
6. Is it necessary for Christians to have Christian friends? How does this chapter illustrate this? What kind of friends do you have? (See Psalm 119:63; Proverbs 17:17; 27:17; Ecclesiastes 4:9–10; Acts 2:42; Romans 1:12; Philippians 1:3–5; 2 Timothy 1:16–18.)
7. Is your character more like Luther's or Melanchthon's? What should you pray for in light of this?

Chapter 7: The Protest at Speyer

1. Discuss the purpose of the Diet of Speyer.
2. Why did the German princes protest and what impact did their protest have?
3. What is the Augsburg Confession?
4. How did God bless this confession?
5. In this chapter, we see good coming out of evil. Has God ever brought good in your life out of something that seemed all wrong? Have you thanked Him for it? (See Genesis 50:20; Psalm 76:10; Acts 8:1–4; Romans 9:17.)

Chapter 8: Martin Bucer

1. Whose writings did God use to convert Bucer?
2. How did God use Bucer for the Reformation?
3. Why did some people criticize him?
4. What was Bucer's view of the Lord's Supper and how was it different from Luther's and Zwingli's views?
5. Are you willing to give yourself to God and His service? Has the Holy Spirit renewed your heart? How can children and young people be used in God's service? (See Genesis 22:1–14; Judges 11:36–39; 1 Samuel

3:1; 16:14–23; 17:32–54; 2 Kings 5:2–4; 2 Chronicles 34:1–3; Matthew 19:14; Luke 1:38; John 6:5–13.)

Chapter 9: Ulrich Zwingli

1. What was the focus of Zwingli's preaching?
2. What important errors did Zwingli contradict?
3. What sad incident occurred between Zwingli and Luther? What can we learn from this? (See Romans 15:1–7; 1 Peter 4:8.)
4. Not all God's people are correct on all their beliefs. Does this mean God cannot use them in His kingdom? How do you know this? (See Mark 9:38–42.)

Chapter 10: Heinrich Bullinger

1. In what two ways did God spare Bullinger's life as a child? How did He spare him as an adult?
2. What was Bullinger's character like and how did God use that to further the Reformation?
3. What were some of Bullinger's contributions to the Reformation?
4. What was Bullinger's parting message to his friends and to the pastors and professors?
5. Bullinger was ready to yield to God's will, whether that meant that he lived or died. Are you willing to say, "Thy will be done"? Why is it difficult to truly mean that? (See 1 Samuel 3:18; 2 Samuel 12:23; Job 1:20–22; Matthew 6:10; 26:39, 42; Luke 1:38; Romans 6:13; James 4:7.)

Chapter 11: William Tyndale

1. What was Tyndale's great desire?
2. Why did the Roman Catholic Church not want the people to have the Bible in their own language?

3. Why was Wycliffe's translation no longer used?
4. What great invention aided Tyndale in his work?
5. Why has there always been persecution of God's children? Do you pray for those who are tortured and imprisoned for Christ's sake? (See Genesis 3:15; Deuteronomy 8:2–3; Zechariah 13:9; Malachi 3:3; James 1:2–4; 1 Peter 1:7.)

Chapter 12: King Edward VI

1. Who were some of Prince Edward's teachers?
2. Do godly teachers ensure salvation? Why not? (See Psalm 49:7; Ezekiel 18:20; John 3:3.)
3. How old was Edward when he became king? Would you like to be a king or queen? Why or why not?
4. List three things King Edward did during his reign.
5. Sometimes God does things that we cannot understand. Discuss this in connection with King Edward's early death.
6. Do you always trust God? Do you always believe that what He does is best? Why is it foolish to doubt Him? (See Deuteronomy 32:4; Psalm 18:30.)

Chapter 13: Thomas Cranmer

1. Describe Cranmer's character.
2. How was Cranmer's character a benefit to the Reformation? How was it a hindrance?
3. What sin troubled Cranmer most?
4. It is easy to criticize Cranmer, but think about the circumstances he faced and the consequences for his faith. Would you have dared to stand up to Queen Mary knowing what she was capable of doing?
5. Think of people whom you look down on. In light of this chapter, is God asking you to reconsider your

disdain? Why must we be slow to criticize others, especially God's children? What sin are we guilty of when we look down on others? (See Matthew 7:1–5; Luke 18:11; John 9:41.)

Chapter 14: Hugh Latimer and Nicholas Ridley

1. How was Latimer converted? What does this teach us about reaching others with the gospel? Do you ask God to bless you with opportunities to reach out to others? (See Exodus 4:10–12; Isaiah 50:4; 1 Corinthians 2:12–13.)
2. Why did King Henry respect Latimer?
3. How were Cranmer and Latimer different? How were they similar?
4. Latimer did not flee upon hearing the news that Queen Mary sought his life. Some people agreed with him, but as you read on page 84, some did not. What do you think? Can you think of someone in the Bible who faced a similar situation? (See Acts 21:10–12.)
5. Why did people love Ridley?
6. How could some people rejoice in their suffering and even sing in the flames? (See Habakkuk 3:17–18; Romans 5:3; 2 Corinthians 7:4.)
7. Latimer died quickly but Ridley suffered terribly. Why do you think God allows some of His children to suffer more than others? Would you be willing to suffer like Ridley did? What is needed in order to be victorious? (See Deuteronomy 8:2–3; John 15:2; James 1:2, 4; 1 Peter 1:6–7; also Psalm 124; Isaiah 41:10–14, 17.)

Chapter 15: John Foxe

1. Why did Foxe begin to study the Bible? What was the result?
2. Do you study your Bible? What effect does it have on you? (See Deuteronomy 17:19; Psalm 19:8; 119:9, 105, 130; John 5:39; Romans 15:4; 2 Timothy 3:16; 1 Peter 2:2; also 2 Chronicles 36:16; Isaiah 5:24; Jeremiah 6:10; Zechariah 7:11–12; John 12:48; Hebrews 12:25.)
3. What was Foxe's greatest work? How do you think it was (and still is) a blessing?
4. What else was Foxe known for? How would people characterize you?
5. What can we learn from John Foxe?

Chapter 16: John Knox

1. In what country did Knox work?
2. Why did Knox become discouraged early in life? How did God restore his faith?
3. How was Knox convinced to preach?
4. What interrupted his preaching?
5. How was Knox's strong character a help in his work?
6. Knox feared nothing and no one but God. What and whom do you fear? (Notice the different meanings of *fear*: Job 28:28; Psalm 19:9; 23:4; 27:1; 34:4, 9; 56:3–4; 76:7; Proverbs 8:13; 14:26–27; Isaiah 35:4; Matthew 10:28; 2 Timothy 1:7–8; 1 John 4:18; Revelation 2:10.)

Chapter 17: Guido de Brès

1. Why did de Brès have to use other names and even wear disguises?
2. What was his greatest work?
3. How did the people of his congregation bring trouble upon themselves? When is it good to stand up for your beliefs and when is it best to be silent? Is there always a clear answer? (See Ecclesiastes 3:7; Amos 5:13; also Isaiah 62:6; Matthew 12:16; 16:20; Mark 3:12; 8:30; Acts 4:20; 18:9–10; 2 Timothy 1:7–8; Titus 2:15.)

4. What can we learn from de Brès? How do you spend your free time? In what ways can you improve your use of free time?

5. Some people believe that the only book we need to study is the Bible. Why is it beneficial to study the works of the Reformers and other godly writers alongside the Bible?

Chapter 18: The Heidelberg Catechism

1. What tragedy encouraged Olevianus to enter the ministry?

2. What prompted Ursinus to go to Zurich?

3. How was Frederick led to study the Scriptures? (See Acts 17:11.)

4. Why did Frederick ask Olevianus and Ursinus to write a catechism? Why do you think God's people love the catechism?

5. Why was Frederick called "Frederick the Pious?" Would you be pleased to have a nickname like that? Why or why not? (See Proverbs 20:11.)

Chapter 19: Peter Martyr Vermigli

1. In what country was Vermigli born?

2. Why did the Roman Catholic Church not trust Vermigli?

3. What were some of the sorrows in his life?

4. What was his contribution to the spread of the Reformation?

5. What was important to Vermigli? What is important to you? (See Psalm 2:12; 90:12; 119:139; Ecclesiastes 12:1; Matthew 6:33; Luke 14:18–20; John 3:3; Ephesians 5:16; Hebrews 4:11; 2 Peter 1:10.)

Chapter 20: John Calvin

1. How was Calvin led to realize the Roman Catholic Church was in error?

2. What is the *Institutes of the Christian Religion* and why was it such a help during the Reformation? Why is it still valuable today?

3. How did God use Farel in Calvin's life?

4. Why was it hard for Calvin to return to Geneva?

5. Even today most people think of Calvin as a stern, harsh man. Give some examples that prove otherwise. What was Calvin's goal for the people of Geneva? (See 2 Samuel 7:18; Psalm 8:4; 51:13; Isaiah 66:2; Matthew 8:8; Acts 20:31; Romans 10:1; 1 Timothy 1:15; 5:20; James 4:6.)

6. Calvin did not want his grave to be marked. Why not? What does this teach us?

Chapter 21: Theodore Beza

1. Why did Beza become ill? How did God use this illness for his good?

2. Whom did Beza succeed in Geneva?

3. How did he help the Huguenots? How should we treat strangers? (See Leviticus 19:33–34; Matthew 22:39; John 13:34–35.)

4. The Calvinists and Lutherans disagreed vehemently about the Lord's Supper. Discuss what each of them believed. Do you remember what Zwingli taught about this sacrament? Why is Calvin's and Beza's view more comforting for God's people than Luther's and Zwingli's views?

5. What can we learn from both Calvin's and Beza's tireless zeal for the Lord? (See Jeremiah 20:9; Amos 3:8; Luke 4:43; 8:39; 12:50; John 4:34–38; 9:4; Acts 4:20; 18:5; 20:22, 31; 1 Corinthians 9:16.)

Chapter 22: Jan Łaski

1. Whom did God use to influence young Łaski?
2. Why did he (and many other Reformers) not leave the Roman Catholic Church immediately?
3. What made Łaski finally break with the church?
4. What kind of work did he do in the Netherlands and in England?
5. What tempting offer had Łaski turned down? Who and what must be our guides in making decisions? Are these decisions always easy? Do they always result in wealth and fame? (See Psalm 5:8; 25:4–5, 8–9; 27:11; 48:14; 73:23–24; 143:10; Luke 1:79; John 16:13–15.)

Chapter 23: The Duke of Alva and William, Prince of Orange

1. What kind of a person was the Duke of Alva?
2. What were some of the obstacles William of Orange faced in fighting the Spanish?
3. How did William die?
4. How do Psalms 10 and 79 apply to this chapter?
5. Have you ever experienced God's delivering power in a time of great need? Did it draw you close to God or did you continue unchanged?

Chapter 24: Petrus Dathenus

1. Why did Dathenus flee the monastery?
2. Why did many Calvinists leave Frankfurt? What can we learn from this incident? (See John 13:34–35; 15:8–12; Romans 12:9–10; 13:9–10; 1 Corinthians 13:13; Ephesians 3:17–19; 5:1–2; Colossians 3:14; 1 Peter 1:22; 1 John 4:7–11.)

3. Why did William of Orange imprison Dathenus and later exile him?
4. What was the low point in Dathenus' life?
5. What did Dathenus contribute to the Reformation?
6. What character traits were stumbling blocks for Dathenus? Do you have character traits that lead you into sin, or do you find excuses for your behaviors? Does this drive you to God to seek forgiveness and deliverance? Is one's character ever an excuse for sin? (See Job 9:20; Proverbs 20:9; Ecclesiastes 7:20; Romans 6–7; Ephesians 4:20–24; Philippians 3:8–21; Hebrews 12:1–4.)

Chapter 25: Queen Marguerite of Navarre

1. Who was Marguerite's brother? Even though he was a Roman Catholic, how did he benefit the Protestants?
2. Why was the church offended by Marguerite's writings?
3. How did her brother want to defend Marguerite against King Henry?
4. How was King Henry converted?
5. What makes a happy marriage? If you are not married, do you ask the Lord to show you His will for your life, whether it is to be married to the person of His choosing, or to serve Him as a single person? If you are married, do you pray for your spouse? Do you set a godly example? Do you encourage your spouse to walk in God's ways? Are you a hindrance to your spouse or a blessing? (See Proverbs 31:10–31; 2 Corinthians 6:14–18; Ephesians 5:20–33; Colossians 3:18–19; 1 Peter 3:1–7.)

Chapter 26: Queen Jeanne d'Albret of Navarre

1. Was Jeanne right in protesting her marriage to the Duke of Cleves? Should she have meekly accepted

her parents' decision? When is it right to disobey one's parents? (See Deuteronomy 5:16; Proverbs 1:8; 23:22; Daniel 1:8; Luke 2:49–51; 2 Corinthians 6:14; Ephesians 6:1–4; Colossians 3:20–21.)

2. Why did Catherine de Medici want to separate Jeanne and her husband, Antoine? Was she successful?

3. What brave act did Jeanne perform? How did God help her?

4. Why did the pope issue a papal bull against her?

5. Whom did she rescue? Why did she do this?

6. Why did Jeanne join in the fight alongside the French Huguenots?

7. What other things did she do for the Reformation?

8. What lessons can you learn from Queen Jeanne? (See Exodus 14:13–14; Deuteronomy 31:6; 2 Chronicles 16:9; 32:7–8; Psalm 3; 27:1–3, 5–6, 12–14; 34:4–8; 91; 125:1–2; Proverbs 29:25.)

Chapter 27: Admiral Coligny and the Tragedy of St. Bartholomew's Day

1. Who were the Huguenots?

2. Who was Admiral Gaspard de Coligny?

3. What was the plan for the massacre?

4. What effect did it have on King Charles IX?

5. How did it seem that Satan was victorious? (Think back to Psalms 10 and 79 that you reflected on for Chapter 23, Study Question 4.) Can you think of other times in the Bible or in history when Satan seemed victorious?

6. How did God bring good out of this horrific event?

7. What would you say to people who claim to be atheists because they cannot believe a God of love would allow such awful things? (See Deuteronomy 29:29; Job 5:9; 11:6–8; Jeremiah 12:1; John 13:7; Romans 11:33–36; 1 Corinthians 2:16.)

8. This is a difficult question: would you say that God *planned* the St. Bartholomew's Day massacre or simply *allowed* it? (See Job 9:10, 12; Psalm 18:30; Isaiah 40:12–28; 45:7; 55:8–9; Daniel 12:8–9; Amos 3:6; Matthew 18:7; Hebrews 11:1; Revelation 15:3.)

Chapter 28: Charlotte, the Nun of Jouarre

1. What sad decision did Charlotte's father make?

2. What did God use to convert Charlotte?

3. How did Charlotte and the other nuns escape the convent?

4. Why was her father angry with her? Why did he approve of her marriage to William?

5. Compare Charlotte's life with Joseph's. What are the similarities? (See Genesis 50:20; Psalm 126:3; 146:9.)

6. What can you learn from Charlotte's life? (See Genesis 18:14; Psalm 27:10; 68:5–6; 127:3–4; Jeremiah 32:17, 27; 49:11; Joel 2:22, 25–27.)

Chapter 29: William Perkins

1. How was Perkins converted?

2. What was unique about his preaching?

3. What did Perkins mean by "inward cleansing"? Why is this necessary? Have you been inwardly cleansed by the Holy Spirit? (Psalm 19:12; Psalm 51; Isaiah 1:16; Ezekiel 36:25–27; Zechariah 3; Mark 7:14–23; 1 Corinthians 6:11; 2 Corinthians 7:1; Ephesians 5:25–27; Hebrews 9:14; James 4:8; 1 Peter 1:2.)

4. Why was Perkins called "the father of Puritanism"?

Chapter 30: William Ames

1. What was the Edict of Tolerance and how did it affect the Puritans?
2. Why were Ames's degrees suspended by Cambridge University?
3. What is Arminianism? Why did Ames oppose it? Is this error still prevalent today? Why do you think it appeals to people? (Genesis 6:5; Psalm 53:1–3; Isaiah 53:6; 64:6–7; Jeremiah 10:23; Ephesians 2:8–9.)
4. What does TULIP stand for?
5. What was Ames's (like other Puritans') main focus in his teachings and writings? Why was it so important to him? Is it important to you? Why or why not?
6. Why is it important to "watch and pray" regarding sound doctrine? Do you think you are correct in all your beliefs? (See Proverbs 28:26; John 3:27; 6:44; 15:5; 1 Corinthians 10:12; 16:13; Ephesians 4:14; Colossians 4:2; 1 Thessalonians 5:21; Hebrews 10:23; 13:9–10; 1 Peter 5:8.)

Chapter 31: Willem Teellinck

1. Why did the Puritans live strict, simple lives?
2. What did Teellinck stress in his preaching?
3. Why did people become frustrated with Teellinck and other Puritans?
4. How is Teellinck's message relevant to us?
5. Do you strive for holiness? Are there things (or even people) that interfere with your relationship with the Lord? Do you have a relationship with the Lord? If not, are there actions you can take to make use of the means of grace? (See 2 Chronicles 7:14; Hosea 14:1–3; Joel 2:12–14; Luke 11:9.)

Chapter 32: The Anabaptists

1. What did the Anabaptists believe about baptism? How was that different from the Roman Catholic Church's and the Reformers' views?
2. What did the Anabaptists believe about the Lord's Supper? How was that different from the Roman Catholic Church's and the Reformers' views?
3. What were some of their other teachings? Why do you think people found some of these teachings appealing?
4. Several Anabaptists held very radical beliefs. How did this come about, that is, what common errors did these people make? How can we keep ourselves from straying from the truth? Why must we always be on our guard? (See Matthew 22:29; Mark 13:33–37; Luke 12:35–40; 21:36; John 7:16–18, 8:31, 32; Acts 17:11; 20:28–31; 1 Corinthians 16:13; Ephesians 6:18; 1 Thessalonians 5:21; Hebrews 13:9; 1 Peter 4:7; 1 John 4:1–3.)
5. Many Anabaptists died for their faith. Do all people who die for their faith go to heaven? What does this teach us? (See Psalm 51:16–17; Hosea 6:6; John 17:3; 1 Corinthians 13:3).

Chapter 33: The Counter Reformation

1. What was the Counter Reformation? What kind of "reforms" or changes did the Roman Catholic Church make? Was this sufficient for salvation?
2. What was the Inquisition? Why is it most often connected to Spain?
3. What were some of the decisions made at the Council of Trent?
4. How did Loyola try to find peace? What did he not understand? Compare him to Martin Luther. Have

you been justified by faith in Jesus Christ? (See Romans 1:17; 5:1; Philippians 3:9; Hebrews 11:6.)

5. Who are the Jesuits? What "good things" did they do? People often say that someone is a "good person." How does God judge people? (See 1 Samuel 16:7; Psalm 14:1–3; Matthew 7:21–23; 19:16–17, 23:23–27; Romans 3:20; also Galatians 5:22–23; Ephesians 2:8–10; Titus 3:5.)

Chapter 34: The Influence of the Reformation

1. Why did the Reformers desire education for all people? How does your education benefit you? Who is the perfect Teacher? (See John 14:26.)

2. In medieval times (and throughout much of history) government was set up with one person being the sole ruler; for example, a king, the pope, a lord, etc. In some passages, the Bible seems to encourage this. (See Ecclesiastes 8:2; Romans 13:1–7; Ephesians 6:5–8; 1 Peter 2:13–18.) Compare this with other passages of Scripture. (See Deuteronomy 27:19; 2 Chronicles 19:6; Nehemiah 5; Proverbs 16:12; Isaiah 1:23; 3:14–15; 10:1–2; 33:15; Ezekiel 22:25–29; Ephesians 6:9.) What is the godly balance? Why is this rare? Why did the Reformers promote democracy? Why is it good to be surrounded with godly counselors? (See Proverbs 11:14; 12:15; 15:22; 24:6.)

3. Throughout history, the rich upper class did no physical labor. What danger is there in not working? (See Proverbs 18:9; 2 Thessalonians 3:10–12.) What was the Puritan view on work? What is the blessing of work? (See Genesis 3:19; Leviticus 23:3; Proverbs 12:11; 14:23; 20:13; 31:13–31; Ecclesiastes 9:10; Romans 12:11; Ephesians 4:28; 1 Thessalonians 4:11–12.)

4. What are the five *solas* of the Reformation?

5. List ways your life has been affected by the Reformation. Imagine what your life would be like had the Reformation never taken place. What are you most thankful for?

Selected English Bibliography

This selected bibliography begins with a sampling of books on the Reformation as a whole, and then follows the order of the chapters of this book. The bibliography includes books written for adults as well as for older children and teens, so that parents can pursue further studies with their children. Books of a highly academic nature are often not included. Only a small sampling of books can be given for major Reformers like Luther and Calvin.

The Reformation

Alexander, J. H. *Ladies of the Reformation: Short Biographies of Distinguished Ladies of the Sixteenth Century.* Harpenden, U.K.: Gospel Standard Strict Baptist Trust, 1978.

Anderson, James. *Ladies of the Reformation, Memoirs of Distinguished Female Characters, Belonging to the Period of the Reformation in the Sixteenth Century.... England, Scotland, and the Netherlands.* London: Blackie and Son, 1855.

Anecdotes of Luther and the Reformation. London: Hodder and Stoughton, 1883.

Bagchi, David V. N., and David Curtis Steinmetz. *The Cambridge Companion to Reformation Theology.* Cambridge: Cambridge University Press, 2004.

Bainton, Roland Herbert. *The Age of the Reformation.* Princeton, N.J.: Van Nostrand, 1956.

———. *The Reformation of the Sixteenth Century.* Boston, Mass.: Beacon Press, 1952.

Barker, William Pierson. *Who's Who in Church History.* Old Tappan, N.J.: F. H. Revell Co., 1969.

Beckett, W. H. *The English Reformation of the Sixteenth Century: With Chapters on Monastic England and the Wycliffite Reformation.* London: Religious Tract Society, 1890.

Belloc, Hilaire. *How the Reformation Happened.* Whitefish, Mont.: Kessinger, 2003.

———. *Characters of the Reformation.* New York: Image Books, 1958.

Benedict, Philip. *Christ's Churches Purely Reformed: A Social History of Calvinism.* New Haven, Conn.: Yale University Press, 2002.

Bennink, B. J. *Sketches from Church History: A Supplementary Reader for History Classes in Christian Schools.* Grand Rapids: Eerdmans, 1926.

Bergin, Thomas Goddard, and Jennifer Speake. *Encyclopedia of the Renaissance and the Reformation.* New York: Facts On File, 2004.

Cameron, Euan. *The European Reformation.* Oxford: Clarendon Press, 1991.

Catherwood, Christopher. *Five Leading Reformers.* Fearn: Christian Focus, 2000.

Chadwick, Owen. *The Early Reformation on the Continent.* Oxford: Oxford University Press, 2001.

———. *The Reformation.* Baltimore, Md.: Penguin Books, 1964.

Characters, Scenes, and Incidents of the Reformation; From the Rise of the Culdees to the Close of the Sixteenth Century. London: The Religious Tract Society, 1874.

Chaunu, Pierre. *The Reformation.* New York: St. Martin's Press, 1990.

Collinson, Patrick. *The Reformation: A History.* New York: Modern Library, 2004.

Cross, F. L. and E. A. Livingstone. *The Oxford Dictionary of the Christian Church.* Oxford: Oxford University Press, 2005.

Crosse, Gordon. *A Short History of the English Reformation.* New York: Morehouse Gorham Co., 1950.

Crosse, J. H. *Historical Tales for Young Protestants.* London: Religious Tract Society, 1857.

The Days of Queen Mary; or, Annals of Her Reign; Containing Particulars of the Restoration of Romanism and the Sufferings of the Martyrs, During That Period. London: The Religious Tract Society, 1826.

DeMolen, Richard L. *Leaders of the Reformation.* Selinsgrove, Pa.: Susquehanna University Press, 1984.

Dickens, Geoffrey, John Tonkin, and Kenneth Powell. *The Reformation in Historical Thought.* Cambridge, Mass.: Harvard University Press, 1985.

Duke, A. C. *Reformation and Revolt in the Low Countries.* London: Hambledon and London, 2003.

Eisenstein, Elizabeth L. *The Printing Revolution in Early Modern Europe.* Cambridge: Cambridge University Press, 1983.

Fuller, Thomas. *Abel Redevivus: Or, the Dead yet Speaking. The Lives and Deaths of the Moderne Divines.* London: Printed by Tho. Brudenell for John Stafford, 1651.

Ganzer, Klaus, and Bruno Steimer. *Dictionary of the Reformation.* New York: Crossroad Publishing Co., 2004.

Gerrish, B. A. *Reformers in Profile.* Eugene, Oreg.: Wipf & Stock, 2004.

Godfrey, W. Robert. *Reformation Sketches: Insights into Luther, Calvin, and the Confessions.* Phillipsburg, N.J.: P&R Publishing, 2003.

Good, James I. *Women of the Reformed Church.* Philadelphia: Sunday-School Board of the Reformed Church in the United States, 1901.

Gray, Madeleine. *The Protestant Reformation: Belief, Practice, and Tradition.* Brighton, U.K.: Sussex Academic Press, 2003.

Hagstotz, Gideon David. *Heroes of the Reformation.* Mountain View, Calif.: Pacific Press Publishing Association, 1951.

Hannah, John D. *Charts of Reformation and Enlightenment Church History.* Grand Rapids: Zondervan, 2004.

Hillerbrand, Hans Joachim. *The Oxford Encyclopedia of the Reformation.* Oxford: Oxford University Press, 1996.

———. *The Protestant Reformation.* New York: Harper Perennial, 2007.

———. *The Reformation: A Narrative History Related by Contemporary Observers and Participants.* Grand Rapids: Baker Book House, 1987.

———. *The World of the Reformation.* New York: Scribner, 1973.

Historical Tales for Young Protestants. Philadelphia: Presbyterian Board of Publications, n.d.

Holt, Mack P. *Renaissance and Reformation France, 1500–1648.* Oxford: Oxford University Press, 2002.

Houghton, S. M., and B. J. Bennink. *Sketches from Church History.* Carlisle, Pa.: Banner of Truth Trust, 1980.

Jackson, Samuel Macauley, and Lefferts Augustine Loetscher, ed. *The New Schaff-Herzog Encyclopedia of Religious Knowledge.* 15 vols. Grand Rapids: Baker Book House, 1955.

Kidder, Daniel and Thomas Summers. *Characters, Scenes, and Incidents, of the Reformation.* London: Religious Tract Society, 1850.

Kuiper, B. K. *The Church in History.* Grand Rapids: Eerdmans, 1951.

Lambert, Malcolm. *Medieval Heresy: Popular Movements from the Gregorian Reform to the Reformation.* Oxford, U.K.: Blackwell Publishers, 2002.

Levi, Anthony. *Renaissance and Reformation: The Intellectual Genesis.* New Haven, Conn.: Yale University Press, 2002.

Lindberg, Carter. *The European Reformations.* Cambridge, Mass.: Blackwell Publishers, 1996.

———. *The European Reformations Sourcebook.* Oxford, U.K.: Blackwell Publishers, 2000.

———. *The Reformation Theologians: An Introduction to Theology in the Early Modern Period.* Oxford: Blackwell Publishers, 2002.

Loetscher, Lefferts Augustine. *Twentieth Century Encyclopedia of Religious Knowledge: An Extension of the New Schaff-Herzog Encyclopedia of Religious Knowledge.* 2 vols. Grand Rapids: Baker Book House, 1955.

Longford, Elizabeth, ed. *The Oxford Book of Royal Anecdotes.* Oxford: Oxford University Press, 1989.

Lucas, Henry Stephen. *The Renaissance and the Reformation.* New York: Harper & Row, 1960.

MacCulloch, Diarmaid. *Reformation: Europe's House Divided, 1490–1700.* London: Allen Lane, 2003.

———. *The Reformation.* New York: Viking Press, 2004.

Macdonald, Fiona. *The Reformation.* Austin, Tex.: Raintree Steck-Vaughn, 2003.

Maltby, William S. *Reformation Europe: A Guide to Research.* St. Louis: Center for Reformation Research, 1992.

Mansfield, Bruce. *Man on His Own: Interpretations of Erasmus, c. 1750–1920.* Toronto, Ont.: University of Toronto Press, 1992.

———. *Phoenix of His Age: Interpretations of Erasmus c. 1550–1750.* Toronto, Ont.: University of Toronto Press, 1979.

Marshall, Peter, and Alec Ryrie. *The Beginnings of English Protestantism.* Cambridge: Cambridge University Press, 2002.

Matthew, H. C. G., and Brian Howard Harrison, eds. *Oxford Dictionary of National Biography: In Association with the British Academy: from the Earliest Times to the Year 2000.* 60 vols. Oxford: Oxford University Press, 2004.

McGrath, Alister E. *In the Beginning: The Story of the King James Bible and How It Changed a Nation, a Language, and a Culture.* New York: Anchor Books, 2002.

———. *The Intellectual Origins of the European Reformation.* Malden, Mass.: Blackwell Publishers, 2004.

McManners, John. *The Oxford Illustrated History of Christianity.* Oxford: Oxford University Press, 1990.

Merle d'Aubigné. *The Reformation in England.* 2 vols. London: Banner of Truth Trust, 1962.

Middleton, Erasmus. *Evangelical Biography; or, An Historical Account of the Lives and Deaths of the Most Eminent and Evangelical Authors or Preachers, Both British and Foreign, in the Several Denominations of Protestants, from the Beginning of the Reformation to the Present Time.* 4 vols. London: W. Baynes, 1816.

Naphy, William G. *Documents on the Continental Reformation.* New York: St. Martin's Press, 1996.

Newton, Richard. *Heroes of the Reformation.* Philadelphia: American Sunday School Union, 1897.

Oaks, Sarah, and Tom Waldecker. *Heroes of the Reformation.* Tucker, Ga.: Children's Ministry International, 2005.

Oberman, Heiko Augustinus. *Forerunners of the Reformation: The Shape of Late Medieval Thought.* New York: Holt, Rinehart and Winston, 1966.

O'Day, Rosemary. *The Debate on the English Reformation.* London: Methuen, 1986.

100 Portretten van Godgeleerden in Nederland uit de 16e, 17e, 18e Eeuw. Utrecht: DenHertog, 1982.

The Oxford Book of Royal Anecdotes, ed. Elizabeth Longford. Oxford: Oxford University Press, 1989.

Ozment, Steven E. *Reformation Europe: A Guide to Research.* St. Louis: Center for Reformation Research, 1982.

———. *The Age of Reform (1250–1550): An Intellectual and Religion History of Late Medieval and Reformation Europe.* New Haven, Conn.: Yale University Press, 1980.

Parish, Helen L., and William G. Naphy. *Religion and Superstition in Reformation Europe.* Manchester: Manchester University Press, 2002.

Pettegree, Andrew. *The Early Reformation in Europe.* Cambridge: Cambridge University Press, 1992.

———. *The Reformation World.* London: Routledge, 2000.

Reardon, Bernard M. G. *Religious Thought in the Reformation.* London: Longman, 1981.

Rublack, Ulinka. *Reformation Europe.* Cambridge: Cambridge University Press, 2005.

Saari, Peggy, Aaron Maurice Saari, and Julie Carnagie. *Renaissance & Reformation.* Detroit: UXL, 2002.

Schaff, Philip. *History of the Christian Church.* 8 vols. Peabody, Mass: Hendrickson Publishers, 1996.

Schwiebert, Ernest G. *The Reformation.* Minneapolis, Minn.: Fortress Press, 1996.

Scribner, R. W. *The German Reformation.* London: Macmillan, 1986.

A Short History of the Reformation. London: The Protestant Truth Society, 1965.

Spalding, M. J. *The History of the Protestant Reformation: In Germany and Switzerland and in England, Ireland, Scotland, the Netherlands, France, and Northern Europe.* Whitefish, Mont.: Kessinger, 2003.

Spitz, Lewis William. *The Protestant Reformation, 1517–1559.* New York, N.Y.: Harper & Row, 1985.

———. *The Reformation: Basic Interpretations. Problems in European civilization.* Lexington, Mass.: Heath, 1972.

Stokes, George. *Lives of the British Reformers. From Wickliff to Foxe.* London: Religious Tract Society, 1873.

Strauss, Gerald. *Law, Resistance, and the State: The Opposition to Roman Law in Reformation Germany.* Princeton, N.J.: Princeton University Press, 1986.

Thompson, Stephen P. *The Reformation.* San Diego, Calif.: Greenhaven Press, 1999.

Vance, Laurence M. *A Brief History of English Bible Translations.* Pensacola, Fla.: Vance Publications, 1993.

Vreugdenhil, John. *God's Care and Continuance of His Church: Church History Told to Young and Old.* 3 vols. Grand Rapids: Netherlands Reformed Publishing, 1999.

Wabuda, Susan. *Preaching During the English Reformation.* Cambridge: Cambridge University Press, 2002.

Wallace, Peter George. *The Long European Reformation: Religion, Political Conflict, and the Search for Conformity, 1350-1750.* Houndmills, U.K.: Palgrave Macmillan, 2004.

Withrow, W. H. *Beacon Lights of the Reformation.* Toronto, Ont.: W. Briggs, 1899.

Wylie, J. A. *The History of Protestantism.* London: Cassell, Petter & Galpin, 1899.

Peter Waldo

Abella, Gilberto V. "The Waldenses and the Reformation." M.A. Thesis, Loma Linda University, 1982.

Audisio, Gabriel. *Preachers by Night: The Waldensian Barbes, 15th–16th Centuries.* Leiden: Brill, 2007.

———. *The Waldensian Dissent: Persecution and Survival, c. 1170–c. 1570.* Cambridge: Cambridge University Press, 1999.

Biller, Peter. *The Waldenses, 1170–1530: Between a Religious Order and a Church.* Aldershot, U.K.: Ashgate, 2001.

Cameron, Euan. *Waldenses: Rejections of Holy Church in Medieval Europe.* Oxford: Blackwell Publishers, 2000.

———. *The Reformation of the Heretics: The Waldenses of the Alps, 1480–1580.* Oxford: Clarendon Press, 1984.

Evans, G. R. *The Medieval Theologians.* Oxford: Blackwell Publishers, 2001.

Goodich, Michael. *Other Middle Ages: Witnesses at the Margins of Medieval Society.* Philadelphia, Pa.: University of Pennsylvania Press, 1998.

Kaelber, Lutz. *Schools of Asceticism: Ideology and Organization in Medieval Religious Communities.* University Park, Pa.: Pennsylvania State University Press, 1998.

Stephens, Prescot. *The Waldensian Story: A Study in Faith, Intolerance and Survival.* Lewes, U.K.: Book Guild, 1998.

Stevens, R. M. *Never Failing Light: The Waldensian Story.* Torre Pellice, Libreria Editrice Claudiana, 1957.

Tourn, Giorgio, et al. *You Are My Witnesses: The Waldensians Across 800 Years.* Torino: Claudiana, 1989.

Wakefield, Walter L., and Austin P. Evans. *Heresies of the High Middle Ages.* New York: Columbia University Press, 1991.

Worsfold, J. N., and B. Tron. *Peter Waldo: The Reformer of Lyons: His Life and Labours.* London: John F. Shaw, 1880.

Wylie, J. A. *The Story of the Waldenses.* Altamont, Tenn.: Pilgrim Books, 1995.

John Wycliffe

Bobrick, Benson. *Wide As the Waters: The Story of the English Bible and the Revolution It Inspired.* New York: Simon & Schuster, 2001.

Caughey, Ellen W. *John Wycliffe: Herald of the Reformation.* Ulrichsville, Ohio: Barbour Publishing, 2001.

Evans, G. R. *John Wyclif: Myth & Reality.* Downers Grove, Ill.: IVP Academic, 2005.

Fountain, David G. *John Wycliffe: The Dawn of the Reformation.* Southampton: Mayflower Christian, 1984.

Hammond, Rebecca. *John Wycliffe: Man of Courage.* Greenville, S.C.: Ambassador Emerald International, 2004.

Hayes, Alan Lauffer, Reginald Stackhouse, and Maurice P. Wilkinson. *A New Introduction to John Wycliffe.* Toronto, Ont.: Wycliffe College, 1994.

Hudson, Anne, and Michael Wilks. *From Ockham to Wyclif.* Oxford: for the Ecclesiastical History Society by B. Blackwell, 1987.

Kenny, Anthony John Patrick. *Wyclif in His Times.* Oxford: Clarendon Press, 1986.

Levy, Ian Christopher. *A Companion to John Wyclif: Late Medieval Theologian*. Leiden: Brill, 2006.

Long, John Douglas. *The Bible in English: John Wycliffe and William Tyndale*. Lanham, Md.: University Press of America, 1998.

Marshall, William. *Wycliffe and the Lollards*. Edinburgh: Oliphant, Anderson, & Ferrier, 1884.

Parker, G. H. W. *The Morning Star: Wycliffe and the Dawn of the Reformation*. Grand Rapids: Eerdmans, 1966.

Richardson, David. *John Wycliffe: The First Reformer?* Belfast: GOLI Publications, 1996.

Robertson, Edwin. *John Wycliffe: Morning Star of the Reformation*. Basingstoke, U.K.: Marshall, 1984.

Somerset, Fiona, Jill C. Havens, and Derrick G. Pitard. *Lollards and Their Influence in Late Medieval England*. Woodbridge, U.K.: Boydell Press, 2003.

Stewart, Clara H. *John Wycliffe's Lengthening Shadow: Roots of the English Evangelical Heritage (1385–1536)*. Wilmore, Ky.: Francis Asbury Society, 2004.

Wood, Douglas C. *The Evangelical Doctor: John Wycliffe and the Lollards*. Welwyn, U.K.: Evangelical Press, 1984.

Anne of Bohemia

Opfell, Olga S. *Queens, Empresses, Grand Duchesses, and Regents: Women Rulers of Europe, A.D. 1328–1989*. Jefferson, N.C.: McFarland, 1989.

Wilson, Katharina M., and Nadia Margolis. *Women in the Middle Ages: An Encyclopedia*. Westport, Conn.: Greenwood Press, 2004.

John Huss

Bracciolini, Poggio. *The Trial and Burning of John Huss: An Eye-Witness Account*. Toronto, Ont.: Wittenburg Publications, 1991.

Fudge, Thomas A. "Myth, Heresy and Propaganda in the Radical Hussite Movement, 1409–1437." Ph.D. diss., University of Cambridge, 1992.

Gillett, E. H. *The Life and Times of John Huss: Or, The Bohemian Reformation of the Fifteenth Century*. New York: AMS Press, 1978.

Grier, Rev. W. J. *Hus and Farel: Heroic Pioneers of the Reformation*. Annual Lecture of the Evangelical Library, 1965.

Hus, Jan. *The Letters of John Hus*. Translated by Matthew Spinka. Manchester: Manchester University Press, 1972.

Lindsay, Gordon. *Men Who Changed the World. The Reformers—Wycliffe, Hus, Savonarola, Knox*. Vol. 2. Dallas, Tex.: Christ for the Nations, 1992.

Mladenovic, Peter. *John Hus at the Council of Constance*. Translated by Matthew Spinka. New York: Columbia University Press, 1966.

Neilson, G. A. *Twelve Reformation Heroes*. London: Pickering & Inglis, 1960.

Poggius, Fra. *The Trial and Burning of John Huss! An Eye-Witness Account by Fra Poggius, Member of the Council of Constance, Taken from: The Lives of the Principal Reformers (1360–1600) by Richard Rolt, 1759*. Toronto: Wittenburg Publications, 1991.

Rabb, Theodore K. *Renaissance Lives: Portraits of an Age*. New York: Pantheon Books, 1993.

Spinka, Matthew. *John Hus, a Biography*. Westport, Conn.: Greenwood Press, 1979.

———. *John Hus' Concept of the Church*. Princeton, N.J.: Princeton University Press, 1966.

Withrow, Mindy, and Brandon Withrow. *Monks and Mystics: Chronicles of the Medieval Church*. Fearn, Scotland: Christian Focus, 2005.

Zeman, Jarold Knox. *The Hussite Movement and the Reformation in Bohemia, Moravia, and Slovakia (1350–1650): A Bibliographical Study Guide (with Particular Reference to Resources in North America)*. Ann Arbor, Mich.: Michigan Slavic Publications, 1977.

Martin Luther

Althaus, Paul. *The Ethics of Martin Luther*. Philadelphia, Pa.: Fortress Press, 1972.

———. *The Theology of Martin Luther*. Philadelphia, Pa.: Fortress Press, 1966.

Bainton, Roland Herbert. *Here I Stand: A Life of Martin Luther*. Nashville, Tenn.: Abingdon Press, 1990.

Bornkamm, Heinrich, and Karin Bornkamm. *Luther in Mid-Career, 1521–1530*. Philadelphia, Pa.: Fortress Press, 1983.

Brecht, Martin. *Martin Luther*. Minneapolis, Minn.: Fortress Press, 1985.

Ebeling, Gerhard. *Luther: An Introduction to His Thought*. Philadelphia, Pa.: Fortress Press, 1970.

Gritsch, Eric W. *Martin—God's Court Jester: Luther in Retrospect*. Philadelphia, Pa.: Fortress Press, 1983.

Kittelson, James M. *Luther the Reformer: The Story of the Man and His Career*. Minneapolis: Augsburg Publishing House, 1986.

Lehmann, Hartmut. *Martin Luther in the American Imagination*. München: W. Fink, 1988.

Lohse, Bernhard. *Martin Luther: An Introduction to His Life and Work*. Philadelphia, Pa.: Fortress Press, 1986.

Macaulay. *Luther Anecdotes: Memorable Sayings and Doings of Martin Luther, Gathered from his Books, Letters, and History; and Illustrating his Life and Work*. London: The Religious Tract Society, n.d.

MacCuish, Dolina. *Luther and His Katie*. Fearn, Scotland: Christian Focus Publications, 1983.

Manns, Peter. *Martin Luther: An Illustrated Biography*. New York: Crossroad, 1982.

Oberman, Heiko A. *Luther: Man between God and the Devil*. London: Fontana, 1993.

Pelikan, Jaroslav and Helmut T. Lehman, eds. *Luther's Works*. St. Louis, Mo.: Concordia, 1955.

Todd, John Murray. *Luther: A Life*. London: Hamilton, 1982.

Zeeden, Ernst Walter. *The Legacy of Luther; Martin Luther and the Reformation in the Estimation of the German Lutherans from Luther's Death to the Beginning of the Age of Goethe*. Westminster, Md.: Newman Press, 1954.

Philip Melanchthon

Deane, David J. *Philip Melancthon: The Wittenberg Professor and Theologian of the Reformation*. London: S.W. Partridge, 1897.

Green, Lowell C., et al. *Melanchthon in English: New Translations into English with a Registry of Previous Translations: a Memorial to William Hammer (1909–1976)*. St. Louis, Mo.: Center for Reformation Research, 1982.

Maag, Karin, ed. *Melanchthon in Europe: His Work and Influence Beyond Wittenberg*. Carlisle, U.K.: Paternoster, 1999.

Meijering, E. P. *Melanchthon and Patristic Thought: The Doctrines of Christ and Grace, the Trinity, and the Creation*. Leiden: E.J. Brill, 1983.

Richard, James William. *Philip Melanchthon, the Protestant Preceptor of Germany, 1497–1560*. New York and London: G.P. Putnam's Sons, 1898.

Rogness, Michael. *Philip Melanchthon; Reformer Without Honor*. Minneapolis, Minn.: Augsburg Publishing House, 1969.

Wilson, George. *Philip Melanchthon, 1497–1560*. London: The Religious Tract Society, 1897.

The Protest at Speyer

Hillerbrand, Hans Joachim. *The Oxford Encyclopedia of the Reformation*. Vol. 4. New York: Oxford University Press, 1996.

Lindberg, Carter. *The European Reformations*. Oxford: Blackwell Publishers, 1996.

Martin Bucer

Baukol, Bard. "The Reformation of Martin Bucer." M.A. Thesis, Arizona State University, 2002.

Burnett, Amy Nelson. *The Yoke of Christ: Martin Bucer and Christian Discipline*. Kirksville, Mo.: Northeast Missouri State University, 1994.

Chrisman, Miriam Usher. *Strasbourg and the Reform: A Study in the Process of Change*. New Haven, Conn.: Yale University Press, 1967.

Greschat, Martin. *Martin Bucer: A Reformer and His Times*. Louisville, Ky.: Westminster John Knox Press, 2004.

Hopf, Constantin. *Martin Bucer and the English Reformation*. Oxford: Basil Blackwell, 1972.

Krieger, Christian, and Marc Lienhard. *Martin Bucer and Sixteenth Century Europe*. Leiden: E.J. Brill, 1993.

Pils, Holger, et al. *Martin Bucer (1491–1551): Bibliographie.* Gütersloh: Gütersloher Verlagshaus, 2005.

Selderhuis, H. J. *Marriage and Divorce in the Thought of Martin Bucer.* Kirksville, Mo.: Thomas Jefferson University Press at Truman State University, 1999.

Spijker, W. van 't. *The Ecclesiastical Offices in the Thought of Martin Bucer.* Leiden: E.J. Brill, 1996.

Steinmetz, David Curtis. *Reformers in the Wings: From Geiler Von Kaysersberg to Theodore Beza.* Oxford: Oxford University Press, 2001.

Stephens, William Peter. *The Holy Spirit in the Theology of Martin Bucer.* London: Cambridge University Press, 1970.

Thompson, Nicholas. *Eucharistic Sacrifice and Patristic Tradition in the Theology of Martin Bucer, 1534–1546.* Leiden: E.J. Brill, 2005.

Wright, David F. *Martin Bucer: Reforming Church and Community.* Cambridge: Cambridge University Press, 1994.

Ulrich Zwingli

Aland, Kurt. *Four Reformers: Luther, Melanchthon, Calvin, Zwingli.* Minneapolis: Augsburg Publishing House, 1979.

Bromiley, Geoffrey William, ed. *Zwingli and Bullinger: Selected Translations with Introductions and Notes.* Philadelphia: Westminster Press, 1953.

Farner, Oskar. *Zwingli the Reformer: His Life and Work.* London: Lutterworth Press, 1968.

Furcha, Edward J., and H. Wayne Pipkin. *Prophet, Pastor, Protestant: The Work of Huldrych Zwingli After Five Hundred Years.* Allison Park, Pa.: Pickwick Publications, 1984.

Gäbler, Ulrich. *Huldrych Zwingli: His Life and Work.* Philadelphia: Fortress Press, 1986.

Gordon, Bruce. *The Swiss Reformation.* Manchester, U.K.: Manchester University Press, 2002.

Hardin, James N., and Max Reinhart. *German Writers of the Renaissance and Reformation, 1280–1580.* Detroit: Gale Research, 1997.

Locher, Gottfried Wilhelm. *Zwingli's Thought: New Perspectives.* Leiden: Brill, 1981.

Merle d'Aubigne, J. H., and Mark Sidwell. *For God and His People: Ulrich Zwingli and the Swiss Reformation.* Greenville, S.C.: BJU Press, 2000.

Potter, G. R., ed. *Huldrych Zwingli.* New York: St. Martin's Press, 1978.

Rilliet, Jean Horace. *Zwingli: Third Man of the Reformation.* Philadelphia: Westminster Press, 1964.

Stephens, W. P. *The Theology of Huldrych Zwingli.* Oxford: Clarendon Press, 1986.

———. *Zwingli: An Introduction to His Thought.* Oxford: Clarendon Press, 1992.

Widmer, Sigmund, and Eduard Widmer. *Zwingli, 1484–1984: Reformation in Switzerland.* Zürich: Theologischer Verlag, 1983.

Heinrich Bullinger

Berthoud, Jean-Marc. *Heinrich Bullinger & the Reformation.* London: The Library, 2004.

Biel, Pamela. *Doorkeepers at the House of Righteousness: Heinrich Bullinger and the Zurich Clergy 1535–1575.* Bern, N.Y.: Peter Lang, 1991.

Bromiley, Geoffrey William. *Zwingli and Bullinger: Selected Translations with Introductions and Notes.* Philadelphia, Pa.: Westminster Press, 1953.

Ella, George M. *Henry Bullinger: Shepherd of the Church.* Durham, UK: Go Publications, 2007.

Gordon, Bruce, and Emidio Campi. *Architect of Reformation: An Introduction to Heinrich Bullinger, 1504–1575.* Grand Rapids: Baker Academic, 2004.

Harding, Thomas, ed. *The Decades of Henry Bullinger.* Introductions by George Ella and Joel R. Beeke. 2 vols. Grand Rapids: Reformation Heritage Books, 2006.

McCoy, Charles S., and J. Wayne Baker. *Fountainhead of Federalism: Heinrich Bullinger and the Covenantal Tradition.* Louisville, Ky.: Westminster/John Knox Press, 1991.

Raitt, Jill. *Shapers of Religious Traditions in Germany, Switzerland, and Poland, 1560–1600.* New Haven, Conn.: Yale University Press, 1981.

Rorem, Paul. *Calvin and Bullinger on the Lord's Supper*. Bramcote, U.K.: Grove Books, 1989.

Venema, Cornelis P. *Heinrich Bullinger and the Doctrine of Predestination: Author of "The Other Reformed Tradition?"* Grand Rapids: Baker Academic, 2002.

William Tyndale

Baker, Derek, and C. W. Dugmore. *Reform and Reformation: England and the Continent c. 1500–c. 1750*. Oxford: for the Ecclesiastical History Society by Basil Blackwell, 1979.

Daniell, David. *The Bible in English: Its History and Influence*. New Haven, Conn.: Yale University Press, 2003.

———. *William Tyndale: A Biography*. New Haven, Conn.: Yale University Press, 1994.

Edwards, Brian. *God's Outlaw*. Welwyn, U.K.: Evangelical Press, 1976.

Gehring, David S. "William Tyndale: A Lutheran?" M.A. Thesis, University of Wisconsin, Madison, 2004.

Jackson, Dave, and Neta Jackson. *The Queen's Smuggler*. Minneapolis, Minn.: Bethany House Publishers, 1991.

Moynahan, Brian. *God's Bestseller: William Tyndale, Thomas More, and the Writing of the English Bible— a Story of Martyrdom and Betrayal*. New York: St. Martin's Press, 2003.

Rees, Fran. *William Tyndale: Bible Translator and Martyr*. Minneapolis, Minn.: Compass Point Books, 2006.

Rich, Lori. *The Smuggler's Flame: William Tyndale*. Fearn, Scotland: Christian Focus, 2004.

Rudge, M. A. *William Tyndale*. Gloucester, U.K.: M.A. Rudge, 1998.

Tyndale, William. *The Obedience of a Christian Man*. Ed. David Daniell. London: Penguin Books, 2000.

Werrell, Ralph S. *The Theology of William Tyndale*. Cambridge, U.K.: J. Clarke, 2006.

Williams, C. H. *William Tyndale*. London: Nelson, 1969.

Edward VI

Davies, Catharine. *A Religion of the Word: The Defence of the Reformation in the Reign of Edward VI*. Manchester, U.K.: Manchester University Press, 2002.

Dickens, A. G. *The English Reformation*. University Park, Pa.: Pennsylvania State University Press, 1991.

Elton, G. R. *Reform and Reformation—England, 1509–1558*. The New History of England. Cambridge, Mass.: Harvard University Press, 1977.

Jordan, W. K. *Edward VI: the Young King; The Protectorship of the Duke of Somerset*. Cambridge, Mass.: Belknap Press of Harvard University Press, 1971.

Lee, Stephen J. *The Mid Tudors Edward VI and Mary, 1547–1558*. London: Routledge, 2007.

MacConica, James Kelsey. *English Humanists and Reformation Politics Under Henry VIII and Edward VI*. Oxford: Clarendon Press, 1965.

MacCulloch, Diarmaid. *The Boy King: Edward VI and the Protestant Reformation*. New York: Palgrave, 2001.

Shagan, Ethan H. *Popular Politics and the English Reformation*. Cambridge: Cambridge University Press, 2003.

Smyth, Charles Hugh Egerton. *Cranmer and the Reformation Under Edward VI*. London: S.P.C.K., 1973.

Thomas Cranmer

Ayris, Paul, ed. *Thomas Cranmer's Register: A Record of Archepiscopal Administration in Diocese and Province*. Cambridge: University of Cambridge Press, 1984.

———, and D. G. Selwyn. *Thomas Cranmer: Churchman and Scholar*. Woodbridge, U.K.: Boydell Press, 1999.

Bromiley, Geoffrey William. *Thomas Cranmer, Archbishop and Martyr*. London: Church Book Room Press, 1956.

Brooks, Peter Newman. *Cranmer in Context: Documents from the English Reformation*. Minneapolis: Fortress, 1989.

———. *Thomas Cranmer's Doctrine of the Eucharist; An Essay in Historical Development*. London: Macmillan & Co. Ltd, 1965.

Cox, J.E., ed. *Writings and Disputations of Thomas Cranmer, Archbishop of Canterbury, Martyr, 1556: Relative to the Sacrament of the Lord's Supper.* Cambridge: University Press, 1844.

Cox, J.E., ed. *The Works of Thomas Cranmer.* Cambridge: University Press, 1844.

Duffield, G.E., ed. *The Work of Thomas Cranmer.* Philadelphia: Fortress Press, 1965.

Loades, D. M. *The Oxford Martyrs.* London: Batsford, 1970.

MacCulloch, Diarmaid. *Thomas Cranmer: A Life.* New Haven, Conn.: Yale University Press, 1996.

Null, Ashley. *Thomas Cranmer's Doctrine of Repentance: Renewing the Power to Love.* Oxford: Oxford University Press, 2000.

Pollard, A. F. *Thomas Cranmer and the English Reformation, 1489–1556.* Hamden, Conn.: Archon Books, 1965.

Ridley, Jasper Godwin. *Bloody Mary's Martyrs: The Story of England's Terror.* New York: Carroll & Graf Publishers, 2001.

Smyth, Charles Hugh Egerton. *Cranmer and the Reformation Under Edward VI.* London: S.P.C.K., 1973.

Hugh Latimer and Nicholas Ridley

Bromiley, Geoffrey William. *Nicholas Ridley, 1500–1555: Scholar, Bishop, Theologian, Martyr.* London: Church Book Room Press, 1953.

Butler, Arthur F. *Hugh Latimer: The Religious Thought of a Reformation Preacher.* Kent, Ohio: Ohio State University, 1977.

Chester, Allan G. *Hugh Latimer, Apostle to the English.* Philadelphia: University of Pennsylvania Press, 1954.

Demaus, R. *Hugh Latimer: a Biography.* London: Religious Tract Society, 1922.

Latimer, Hugh. *Sermons.* London: Dent & Co, 1906.

Loades, D. M. *The Oxford Martyrs.* Bangor, U.K.: Headstart History, 1992.

McGrath, Alister E. *Passion for the Gospel: Hugh Latimer (1485–1555) Then and Now: a Commemorative Lecture to Mark the 450th Anniversary of His Martyrdom in Oxford.* London: The Latimer Trust, 2005.

Pasquarello, Michael. "God's Ploughman, Hugh Latimer, A Preaching Life (1490–1555)." Ph.D. Thesis, University of North Carolina at Chapel Hill, 2002.

Ridley, Jasper Godwin. *Nicholas Ridley, A Biography.* London: Longmans, Green, 1957.

Ridley, Nicholas, and Henry Christmas, ed. *The Works of Nicholas Ridley.* Cambridge: University Press, 1841.

Ridley, Nicholas. *Treatises and Letters of Doctor Nicholas Ridley, Bishop of London, and Martyr, 1555.* London: Religious Tract Society, 1883.

Ridley, Nicholas, and John Ponet, ed. *A Brief Declaration of the Lord's Supper With Some Other Determinations and Disputations Concerning the Same Argument by the Same Author.* London: for Richard Chiswell, 1983.

Ryle, J. C. *Five English Reformers.* London: Banner of Truth Trust, 1960.

Stokes, George. *Days of Queen Mary; or, Annals of Her Reign: Containing Particulars of the Restoration of Romanism, and the Sufferings of Martyrs During That Period.* London: Religious Tract Society, 1839.

Stuart, Clara H. *Latimer, Apostle to the English.* Grand Rapids: Zondervan Books, 1986.

Wood, Douglas C. *Such a Candle: The Story of Hugh Latimer.* Welwyn, U.K.: Evangelical Press, 1980.

John Foxe

Foxe, John, and Charles Henry Hamilton Wright, ed. *Foxe's Book of Martyrs: A Complete and Accurate Account of the Lives, Sufferings, and Triumphant Deaths of the Primitive and Protestant Martyrs in All Parts of the World.* London: Morgan & Scott, 1929.

———, and George Townsend, ed. *The Acts and Monuments of John Foxe; With a Life of the Martyrologist, and Vindication of the Work.* New York: AMS Press, 1965.

Haller, William. *The Elect Nation: The Meaning and Relevance of Foxe's Book of Martyrs.* New York: Harper & Row, 1963.

Helgerson, Richard. *Forms of Nationhood: The Elizabethan Writing of England*. Chicago: University of Chicago Press, 1992.

Highley, Christopher, and John N. King. *John Foxe and His World*. Aldershot, U.K.: Ashgate, 2002.

Knott, John Ray. *Discourses of Martyrdom in English Literature, 1563–1694*. Cambridge: Cambridge University Press, 1993.

Loades, D. M. *John Foxe: An Historical Perspective*. Brookfield, Vt.: Ashgate, 1999.

———. *John Foxe and the English Reformation*. Aldershot, U.K.: Scholar Press, 1997.

———. *John Foxe at Home and Abroad*. Aldershot, U.K.: Ashgate, 2004.

———. *John Foxe: Essays I*. Oxford: Davenant Press, 2001.

Mozley, James Frederic. *John Foxe and His Book*. New York: Octagon Books, 1970.

Olsen, V. Norskov. *John Foxe and the Elizabethan Church*. Berkeley, Calif.: University of California Press, 1973.

Penny, D. Andrew. *John Foxe, Evangelicalism, and the Oxford Movement: Dialogue Across the Centuries*. Lewiston, N.Y.: E. Mellen Press, 2002.

White, Helen Constance. *Tudor Books of Saints and Martyrs*. Madison, Wisc.: University of Wisconsin Press, 1963.

John Knox

Brown, William. *The Life-Story of John Knox*. Edinburgh: W.P. Nimmo, Hay, & Mitchell, 1905.

Cowan, Henry. *John Knox, the Hero of the Scottish Reformation*. New York: AMS Press, 1970.

Greaves, Richard L. *Theology and Revolution in the Scottish Reformation: Studies in the Thought of John Knox*. Grand Rapids: Christian University Press, 1980

Knox, John, and David Laing, ed. *The Works of John Knox*. 6 vols. Edinburgh: J. Thin, 1895.

———, and Roger A. Mason, ed. *On Rebellion*. Cambridge: Cambridge University Press, 1994.

———, and William Croft Dickinson, ed. *John Knox's History of the Reformation in Scotland*. Wilmington, Del.: International Academic Publishing, 1979.

Kyle, Richard G. *The Ministry of John Knox: Pastor, Preacher, and Prophet*. Lewiston, N.Y.: E. Mellen Press, 2002.

Lang, Andrew. *John Knox and the Reformation*. Port Washington, N.Y.: Kennikat Press, 1967.

Marshall, Rosalind Kay. *John Knox*. Edinburgh: Birlinn, 2000.

Mason, Roger A. *John Knox and the British Reformations*. Aldershot, U.K.: Ashgate, 1998.

Murray, Iain Hamish. *John Knox*. London: Evangelical Library, 1973.

Percy, Eustace. *John Knox*. Richmond: John Knox Press, 1965.

Reid, W. Stanford. *Trumpeter of God; A Biography of John Knox*. New York: Scribner, 1974.

Wilson, Douglas. *For Kirk & Covenant: The Stalwart Courage of John Knox*. Nashville, Tenn.: Cumberland House, 2000.

Wylie, J. A. *The History of Protestantism in Scotland*. Edmonton, Alta.: Still Waters Revival Books, 1992.

Guido de Brès

Beeke, Joel R., and Sinclair B. Ferguson, eds. *Reformed Confessions Harmonized*. Grand Rapids, Mich.: Baker Books, 1999.

Cochrane, Arthur C. *Reformed Confessions of the 16th Century*. Philadelphia: Westminster Press, 1966.

Van Halsema, Thea B. *Three Men Came to Heidelberg; And, Glorious Heretic: The Story of Guido de Brès*. Grand Rapids: I.D.E.A., 1996.

The Heidelberg Catechism

Beeke, Joel R. "Faith and Assurance in the Heidelberg Catechism and Its Primary Composers." *Calvin Theological Journal* 27 (1992): 39–67.

Benrath, Gustav Adolf. *Zacharias Ursinus (1534–1583): His Life, Work and Significance*. Collegeville, Pa.: Ursinus College, 1970.

Bierma, Lyle D., et al. *An Introduction to the Heidelberg Catechism: Sources, History, and Theology: with a Translation of the Smaller and Larger Catechisms of Zacharias Ursinus.* Grand Rapids: Baker Academic, 2005.

———. *A Firm Foundation: An Aid to Interpreting the Heidelberg Catechism.* Carlisle, U.K.: Paternoster Press, 1995.

———. *The Covenant Theology of Caspar Olevianus.* Grand Rapids: Reformation Heritage Books, 2005.

Clasen, Claus Peter. *The Palatinate in European History, 1555–1618.* Oxford: Blackwell, 1966.

Cohn, Henry J. *The Government of the Rhine Palatinate in the Fifteenth Century.* London: Oxford University Press, 1965.

Klooster, Fred H. *The Heidelberg Catechism: Origin and History.* Grand Rapids: Calvin Theological Seminary, 1981.

Prestwich, Menna. *International Calvinism, 1541–1715.* Oxford: Clarendon Press, 1985.

Toft, Daniel John. "Zacharias Ursinus: A Study in the Development of Calvinism." M.S. Thesis, University of Wisconsin, Madison, 1962.

Ursinus, Zacharias. *The Commentary of Dr. Zacharias Ursinus on the Heidelberg Catechism.* Grand Rapids: Eerdmans, 1954.

Van Halsema, Thea B. *Three Men Came to Heidelberg; and, Glorious Heretic: The Story of Guido de Brès.* Grand Rapids: Baker, 1982.

Visser, Derk. *Controversy and Conciliation: The Reformation and the Palatinate, 1559–1583.* Allison Park, Pa.: Pickwick Publications, 1986.

———. *Zacharias Ursinus: The Reluctant Reformer: His Life and Times.* New York: United Church Press, 1983.

Peter Martyr Vermigli

Anderson, Marvin Walter. *Peter Martyr, a Reformer in Exile (1542–1562): A Chronology of Biblical Writings in England & Europe.* Nieuwkoop: De Graaf, 1975.

Campi, Emidio. *Peter Martyr Vermigli: Humanism, Republicanism, Reformation.* Genève: Droz, 2002.

Di Gangi, Mariano. *Peter Martyr Vermigli, 1499–1562: Renaissance Man, Reformation Master.* Lanham, Md.: University Press of America, 1993.

Donnelly, John Patrick. *Calvinism and Scholasticism in Vermigli's Doctrine of Man and Grace.* Leiden: Brill, 1976.

Donnelly, John Patrick, Robert McCune Kingdon, and Marvin Walter Anderson. *A Bibliography of the Works of Peter Martyr Vermigli.* Kirksville, Mo.: Sixteenth Century Journal Publishers, 1990.

James, Frank A. *Peter Martyr Vermigli and the European Reformations: Semper Reformanda.* Leiden: Brill, 2004.

———. *Peter Martyr Vermigli and Predestination: The Augustinian Inheritance of an Italian Reformer.* Oxford: Clarendon Press, 1998.

McLelland, Joseph C. *Peter Martyr Vermigli and Italian Reform.* Waterloo, Ont.: Wilfred Laurier University Press, 1980.

McLelland, Joseph C. and Gervase Elwes Duffield. *The Life, Early Letters and Eucharistic Writings of Peter Martyr.* Abingdon, U.K.: Sutton Courtenay Press, 1989.

McLelland, Joseph C. *The Visible Words of God: An Exposition of the Sacramental Theology of Peter Martyr Vermigli, A.D. 1500–1562.* Grand Rapids: Eerdmans, 1957.

McNair, Philip Murray Jourdan. *Peter Martyr in Italy: An Anatomy of Apostasy.* Oxford: Clarendon Press, 1967.

Stoughton, John. *Footprints of Italian Reformers.* London: Religious Tract Society, 1881.

Vermigli, Pietro Martire. *The Political Thought of Peter Martyr Vermigli: Selected Texts and Commentary.* Ed. R.M. Kingdon. Genève: Librairie Droz, 1980.

Vermigli, Pietro Martire, John Patrick Donnelly, and Joseph C. McLelland. *The Peter Martyr Library.* Kirksville, Mo.: Thomas Jefferson University Press, 1994-.

Zuidema, Jason Nathanael. "Peter Martyr Vermigli (1499–1562) and the Outward Instruments of Divine Grace." Ph.D. Thesis, McGill University, 2006.

John Calvin

Arnold, Jack L. "John Calvin: From Birth to Strassburg (1509–1541)." Reformation Men and Theology, Lesson 7 of 11.

Bevan, Frances A. *The Life of William Farel: A Spiritual Force in the Great Reformation Who Nobly Endured "The Reproach of Christ."* Oak Park, Ill.: Bible Truth Publishers, 1975.

Beveridge, Henry, and Jules Bonnet, eds. *Selected Works of John Calvin, Tracts and Letters.* 7 vols. Grand Rapids: Baker Book House, 1983.

Beza, Theodore. *The Life of John Calvin.* Darlington, U.K.: Evangelical Press, 1997.

Bouwsma, William James. *John Calvin: A Sixteenth-Century Portrait.* New York: Oxford University Press, 1988.

Breen, Quirinus. *John Calvin; A Study in French Humanism.* Hamden, Conn.: Archon Books, 1968.

Calvin, Jean. *Calvin's Commentaries.* 22 vols. Grand Rapids: Baker Book House, 2003.

———. *Concerning the Eternal Predestination of God.* Ed. John Kelman Sutherland Reid. Louisville, Ky.: Westminster John Knox Press, 1997.

———. *John Calvin's Sermons on the Ten Commandments.* Ed. Benjamin Wirt Farley. Grand Rapids: Baker Book House, 1980.

———. *Institutes of the Christian Religion.* 2 vols. Trans. Ford Lewis Battles. Ed. John T. McNeill. Philadelphia: Westminster Press, 1997.

———. *On Prayer: Conversation with God.* Ed. I. John Hesselink. Louisville, Ky.: Westminster John Knox Press, 2006.

———. *The Piety of John Calvin: An Anthology Illustrative of the Spirituality of the Reformer.* Ed. Ford Lewis Battles. Grand Rapids: Baker Book House, 1978.

———. *Sermons on Job.* Edinburgh: Banner of Truth Trust, 1993.

———. *Sermons on the Beatitudes: Five Sermons from the Gospel Harmony, Delivered in Geneva in 1560.* Edinburgh: Banner of Truth Trust, 2006.

Conditt, Marion W. *More Acceptable Than Sacrifice: Ethics and Election As Obedience to God's Will in the Theology of Calvin.* Basel: F. Reinhardt Kommissionsverlag, 1973.

Cunningham, William, James Buchanan, and James Bannerman. *The Reformers and the Theology of the Reformation.* London: Banner of Truth Trust, 1967.

Dowey, Edward A. *The Knowledge of God in Calvin's Theology.* New York: Columbia University Press, 1952.

Forstman, H. Jackson. *Word and Spirit; Calvin's Doctrine of Biblical Authority.* Stanford, Calif.: Stanford University Press, 1962.

Gamble, Richard C. *Articles on Calvin and Calvinism: A Fourteen-Volume Anthology of Scholarly Articles.* New York: Garland Publishers, 1992.

Ganoczy, Alexandre. *The Young Calvin.* Philadelphia, Pa.: Westminster Press, 1987.

Greef, W. de. *The Writings of John Calvin: An Introductory Guide.* Grand Rapids: Baker Books, 1993.

Hancock, Ralph Cornel. *Calvin and the Foundations of Modern Politics.* Ithaca, N.Y.: Cornell University Press, 1989.

Hesselink, I. John. *Calvin's Concept of the Law.* Allison Park, Pa.: Pickwick Publications, 1992.

Höpfl, Harro. *The Christian Polity of John Calvin.* Cambridge: Cambridge University Press, 1982.

Jansen, John Frederick. *Calvin's Doctrine of the Work of Christ.* London: J. Clark, 1956.

Johnson, Elsie May. *The Man of Geneva: The Story of John Calvin.* Edinburgh: Banner of Truth Trust, 1977.

McGrath, Alister E. *A Life of John Calvin: A Study in the Shaping of Western Culture.* Oxford: Blackwell Publishers, 1990.

McKim, Donald K., ed. *The Cambridge Companion to John Calvin.* Cambridge: Cambridge University Press, 2004.

McNeill, John Thomas. *The History and Character of Calvinism.* New York: Oxford University Press, 1954.

Monter, E. William. *Calvin's Geneva.* New York: Wiley, 1967.

Muller, Richard A. *The Unaccommodated Calvin: Studies in the Foundation of a Theological Tradition.* Oxford: Oxford University, 2000.

Parker, T. H. L. *Calvin's Preaching.* Louisville, Ky.: Westminster John Knox Press, 1992.

———. *John Calvin: A Biography.* Philadelphia: Westminster Press, 1975.

Penning, L. *John Calvin: Genius of Geneva: a Popular Account of the Life and Times of John Calvin.* Neerlandia, Alta.: Inheritance Publications, 2006.

Richard, Lucien. *The Spirituality of John Calvin.* Atlanta, Ga.: John Knox Press, 1974.

Wendel, François. *Calvin; The Origins and Development of His Religious Thought*. New York: Harper & Row, 1963.

Theodore Beza

Archibald, Paul Noel. "A Comparative Study of John Calvin and Theodore Beza on the Doctrine of the Extent of the Atonement." Ph.D. Thesis, Westminster Theological Seminary, Philadelphia, 1998.

Backus, Irena Dorota. *The Reformed Roots of the English New Testament: The Influence of Theodore Beza on the English New Testament*. Pittsburgh, Pa.: Pickwick Press, 1980.

Baird, Henry Martyn. *Theodore Beza: The Counsellor of the French Reformation, 1519–1605*. New York: B. Franklin, 1970.

Bray, John S. *Theodore Beza's Doctrine of Predestination*. Nieuwkoop: De Graaf, 1975.

Conradt, Nancy Marilyn. "John Calvin, Theodore Beza and the Reformation in Poland." Ph.D. Thesis, University of Wisconsin, 1974.

Mallinson, Jeffrey. *Faith, Reason, and Revelation in Theodore Beza, 1519–1605*. Oxford: Oxford University Press, 2003.

Manetsch, Scott M. *Theodore Beza and the Quest for Peace in France, 1572–1598*. Leiden: Brill, 2000.

Maruyama, Tadataka. *The Ecclesiology of Theodore Beza: The Reform of the True Church*. Genève: Droz, 1978.

McCrie, C. G., ed. *Contemporary Portraits of Reformers of Religion and Letters; Being Facsimile Reproductions of the Portraits in Beza's Icones (1580), and in Goulard's Edition (1581)*. London: Religious Tract Society, 1906.

Raitt, Jill. *The Eucharistic Theology of Theodore Beza: Development of the Reformed Doctrine*. Chambersburg, Pa.: American Academy of Religion, 1972.

Steinmetz, David Curtis. *Reformers in the Wings: From Geiler Von Kaysersberg to Theodore Beza*. Oxford: Oxford University Press, 2001.

Wright, Shawn D. *Our Sovereign Refuge: The Pastoral Theology of Theodore Beza*. Cumbria, U.K.: Paternoster, 2004.

Jan Łaski

Brown, Harold O. J. "John Łaski: a Theological Biography, A Polish Contribution to the Protestant Reformation." Ph.D. Thesis, Harvard University, 1967.

Brycko, Dariusz Mirosław. "An Ecumenical Movement in Early Modern Europe: A Revision of Jan Łaski's Irenic Efforts Among Polish Protestants." M.A. Thesis, Gordon-Conwell Theological Seminary, 2002.

Dalton, Hermann. *John à Lasco: His Earlier Life and Labours; a Contribution to the History of the Reformation in Poland, Germany, and England*. London: Hodder and Stoughton, 1886.

Hall, Basil. *John à Lasco, 1499–1560: a Pole in Reformation England*. London: Dr. Williams's Trust, 1971.

McAlhaney, Timothy Morris. "Influence of the Continental Reformers Bucer, Vermigli, and Łaski Upon Cranmer and the *Via Media* of the English Reformation." Ph.D. Thesis, Southwestern Baptist Theological Seminary, 2002.

Rodgers, Dirk W. *John à Lasco in England*. New York: P. Lang, 1994.

Smith, James Frantz. *John à Lasco and the Strangers' Churches*. Ann Arbor, Mich.: University Microfilms International, 1981.

Springer, Michael Stephen. *Restoring Christ's Church: John à Lasco and the Forma Ac Ratio*. Aldershot, U.K.: Ashgate, 2007.

The Duke of Alva and William, Prince of Orange

Benedict, Philip. *Reformation, Revolt and Civil War in France and the Netherlands, 1555–1585*. Amsterdam: Royal Netherlands Academy of Arts and Sciences, 1999.

Cohn, Henry J. *Government in Reformation Europe, 1520–1560*. London: Macmillan, 1971.

Darby, Graham. *The Origins and Development of the Dutch Revolt*. London: Routledge, 2001.

Duke, A. C. *Reformation and Revolt in the Low Countries*. London: Hambledon Press, 1990.

Ellemers, Jo Egbert. *The Revolt of the Netherlands: The Part Played by Religion in the Process of Nation-Building*. Amsterdam: Universiteit van Amsterdam, 1967.

Freedberg, David. *Iconoclasm and Painting in the Revolt of the Netherlands, 1566–1609*. New York: Garland, 1988.

Gelderen, Martin van. *The Dutch Revolt*. Cambridge: Cambridge University Press, 1992.

———. *The Political Thought of the Dutch Revolt, 1555-1590*. Cambridge: Cambridge University Press, 1992.

Geyl, Pieter. *History of the Dutch-Speaking Peoples: 1555–1648*. London: Phoenix, 2001.

———. *The Revolt of the Netherlands (1555–1609)*. New York: Barnes & Noble, 1958.

Hibben, C. C. *Gouda in Revolt: Particularism and Pacifism in the Revolt of the Netherlands 1572–1588*. Utrecht: HES, 1983.

Holt, Mack P. *The Duke of Anjou and the Politique Struggle During the Wars of Religion*. Cambridge: Cambridge University Press, 1986.

Janson, Carol. *Public Places, Private Lives: The Impact of the Dutch Revolt on the Reformed Churches in Holland*. Newark, Del.: University of Delaware Press, 2000.

Jardine, Lisa. *The Awful End of Prince William the Silent: The First Assassination of a Head of State with a Handgun*. New York: Harper Collins, 2005.

Kamen, Henry. *The Duke of Alva*. New Haven, Conn.: Yale University Press, 2004.

Kossmann, E. H., and Albert Fredrik Mellink. *Texts Concerning the Revolt of the Netherlands*. London: Cambridge University Press, 1974.

Limm, Peter. *The Dutch Revolt, 1559–1648*. London: Longman, 1989.

Maltby, William S. *Alva: A Biography of Fernando Alvarez De Toledo, Third Duke of Alva, 1507–1582*. Berkeley, Calif.: University of California Press, 1983.

Morgan, Walter, and Duncan Caldecott-Baird. *The Expedition in Holland 1572–1574: The Revolt of the Netherlands: the Early Struggle for Independence: from the Manuscript*. London: Seeley Service, 1976.

Parker, Geoffrey. *The Dutch Revolt*. Ithaca, N.Y.: Cornell University Press, 1977.

Pettegree, Andrew. *Emden and the Dutch Revolt: Exile and the Development of Reformed Protestantism*. Oxford: Clarendon Press, 1992.

Rooney, John W. *Revolt in the Netherlands*. Lawrence, Kan.: Coronado Press, 1982.

Simmons, Dawn Langley. *William, Father of The Netherlands*. Chicago: Rand McNally, 1969.

Swart, K. W., et al. *William of Orange and the Revolt of the Netherlands, 1572–84*. Aldershot, U.K.: Ashgate, 2003.

Wedgwood, C. V. *William the Silent, William of Nassau, Prince of Orange, 1533–1584*. London: J. Cape, 1944.

Petrus Dathenus

Crew, Phyllis Mack. *Calvinist Preaching and Iconoclasm in the Netherlands, 1544–1569*. Cambridge: Cambridge University Press, 1978.

Dathenus, Petrus. *The Pearl of Christian Comfort*. Trans. Arie W. Blok. Grand Rapids: Reformation Heritage Books, 2005.

De Jong, Peter Y. *The Church's Witness to the World*. St. Catharines, Ont.: Paideia Press, 1980.

Queen Marguerite of Navarre

Clive, H. P. *Marguerite de Navarre: An Annotated Bibliography*. London: Grant & Cutler, 1983.

Cottrell, Robert D. *The Grammar of Silence: A Reading of Marguerite de Navarre's Poetry*. Washington, D.C.: Catholic University of America Press, 1986.

Deen, Edith. *Great Women of the Christian Faith*. New York: Harper, 1959.

Hannay, Margaret P. *Silent but for the Word: Tudor Women As Patrons, Translators, and Writers of Religious Works*. Kent, Ohio: Kent State University Press, 1985.

Marguerite, and Marie West King. *Recipe for a Happy Life*. New York: Cosimo Classics, 2004.

Marguerite, and Paul A. Chilton. *The Heptameron*. Harmondsworth, U.K.: Penguin Books, 1984.

Marguerite. *The Prisons of Marguerite de Navarre*. Reading, U.K.: Whiteknights Press, 1989.

Jeanne d'Albret of Navarre

Bryson, David. *Queen Jeanne and the Promised Land: Dynasty, Homeland, Religion, and Violence in Sixteenth-Century France*. Leiden: Brill, 1999.

Farenhorst, Christine. *Wings Like a Dove: The Courage of Queen Jeanne d'Albret*. Phillipsburg, N.J.: P&R Publishing Co., 2006.

Roelker, Nancy L. *Queen of Navarre; Jeanne d'Albret, 1528–1572*. Cambridge, Mass.: Belknap Press of Harvard University Press, 1968.

Admiral de Coligny and St. Bartholomew's Day

DeMolen, Richard L. *Leaders of the Reformation*. Selinsgrove, Pa.: Susquehanna University Press, 1984.

Kingdon, Robert McCune. *Geneva and the Coming of the Wars of Religion in France, 1555–1563*. Genève: Librairie E. Droz, 1956.

———. *Geneva and the Consolidation of the French Protestant Movement, 1564–1572: A Contribution to the History of Congregationalism, Presbyterianism, and Calvinist Resistance Theory*. Madison, Wisc.: University of Wisconsin Press, 1967.

———. *Myths About the St. Bartholomew's Day Massacres, 1572–1576*. Cambridge, Mass.: Harvard University Press, 1988.

Shimizu, J. *Conflict of Loyalties, Politics and Religion in the Career of Gaspard de Coligny, Admiral of France, 1519–1572*. Genève: Droz, 1970.

Sutherland, N. M. *The Huguenot Struggle for Recognition*. New Haven, Conn.: Yale University, 1980.

———. *The Massacre of St. Bartholomew and the European Conflict, 1559–1572*. New York: Barnes & Noble, 1973.

Charlotte, the Nun of Jouarre

Walker, Frances M. Cotton. *Cloister to Court: Scenes from the Life of Charlotte of Bourbon, Abbess of Jouarre, Princess of Orange*. London: Longmans, Green, and Co., 1909.

William Perkins

Beeke, Joel R. *Assurance of Faith: Calvin, English Puritanism, and the Dutch Second Reformation*. New York: P. Lang, 1991.

Beeke, Joel R. and Randall J. Pedersen. *Meet the Puritans: With a Guide to Modern Reprints*. Grand Rapids: Reformation Heritage Books, 2006.

Breward, Ian, ed. *The Work of William Perkins*. Abingdon, U.K.: Sutton Courtenay Press, 1970.

Collinson, Patrick. *The Elizabethan Puritan Movement*. Berkeley, Calif.: University of California Press, 1967.

———. *The Religion of Protestants: The Church in English Society, 1559–1625*. Oxford: Clarendon Press, 1982.

Delbanco, Andrew. *The Puritan Ordeal*. Cambridge, Mass.: Harvard University Press, 1989.

Durston, Christopher, and Jacqueline Eales. *The Culture of English Puritanism: 1560–1700*. New York, N.Y.: St. Martin's Press, 1996.

Haller, William. *The Rise of Puritanism; Or, The Way to the New Jerusalem As Set Forth in Pulpit and Press from Thomas Cartwright to John Lilburne and John Milton, 1570–1643*. New York: Harper, 1957.

Lake, Peter. *Anglicans and Puritans?: Presbyterianism and English Conformist Thought from Whitgift to Hooker*. London: Unwin Hyman, 1988.

———. *Moderate Puritans and the Elizabethan Church*. Cambridge: Cambridge University Press, 1982.

Merrill, Thomas F., ed. *William Perkins, 1558–1602, English Puritanist; His Pioneer Works on Casuistry: "A Discourse of Conscience" and "The Whole Treatise of Cases of Conscience."* Nieuwkoop: B. De Graaf, 1966.

Perkins, William. *The Art of Prophesying; with, The Calling of the Ministry*. Ed. Sinclair B. Ferguson. Carlisle, Pa.: Banner of Truth Trust, 1996.

Pettit, Norman. *The Heart Prepared; Grace and Conversion in Puritan Spiritual Life*. New Haven, Conn.: Yale University Press, 1966.

Porter, H. C. *Reformation and Reaction in Tudor Cambridge*. Cambridge U.K.: Cambridge University Press, 1958.

William Ames

Ames, William. *Conscience with the Power and Cases Thereof*. Amsterdam: Theatrum Orbis Terrarum, 1975.

Anderson, Charles William. "Covenant Theology of Perkins and Ames." S.T.M. Thesis, University of the South, 1972.

Boerkoel, Benjamin J. "Uniqueness Within the Calvinist Tradition, William Ames (1576–1633): Primogenitor of the *Theologia Pietatis* in English-Dutch Puritanism." Th.M. Thesis, Calvin Theological Seminary, 1990.

————. *The Marrow of Theology*. Ed. John D. Eusden. Durham, N.C.: Labyrinth Press, 1983.

Horton, Douglas. *Let Us Not Forget the Mighty William Ames*. Nashville, Tenn.: Abingdon Press, 1960.

Horton, Douglas, et al. *William Ames*. Cambridge Mass.: Harvard Divinity School Library, 1965.

Lindsley, Arthur William. "Conscience and Casuistry in the English Puritan Concept of Reformation." Ph.D. Thesis, University of Pittsburgh, 1982.

Sprunger, Keith L. *The Auction Catalogue of the Library of William Ames*. Utrecht: HES Publishers, 1988.

————. *Dutch Puritanism: A History of English and Scottish Churches of the Netherlands in the Sixteenth and Seventeenth Centuries*. Leiden: Brill, 1983.

————. *The Learned Doctor William Ames; Dutch Backgrounds of English and American Puritanism*. Urbana, Ill.: University of Illinois Press, 1972.

Van Vliet, Jan. "William Ames: Marrow of the Theology and Piety of the Reformed Tradition." Ph.D. Thesis, Westminster Theological Seminary, Philadelphia, 2002.

William Teellinck

Teellinck, Willem. *The Path of True Godliness*. Trans. Annemie Godbehere. Ed. and intro. Joel R. Beeke. Grand Rapids: Baker Academic, 2003.

The Anabaptists

Armour, Rollin S. *Anabaptist Baptism: A Representative Study*. Scottdale, Pa.: Herald Press, 1966.

Balke, Willem. *Calvin and the Anabaptist Radicals*. Grand Rapids: Eerdmans, 1981.

Bax, Ernest Belfort. *Rise and Fall of the Anabaptists*. New York: American Scholar Publications, 1966.

Bender, Harold Stauffer. *Conrad Grebel; c. 1498–1526, the Founder of the Swiss Brethren Sometimes Called Anabaptists*. Scottdale, Pa.: Herald Press, 1950.

————. *Conrad Grebel As a Zwinglian, 1522–1523*. Goshen, Ind.: Mennonite Historical Society, 1941.

————. *The Life and Letters of Conrad Grebel*. Goshen, Ind.: Mennonite Historical Society, Goshen College, 1950.

Bergsten, Torsten, and William Roscoe Estep. *Balthasar Hubmaier: Anabaptist Theologian and Martyr*. Valley Forge, Pa.: Judson Press, 1978.

Boyd, Stephen Blake. *Pilgram Marpeck: His Life and Social Theology*. Durham, N.C.: Duke University Press, 1992.

Brunk, Gerald R. *Menno Simons, a Reappraisal: Essays in Honor of Irvin B. Horst on the 450th Anniversary of the Fundamentboek*. Harrisonburg, Va.: Eastern Mennonite College, 1992.

Clasen, Claus Peter. *Anabaptism: A Social History, 1525–1618: Switzerland, Austria, Moravia, South and Central Germany*. Ithaca, N.Y.: Cornell University Press, 1972.

Davis, Kenneth Ronald. *Anabaptism and Asceticism; A Study in Intellectual Origins*. Scottdale, Pa.: Herald Press, 1974.

Deppermann, Klaus, and Benjamin Drewery. *Melchior Hoffman: Social Unrest and Apocalyptic Visions in the Age of Reformation*. Edinburgh: T. & T. Clark, 1987.

Dyck, Cornelius J. *An Introduction to Mennonite History: A Popular History of the Anabaptists and the Mennonites*. Scottdale, Pa.: Herald Press, 1993.

Friedmann, Robert. *The Theology of Anabaptism: An Interpretation*. Scottdale, Pa.: Herald Press, 1975.

Friesen, Abraham. *Thomas Muentzer, a Destroyer of the Godless: The Making of a Sixteenth-Century Religious Revolutionary*. Berkeley, Calif.: University of California Press, 1990.

George, Timothy. *Theology of the Reformers*. Nashville, Tenn.: Broadman Press, 1988.

Grebel, Konrad, and Leland Harder. *The Sources of Swiss Anabaptism: The Grebel Letters and Related Documents*. Scottdale, Pa.: Herald Press, 1985.

Goertz, Hans-Jürgen, and Peter Matheson. *Thomas Müntzer: Apocalyptic, Mystic, and Revolutionary*. Edinburgh: T&T Clark, 1993.

———, and Walter Klaassen. *Profiles of Radical Reformers: Biographical Sketches from Thomas Müntzer to Paracelsus*. Kitchener, Ont.: Herald Press, 1982.

Gritsch, Eric W. *Reformer Without a Church; The Life and Thought of Thomas Muentzer, 1488?–1525*. Philadelphia, Pa.: Fortress Press, 1967.

———. *Thomas Müntzer: A Tragedy of Errors*. Minneapolis: Fortress Press, 1989.

Gross, Leonard. *The Golden Years of the Hutterites: The Witness and Thought of the Communal Moravian Anabaptists During the Walpot Era, 1565-1578*. Scottdale, Pa.: Herald Press, 1980.

Hillerbrand, Hans J., ed. *Anabaptist Bibliography 1520–1630*. St. Louis: Center for Reformation Research, 1991.

Horsch, John. *The Hutterian Brethren, 1528–1931; A Story of Martyrdom and Loyalty*. Goshen, Ind.: The Mennonite Historical Society, 1931.

Hutterian Brethren. *The Chronicle of the Hutterian Brethren*. Rifton, New York: Plough Publishing House, 1987.

Klaassen, Walter. *Living at the End of the Ages: Apocalyptic Expectation in the Radical Reformation*. Lanham, Md.: University Press of America, 1992.

Klassen, William. *Covenant and Community; The Life, Writings, and Hermeneutics of Pilgram Marpeck*. Grand Rapids: Eerdmans, 1968.

———, and Walter Klaassen, eds. and trans. *The Writings of Pilgram Marpeck*. Kitchener, Ont.: Herald Press, 1978.

Krahn, Cornelius. *Dutch Anabaptism. Origin, Spread, Life, and Thought (1450–1600)*. The Hague: Martinus Nijhoff, 1968.

Matheson, Peter, ed. *The Collected Works of Thomas Müntzer*. Edinburgh: T&T Clark, 1988.

Moore, John Allen. *Anabaptist Portraits*. Scottdale, Pa.: Herald Press, 1984.

Oyer, John S. *Lutheran Reformers against Anabaptists: Luther, Melanchton, and Menius, and the Anabaptists of Central Germany*. The Hague: M. Nijhoff, 1964.

Ozment, Steven E. *Mysticism and Dissent; Religious Ideology and Social Protest in the Sixteenth Century*. New Haven, Conn.: Yale University Press, 1973.

Packull, Werner O. *Mysticism and the Early South German-Austrian Anabaptist Movement, 1525–1531*. Scottdale, Pa.: Herald Press, 1977.

Pipkin, Wayne H. and John Howard Yoder, eds. *Balthasar Hubmaier, Theologian of Anabaptism*. Scottdale, Pa.: Herald Press, 1989.

Scott, Tom. *Thomas Müntzer: Theology and Revolution in the German Reformation*. New York: St. Martin's Press, 1989.

Stayer, James M. *Anabaptists and the Sword*. Lawrence, Kan.: Coronado Press, 1972.

———. *The German Peasants' War and Anabaptist Community of Goods*. Montreal: McGill-Queen's University Press, 1991.

Vedder, Henry C. *Balthasar Hubmaier: The Leader of the Anabaptists*. New York: AMS Press, 1971.

Waite, Gary K. *David Joris and Dutch Anabaptism, 1524–1543*. Waterloo, Ont.: Wilfred Laurier University Press, 1990.

Weis, Frederick Lewis. *The Life and Teachings of Ludwig Hetzer, a Leader and Martyr of the Anabaptists, 1500–1529*. Dorchester, Mass.: Underhill Press, 1930.

Wenger, J.C, ed. *The Complete Writings of Menno Simons, c. 1496–1561*. Scottdale, Pa.: Herald Press, 1986.

Williams, George Huntston, and Angel M. Mergal. *Spiritual and Anabaptist Writers: Documents Illustrative of the Radical Reformation*. Philadelphia: Westminster Press, 1957.

Williams, George Huntston. *The Radical Reformation*. 3rd ed. Kirksville, Mo.: Truman State University, 2000.

Yoder, John Howard, ed. and trans. *The Legacy of Michael Sattler*. Scottdale, Pa.: Herald Press, 1973.

The Counter Reformation

Aldama, Antonio M. de. *The Formula of the Institute: Notes for a Commentary*. Rome: Centrum Ignatianum Spiritualitatis, 1990.

Anderson, James Maxwell. *Daily Life During the Spanish Inquisition*. Westport, Conn.: Greenwood Press, 2002.

Bangert, William V. *A History of the Society of Jesus*. St. Louis: Institute of Jesuit Sources, 1972.

Bireley, Robert. *Religion and Politics in the Age of the Counterreformation: Emperor Ferdinand II, William Lamormaini, S.J., and the Formation of Imperial Policy*. Chapel Hill, N.C.: University of North Carolina Press, 1981.

Bossy, John. *Christianity in the West, 1400–1700*. Oxford: Oxford University Press, 1985.

———, ed. *The Spirit of the Counter-Reformation*. Cambridge: Cambridge University Press, 1968.

Châtellier, Louis. *The Europe of the Devout: The Catholic Reformation and the Formation of a New Society*. Cambridge: Cambridge University Press, 1989.

Coxwell, Gene M. "An Evaluation of the Educational Methods of the Jesuits During the Counter-Reformation." Th.M. Thesis, Dallas Theological Seminary, 1964.

Dalmases, Cándido de. *Ignatius of Loyola, Founder of the Jesuits: His Life and Work*. St. Louis, Mo.: Institute of Jesuit Sources in cooperation with Gujarat Sahitya Prakash, Anand, India, 1985.

Delumeau, Jean. *Catholicism between Luther and Voltaire: A New View of the Counter Reformation*. London: Burns & Oates, 1977.

Donnelly, John Patrick. *Ignatius of Loyola: Founder of the Jesuits*. New York: Longman, 2004.

———. *Jesuit Writings of the Early Modern Period, 1540–1640*. Indianapolis, Ind.: Hackett Publishing Co., 2006.

Edwards, John. *The Spanish Inquisition*. Stroud, U.K.: Tempus, 1999.

Garstein, Oskar. *Rome and the Counter-Reformation in Scandinavia: Jesuit Educational Strategy, 1553–1622*. Leiden: E.J. Brill, 1992.

Goldberg, Enid A., and Norman Itzkowitz. *Tomás De Torquemada: Architect of Torture During the Spanish Inquisition*. New York: Franklin Watts, 2007.

Grendler, Paul Frederick. *The Roman Inquisition and the Venetian Press, 1540–1605*. Princeton, N.J.: Princeton University Press, 1977.

Guibert, Joseph de, William J. Young, and George E. Ganss, trans. *The Jesuits: Their Spiritual Doctrine and Practice: a Historical Study*. St. Louis: Institute of Jesuit Sources, 1986.

Headley, John M., and John B. Tomaro, ed. *San Carlo Borromeo: Catholic Reform and Ecclesiastical Politics in the Second Half of the Sixteenth Century*. Washington, D.C.: Folger Shakespeare Library, 1988.

Henningsen, Gustav, John A. Tedeschi, and Charles Amiel. *The Inquisition in Early Modern Europe: Studies on Sources and Methods*. Dekalb, Ill.: Northern Illinois University Press, 1986.

Homza, Lu Ann. *The Spanish Inquisition, 1478–1614: An Anthology of Sources*. Indianapolis, Ind.: Hackett Publishing Co., 2006.

Höpfl, Harro. *Jesuit Political Thought: The Society of Jesus and the State, c. 1540–1640*. New York: Cambridge University Press, 2004.

Hsia, R. Po-chia. *The World of Catholic Renewal, 1540–1770*. Cambridge: Cambridge University Press, 1998.

Jedin, Hubert, and Frederic Clement Eckhoff. *Papal Legate at the Council of Trent, Cardinal Seripando*. St. Louis: B. Herder Book Co., 1947.

Jones, Martin D. W. *The Counter Reformation: Religion and Society in Early Modern Europe*. Cambridge: Cambridge University Press, 1995.

Kamen, Henry. *Inquisition and Society in Spain in the Sixteenth and Seventeenth Centuries*. Bloomington, Ind.: Indiana University Press, 1985.

———. *The Phoenix and the Flame: Catalonia and the Counter Reformation*. New Haven, Conn.: Yale University Press, 1993.

———. *The Spanish Inquisition: A Historical Revision*. London: Folio Society, 1998.

Lacouture, Jean. *Jesuits: A Multibiography*. Washington, D.C.: Counterpoint, 1995.

Martin, A. Lynn. *The Jesuit Mind: The Mentality of an Elite in Early Modern France*. Ithaca, N.Y.: Cornell University Press, 1988.

Meissner, W. W. *Ignatius of Loyola: The Psychology of a Saint*. New Haven, Conn.: Yale University Press, 1992.

Monter, William. *Frontiers of Heresy: The Spanish Inquisition from the Basque Lands to Sicily*. Cambridge: Cambridge University Press, 2002.

O'Donohoe, James A. *Tridentine Seminary Legislation: Its Sources and Its Formation*. Louvain: Publications Universitaires de Louvain, 1957.

Olin, John C. *The Catholic Reformation: Savonarola to Ignatius Loyola*. New York: Fordham University Press, 1992.

O'Malley, John W. *Catholicism in Early Modern History: A Guide to Research*. 2 vols. St. Louis: Center for Reformation Research, 1988.

———. *The First Jesuits*. Cambridge, Mass.: Harvard University Press, 1993.

Pérez, Joseph. *The Spanish Inquisition: A History*. London: Profile, 2004.

Peters, Edward. *Inquisition*. New York: Free Press, 1988.

Plaidy, Jean. *The Spanish Inquisition: Its Rise, Growth, and End*. New York: Citadel Press, 1967.

Ravier, André. *Ignatius of Loyola and the Founding of the Society of Jesus*. San Francisco: Ignatius Press, 1987.

Rawlings, Helen. *The Spanish Inquisition*. Malden, Mass.: Blackwell Publishers, 2006.

Robinson-Hammerstein, Helga. *European Universities in the Age of Reformation and Counter Reformation*. Dublin: Four Courts Press, 1998.

Schroeder, Henry J., ed. *Canons and Decrees of the Council of Trent*. Rockford, Ill.: Tan Books and Publishers, 1978.

Schütte, Josef Franz. *Valignano's Mission Principles for Japan*. St. Louis: Institute of Jesuit Sources, 1980.

Stalcup, Brenda. *The Inquisition*. San Diego, Calif.: Greenhaven Press, 2001.

Wright, A. D. *The Counter-Reformation: Catholic Europe and the Non-Christian World*. New York: St. Martin's Press, 1982.

Wright, Jonathan. *God's Soldiers: Adventure, Politics, Intrigue, and Power: a History of the Jesuits*. New York: Doubleday, 2004.

The Influence of the Reformation

Beery, Dewitt Candler. "Influence of the Reformation on Social Conditions in Germany." M.A. Thesis, Emory University, 1927.

Cummings, Brian. *The Literary Culture of the Reformation: Grammar and Grace*. Oxford: Oxford University Press, 2002.

Douglass, E. Jane Dempsey. *Women, Freedom, and Calvin*. Philadelphia: Westminster Press, 1985.

Edwards, John. *The Jews in Christian Europe, 1400–1700*. London: Routledge, 1988.

Edwards, Mark U. *Printing, Propaganda, and Martin Luther*. Berkeley, Calif.: University of California Press, 1994.

Eisenstein, Elizabeth L. *The Printing Press As an Agent of Change: Communications and Cultural Transformations in Early Modern Europe*. Cambridge: Cambridge University Press, 1979.

Graham, W. Fred, ed. *Later Calvinism: International Perspectives*. Kirksville, Mo.: Sixteenth Century Journal Publishers, 1994.

Greengrass, M., and Peter Baumgart. *Conquest and Coalescence: The Shaping of the State in Early Modern Europe*. London: Edward Arnold, 1991.

Hazard, Paul. *The European Mind, 1680–1715*. London: Hollis and Carter, 1953.

Hodges, Joseph Percy. *The Influence and Implications of the Reformation*. London: J. Heritage, 1938.

Hsia, R. Po-chia. *Social Discipline in the Reformation: Central Europe, 1550–1750*. London: Routledge, 1989.

Lawson, John. *Mediaeval Education and the Reformation*. London: Routledge & K. Paul, 1967.

Lawton, Denis, and Peter Gordon. *A History of Western Educational Ideas*. London: Woburn Press, 2002.

Luke, Carmen. *Pedagogy, Printing, and Protestantism: The Discourse on Childhood*. Albany, N.Y.: State University of New York Press, 1989.

Marshall, Sherrin. *Women in Reformation and Counter-Reformation Europe: Public and Private Worlds*. Bloomington, Ind.: Indiana University Press, 1989.

McGrath, Alister E. *A Life of John Calvin: A Study in the Shaping of Western Culture*. Oxford, U.K.: Basil Blackwell, 1990.

McLelland, Joseph C. *The Reformation and Its Significance Today*. Philadelphia: The Westminster Press, 1962.

Oberman, Heiko Augustinus. *The Roots of Anti-Semitism in the Age of Renaissance and Reformation*. Philadelphia, Pa.: Fortress Press, 1984.

————, and Donald Weinstein. *The Two Reformations: The Journey from the Last Days to the New World*. New Haven, Conn.: Yale University Press, 2003.

Ozment, Steven E. *When Fathers Ruled: Family Life in Reformation Europe*. Cambridge, Mass.: Harvard University Press, 1983.

Pelikan, Jaroslav, and John Henry Newman. *The Idea of the University: A Reexamination*. New Haven, Conn.: Yale University Press, 1992.

Pettegree, Andrew. *Reformation and the Culture of Persuasion*. Cambridge: Cambridge University Press, 2005.

Schilling, Heinz. *Civic Calvinism in Northwestern Germany and the Netherlands: Sixteenth to Nineteenth Centuries*. Kirksville, Mo.: Sixteenth Century Journal Publishers, 1991.

————. *Religion, Political Culture, and the Emergence of Early Modern Society: Essays in German and Dutch History*. Leiden: E.J. Brill, 1992.

Spitz, Lewis William. *The Reformation: Education and History*. Aldershot, U.K. Variorum, 1997.

Trevor-Roper, H. R. *The Crisis of the Seventeenth Century; Religion, the Reformation, and Social Change*. New York: Harper & Row, 1968.

Walzer, Michael. *The Revolution of the Saints; A Study in the Origins of Radical Politics*. Cambridge: Harvard University Press, 1965.

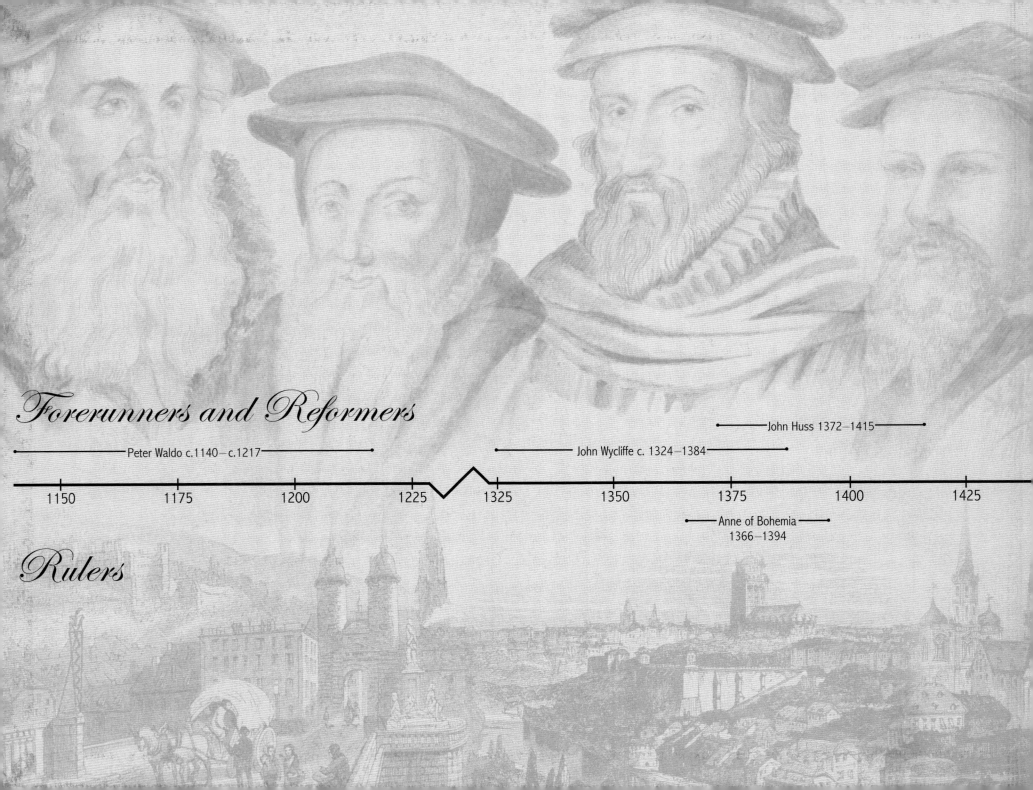

Forerunners and Reformers

Peter Waldo c.1140—c.1217

John Wycliffe c. 1324—1384

John Huss 1372—1415

1150	1175	1200	1225	1325	1350	1375	1400	1425

Anne of Bohemia
1366—1394

Rulers